D0949467

They Heard Georgia Singing

ZELL MILLER

They Heard Georgia Singing
ZELL MILLER

MERCER UNIVERSITY PRESS
Macon, Georgia 1996

ISBN 0-86554-504-9

They Heard Georgia Singing
by
Zell Miller

Copyright © 1996
Mercer University Press
6316 Peake Road
Macon, Georgia 31210-3960

The paper used in this publication meets the minimum requirements of
American National Standard for Information Sciences—Permanence of
Paper for Printed Library Materials,
ANSI Z39.48-1984.

Library of Congress Cataloging-in-Publication Data

[On file with the Library of Congress]

CONTENTS

THIS BOOK IS FOR ALL THOSE SONGWRITERS, ARTISTS, AND musicians who over the years have made my spirits soar, my eyes moisten, my lips smile, and my toes tap . . . from my neighbor Lee Kirby, fiddling on his front porch in the mountains, to my student Ronnie Milsap, playing the piano in the student center at Young Harris College, to my Nashville friend Jack Clement, singing one of his own compositions in the governor's mansion.

ALSO, IN MEMORY OF MARY TALLENT.

INTRODUCTION

From its beginning, Georgia has been in the forefront of musical pioneering. Tin Pan Alley, Hollywood and Vine, Beale Street, and Sixteenth Avenue have had more publicity and have been more commercial over the years, but they were not there first.

When the colony of Georgia was but a few years old, Charles Wesley was writing songs in Savannah during his brief stay there—hymns that have endured more than two centuries. Quite likely, Wesley was the first to hear Georgia singing. But he was not the last.

Sidney Lanier, today known for his poetry, was considered in his lifetime as one of the finest flute players of the nineteenth century and was First Flute for the Peabody Orchestra in Baltimore for seven seasons in the 1870s.

Gertrude "Ma" Rainey of Columbus was the Mother of the Blues, and Thomas A. "Georgia Tom" Dorsey was the Father of Gospel music. And Savannah's Johnny Mercer was the greatest lyricist the nation has produced.

Atlanta's radio station WSB put Fiddlin' John Carson on the air in 1922 and Okeh Records set up a studio in Atlanta to record his "hillbilly" tunes the following year. The Voice of the South under the directional genius of Lambdin Kay set national trends throughout the early days of broadcasting in encouraging musicians to present themselves on the airwaves and built upon that foundation under the far-sighted leadership of J. Leonard Reinsch, who made the WSB Barn Dance and stars like Hank Penny, James and Martha Carson, and the Swanee River Boys models for the programs and performers who would emulate them on other radio, and later television, stations throughout the nation.

Georgia Tech's radio station WGST put Georgia on the road to becoming a recording center by allowing its studios to be used by Bill Lowery to make some of his first recordings, including Ray Charles's first big hit, and set the stage for the development of his music recording and publishing conglomerate, The Lowery Group, and its fabulous string of superstars such as Ray Stevens, Jerry Reed, Brenda Lee, Joe South, the Tams, Tommy Roe, and many others whose careers are treated in this book.

Zenas "Daddy" Sears, the white owner of Atlanta's major black radio station, WAOK, was one of the nation's foremost developers and producers of black rhythm and blues artists, and Phil Walden, of Macon's Capricorn Records, was the national leader in the development of rock bands such as the Allman Brothers, Marshall Tucker, and Dixie Dregs. Buddy Buie built one of the nation's most modern and efficient recording enterprises in his acclaimed Studio One operation in Doraville, Georgia, and was the guiding genius behind the development of the Classics IV, Lynyrd Skynyrd, and the Atlanta Rhythm Section, the superband that, with the promotional assistance of Alex Cooley (whose Southeast Music Hall became the gathering place of the nation's foremost musical groups), filled Georgia Tech's Grant Stadium twice for "Champagne Jam" concerts.

Artists from throughout the world came to Lowery, Buie, and Bob Richardson of Master Sound for professional advice and production assistance, and one of the fastest-rising recording labels in the nation is Atlanta's new Katz Family Records established by entertainment attorney Joel Katz. Katz has built one of the largest entertainment law firms in the nation and represents dozens of superstars in every field.

Perhaps the greatest strength of Georgia's music industry is its diversity, covering the spectrum of black artists from gospel singer Thomas Dorsey and soul singer James Brown to opera singer Jessye Norman and of white artists from country singer Alan Jackson to folk singer Hedy West and symphony and chorale conductors Robert Shaw and Yoel Levi.

Its concerts run the gamut from those of the Atlanta Symphony Orchestra in Chastain Park, to which thousands bring gourmet picnic baskets and candelabra to wine and dine, to a mix of popular and classical music each week during the summer to those by gospel groups at Christian Night Clubs where the strongest beverage served is coffee. There are also the highly successful music parks operated throughout the state attracting sellout crowds to hear top country artists. Country music nightclubs, pioneered by "Mama" Wynette Mitchem, have flourished. All-night gospel sings are popular and followers of the ancient system of singing by shaped notes hold an annual sacred harp sing, using the hymnal first compiled in 1844 by Georgians Franklin White and E. L. King.

Because there exists no ready reference work on the many personalities who have brought Georgia to musical greatness, I endeavored in 1984 to compile brief musical biographies of those men and women who have made major contributions to Georgia musical history either as native sons and daughters or as major personalities within the context of Georgia music.

With the opening of the Georgia Music Hall of Fame in Macon in the summer of 1996, I was encouraged by the good people at Mercer University Press to revise and add to the original volume. It was a challenge because so much has happened during the previous decade: Alan Jackson, Travis Tritt, Doug Stone, and Trisha Yearwood have burst like comets upon the Nashville scene. Atlanta has become even a greater mecca for Afro-American artists like Babyface, Kriss Kross, and "L. A." Reid.

I have endeavored to put these short biographical sketches together in a manner that will be both informative and enjoyable to read and will serve to give readers a better perspective of how Georgia music of today represents a blending of the black rhythm and blues music of the fields of South Georgia and the white traditional music of the mountains of North Georgia into the urban sounds of the metropolitan recording studios that are rapidly being homogenized into a common music embracing classical, country, gospel, rock, soul, and rhythm and blues that is enjoyed, appreciated, and sung by people of all ages and classes regardless of color, economic status, or place of residence.

Zell Miller
February 1996

LEE ROY ABERNATHY

While still in life, Lee Roy Abernathy personified the term "living legend" as if it had been coined for him. The colorful singer, composer, professor, impresario, innovator, and entrepreneur from Canton, Georgia, is called "Gospel Music Patriarch" by the *History of Gospel Music.* His Hall of Fame School of Music attracted drive-and-fly-in students from as far away as California. Lee Roy was larger than life in everything he did during his eighty years—from walking weekly to Atlanta to study conservatory music at the age of fifteen to writing the first singing commercials and devising and offering the world's only "guaranteed-to-play" piano course.

He wrote campaign songs for both Franklin D. Roosevelt and Eugene Talmadge, composed one of the all-time-best-selling gospel songs, was the first publisher of gospel sheet music, invented a typesetting system for setting music, and has been a member of the Gospel Music Hall of Fame since 1973.

Abernathy was literally "born into gospel music." His father, Dee Abernathy, was a gospel songwriter. His mother, Clara, took him in her arms when the three of them went to singing school three weeks after his birth on Friday the 13th of August, 1913, in the little North Georgia textile village of Atco. He had to stand on a Coca-Cola crate to sing first tenor in the Atco Quartet at the age of five and was tenor for the quartet five years later when they cut their first record with Columbia.

Two years later, his singing career was stalled for the next twenty years because of impacted tonsils that required extensive throat surgery. He continued with the group as its piano player when his sister Velma quit that spot to get married. When he was fourteen, a better job for his father at Canton Cotton Mill took him to the town that was to be his home intermittently and finally thereafter. He joined his father as piano player for the Abernathy Quartet, which he founded to sing at funerals in the area, and accompanied the group at the age of fifteen when it recorded "I'm Redeemed" and "Don't Forget to Pray" for RCA Victor. That year he also started his own quartet, the Modern Mountaineers, which made fifty Bluebird Records for fifty dollars each and played an extensive schedule of theater, church, and banquet engagements.

That same year he reached a crisis and turning point in his life when he was invited to play piano for the Electrical Workers Quartet in Atlanta, which sang both popular and gospel music. He quickly discovered to his embarrassment and dismay that he could not read the pop music. He went back home, closeted himself in a dark room for four days as a failure, and emerged with a vow that he would master all kinds of music so "there will never be anyone to set a piece of music in front of me that I can't play." That was the beginning of the development of the force in his life that he called "PMA"—Positive Mental Attitude. He taught PMA to all of his students and defined it in one of his songs in these words: "You can help to change the world if you'll just change, change your attitude."

Abernathy enrolled in the Atlanta conservatory, taking thirty-minute lessons each Saturday for the next three years; lacking any other means of transportation, he walked the forty-nine miles to and from Canton each week, often "trotting the last ten to fifteen miles to get home in time for the play of the Men's Bible Class on Sunday mornings." He paid five dollars for each of his lessons by walking from house to house giving music lessons for twenty-five cents each, an experience that planted in his mind the seeds for his famous mail-order piano course, which he began offering fourteen years later. At the age of nineteen he married Louise Ammons, the sixteen-year-old daughter of the mill supervisor who later would fire him for tardiness. The first piece of furniture they bought for their cotton mill village house was a piano—purchased even before they owned a bed.

Taking unemployment with PMA and as a signal to get on with his music career, Abernathy opened Lee Roy's Music Store in Dalton, where he taught private music lessons, organized and played in his own quartet, and began writing his piano course. He and his father wrote songs together, including "Won't We Have a Good Time" and "My Labor Will Be O'er." One of his father's solo efforts, "Don't Be Knockin'" was recorded by the Kingsmen. He began making movies of talent shows and gospel singings and was the first to use recording equipment and public address systems at gospel sings. He wrote the 1936 campaign song for FDR, "Good Times Are Coming Soon," which had to be shelved after the NRA was declared unconstitutional. He wrote Gene Talmadge's famous "Three-Dollar Tag Song" and personally hawked copies at Talmadge rallies for a nickel each, often making as much as one hundred dollars a Saturday. He recorded the Speer Family's first record in 1936 and conducted the first and only singing school ever taught on radio over station WBLJ in Dalton.

In 1942 he was the first to introduce piano arrangements of gospel music and in 1943 published the first sheet music in the gospel world—his own "I'll Thank My Savior for It." Despite ridicule from other gospel groups, which sold their songs in books rather than individually, he proved he could sell more of his single copies for fifty cents than they could of their books for only thirty-five cents. That same year he and Louise moved to Chattanooga, Tennessee, where he organized the Four Tones, with which he toured the country doing U.S.O. shows for servicemen. When two members of the quartet were drafted, the group was disbanded and Abernathy went to Atlanta, where he joined Billy Carrier, George Hughes, and Bill Lyles in reforming the Swanee River Boys. This was followed by a stint in Richmond, Virginia, playing the piano for the Rangers Quartet featured on station WRVA. In 1945 he completed his mail-order piano course after eight years of work, which, although the subject of many jokes, proved exceedingly popular and profitable and subsequently was offered throughout the world in every country having dependable post offices available to the general public.

It was during this period that he narrowly missed being a victim of Atlanta's tragic Winecoff Hotel fire, about which he wrote the controversial song, "The Burning of the Winecoff," which received the National Fire Protection award in 1946. Although Abernathy had a permanent room at the hotel and usually stayed there because of the gasoline shortage, he had been able to go home on the weekend of the fire because a friend had given him a coupon for three gallons of gas.

In 1946 Lee Roy introduced the "Battle of Songs" in Atlanta between himself and the Rangers and Hovie Lister and the Homeland Harmony Quartet. Later that year he joined the Homeland Harmony group, which subsequently recorded his hit song, "Everybody's Gonna Have a Wonderful Time Up There." The song swept the country under the title of "Gospel Boogie," selling more than five million records and was covered by almost every gospel group in the nation, as well as by such popular and country singers as Pat Boone, Johnny Mathis, and Johnny Cash. He and the group were the subject of much national publicity, including major articles in *Billboard* and *Radio Mirror*. In 1947 he and Homeland Harmony appeared on a closed circuit television show in Atlanta, for which he quickly wrote a special song entitled "Television" after being asked by the producer to do "something different." That also was the year he wrote his book, *it*, which now is out of print but is a classic account of historic gospel events.

Lee Roy Abernathy (left)

Lee Roy and Shorty Bradford, with whom he had worked off and on since 1939, left Homeland Harmony in 1949 to form the Happy Two and make cross-country tours for television shows, recordings, backup work, and commercials. It was during this time that Lee Roy wrote the nation's first singing commercials—the most famous of which was "You'd Better Get Wild Root Cream Oil, Charlie." Other memorable ones were for Halo Shampoo and B-Brand Insect Spray. The popularity of the Happy Two brought them an invitation to do a daily television show on WAGA-TV in Atlanta beginning in 1951. It continued five nights weekly for seven years. At the height of its popularity it was rated Number Three in the nation by both Nielson and *Cash Box*. Virtually every gospel group in the country appeared as guests on the program during its course. Also during this time he formed several other quartets, including the Miracle Men and the Lee Roy Abernathy Quartet. He and Bradford traveled more than five million miles for concerts and personal appearances throughout the United States and abroad.

In 1958 with a campaign chest of only five hundred dollars, Lee Roy became a candidate for governor of Georgia, traveling the byways of the state in a forty-foot road train with a red piano and a Coca-Cola crate for a bench. His campaign song was "Lee Roy's the Boy," sung to the tune of

"Casey Jones." He didn't win the race, but he attracted a lot of attention and much media coverage.

From 1959 until 1961 he studied for his doctorate in music at Golden Temple, Inc., in Knoxville and pursued other graduate studies in Chicago and Cincinnati. He also invented a typesetting system for setting music and in 1973 was elected to the Gospel Music Hall of Fame.

A pinched nerve forced him into temporary retirement for three years in 1969, but he recovered and spent most of his later years giving voice lessons fifty to sixty times a week to students who came from throughout the Southeast and as far away as Texas and California. He constructed a new, modern building, complete with the most modern musical, sound, and recording equipment for his Hall of Fame School of Music located across the road from his house in Canton.

This man, who once said he had "lived four or five lifetimes," died on May 25, 1993, at the age of eighty.

PAT ALGER

Pat Alger is the Georgia-born and -educated songwriter and performer who is regarded as the epitome of the "New Country" music that increasingly has characterized the hard edge of Nashville's output since the mid-eighties.

In a real sense, he is regarded as the major link between the folk and country styles that run the gamut of Nanci Griffith and Lyle Lovett on the extremes with Garth Brooks, Kathy Mattea, and Trisha Yearwood somewhere in between. Proof of his stature and influence in this regard is the fact that he not only is probably the one trendsetter who could have attracted, but also actually is the only one who did get, all five of these superstars and others to make appearances and sing backup on his own albums.

Alger grew up in LaGrange, Georgia, and studied architecture at Georgia Tech in Atlanta. But his interest in designing buildings played second fiddle to his writing of songs and performing at folk clubs. He forsook the drafting table after his first taste of songwriting success in 1980 when Livingston Taylor turned out a two-chart hit—Top Forty Pop and Top Ten Adult Contemporary—with his "First Time Love."

It was straight to Nashville after that where he concentrated on writing a catalog of material that attracted such greats as Brooks; Griffith; Mattea; Lovett; Dolly Parton; the Everly Brothers; Peter, Paul and Mary; Crystal Gayle; and Brenda Lee. He also performed both singly and as the opening act between 1984 through 1988 for the Everly Brothers for virtually all of their appearances in the United States and Europe.

He wrote two Number One hits for Mattea, "Goin' Gone" and "She Came from Fort Worth," plus her Top Five cut, "A Few Good Things Remain." Six of his songs have gone to Number One since January 1991, four of them for Brooks—"Unanswered Prayers," "The Thunder Rolls," "What She's Doing Now," and "That Summer." The other two were "Small Town Saturday Night" for Hal Ketchum and "Like We Never Had a Broken Heart" for Yearwood. Icing on the cake were his "True Love," which made the Top Five for Don Williams, and "Calloused Hands," a Top Twenty for Mark Collie.

Other notable tunes he turned out were Brooks's "The Night I Called the Old Man Out" from the album *In Pieces*, Mattea's "Seeds," Ketchum's

Zell Miller and Pat Alger

"Softer Than a Whisper," and Skip Ewing's "Rodeo Romeo."

Sugar Hill Records released Algar's first solo album, *True Love and Short Stories*, in 1991. It was critically acclaimed and featured appearances by Griffith, Lovett, Mattea, and Yearwood. His second was *Seeds* issued the following year and highlighted backups by Brooks, Mattea, Yearwood, and Tim O'Brien. He released *Notes and Grace Notes* when he switched to Liberty Records in 1994 and had a Liberty-sponsored tour of the United States and Europe.

He has a close relationship with folksingers Happy and Artie Traum and first emerged as a guitarist, vocalist, and songwriter with their Woodstock Mountains Revue. He produced the country-flavored "Ole Time Music" and "Southern Crescent Line" for that loosely knit group of

Woodstock area musicians, performing with such diverse talents as Maria Muldaur and bluegrasser John Herald. He and Griffith joined talents in the mid-eighties, cowriting her hits of "Once in a Very Blue Moon" and "Lone Star State of Mind." Griffith also was his cowriter on the Mattea hit, "Goin' Gone."

These accomplishments have brought Alger many significant recognitions. In 1992 he was named Songwriter of the Year by the Nashville Songwriters Association International and by *Music Row, Radio & Records,* and *Cash Box* magazines. ASCAP that year named him Jukebox Songwriter of the Year and, in 1992, Country Songwriter of the Year. He also has been the recipient of two Triple Play awards, the recognition given by the Country Music Association to those who have three Number One songs in a year.

He holds many leadership positions in the music industry. He is president of the Nashville Songwriters Association International, a member of the boards of directors of the Country Music Association, Leadership Music, and NARAS. He also serves on ASCAP's Writer Advisory Committee.

Alger's guitar style is simple and his vocals are relaxed in keeping with his folkie roots, but his record also proves that he can turn out the eccentric songs and tunes so favored by "New Country" stars of the 1990s.

ALLMAN BROTHERS BAND

Duane and Gregg Allman and the other master musicians who were their compatriots in the Allman Brothers Band struggled for years for the success they finally achieved. In doing so they developed the Macon, Georgia, Sound, which made their organization America's best answer to the British supergroups who had dominated rock music prior to their emergence in the seventies.

That the Allman Brothers Band was more than the "southern-fried boogie band," which some of its critics called it, is evidenced by the facts that it was integrated and that even after the tragic deaths of its two most talented members, Duane Allman and Berry Oakley, it participated in July 1973 at Watkins Glen in the largest rock concert in history, of which they costarred with the Grateful Dead.

In retrospect, the Allman Brothers Band must be credited with bringing rock music back to its no-frills roots of Southern country, soul, rhythm and blues, and jazz basics and establishing the soaring interplay and meticulous counterpoint of two lead guitars as the bedrock of America's new contemporary pop rock music. The group in its varying compositions both helped make and destroy Capricorn Records of Macon, Georgia, as the world's largest independent recording company. Although there have been many imitators of his work and style, no one has come close to equalling Duane as a virtuoso slide guitarist. It is impossible to speculate what the band might have accomplished had it been able to maintain the creative momentum Duane inspired.

Howard Duane and Gregory Lenoir Allman were born within thirteen months of each other in Nashville, Tennessee. After the killing of their soldier father by a hitchhiker, they moved with their mother in 1959 to Daytona Beach, Florida, where she became a CPA. Much to her dismay, they became contemporaries of black blues musicians. Duane first wrecked a motorcycle and then dropped out of school to teach himself to play the guitar as Gregg already did. They soon had their own school dance band, the Y-Teens, and in 1963 joined an integrated rock group called the House Rockers. They then became one of the most popular Daytona bands under the name, the Allman Joys.

When Gregg graduated from high school in 1965, they went to St. Louis where the Allman Joys enjoyed fair success playing honky-tonks and go-go bars. They did two albums, including a psychedelic single of the Willie Dixon blues number, "Spoonful," which were released on Did Records.

When the band folded in 1967, they went to Los Angeles at the suggestion of Bill McKuen, manager of the Nitty Gritty Dirt Band, and joined three Alabama musicians to form Hourglass. They signed a recording contract with Liberty Records that produced two bland, unsuccessful albums and threatened them with prosecution when they headed back home after becoming discouraged and fed up with living in "garbage motels."

In 1968 they teamed up briefly with drummer Butch Truck's band, the 31st of February, before Duane was invited by Rick Hall of Fame Studios to come to Muscle Shoals to back Wilson Pickett and convinced him to do his hit cover of the Beatles' "Hey, Jude." Intimidated by Liberty Records, Gregg returned to California to complete their contract. Hall signed Duane to a contract he sold to Jerry Wexler, of Atlantic Records, who sold it to Phil Walden of Macon, Otis Redding's former manager, as part of a deal in which Walden was to set up Capricorn as a custom label to be distributed by Atlantic.

Walden called Duane and asked him to assemble a band. Taking Jaimoe (Jai Johnny) Johanson, with whom he had played in Alabama, Duane went to Jacksonville where they slept on the floor at Truck's place and jammed with them and two members of a band known as Second Coming, featuring lead guitarist Dickey Betts and bassist Berry Oakley. Afterwards Duane stood in the doorway and declared: "Anybody in this room that's not gonna play in my band, you're gonna have to fight your way out."

It was March 1969 when he sent a telegram to Gregg to come back to be organist and vocalist. Gregg later recalled it arrived just as he was "building up nerve to put a pistol to my head." They moved to Macon where they lived in two rooms with a bath that did not work and slept on the floor on five double mattresses. They recorded their first Capricorn album, *The Allman Brothers Band*, in New York that summer. It won critical acclaim but enjoyed little success. They then hit the road to do five hundred concerts in the next two years. Their resources were so meager that they traveled in an Econoline van with eleven of them sleeping on two mattresses. At one time they were so broke they had to panhandle enough money to pay the toll across the Golden Gate Bridge to do a gig in the Fillmore West.

If it had not been for Duane returning periodically to Muscle Shoals for session work, they might not have made it at all. It was in Alabama that Duane began building his reputation as a top guitarist by backing such stars as Aretha Franklin and doing the slide work on Eric Clapton's "Layla" by Derek and the Dominoes.

They did their second album, *Idlewild South*, in October 1969, but it, too, was disappointing. Deciding they could not capture the awesome power of their concert performances in a studio, they achieved their break-through by doing their third album live. It was a double disc done in New York and titled *At the Fillmore East*. It became the band's first Gold record when released in 1971. It contained only seven songs but among them were the band's classic versions of "Statesboro Blues," "Hot Lanta," "Stormy Monday," "You Don't Love Me," "In Memory of Elizabeth Reed," and "Whipping Post."

With the thunderous bass of Oakley, the climbing call-and-response guitar duets and mercurial solos of Duane and Dickey and Gregg's growling vocals and inventive organ, it captured the All-mans at their

Allman Brothers Band

artistic peak and caused their popularity to soar like wildfire and their income to pyramid accordingly.

It was when they took their first vacation to enjoy the fruits of their labors that Duane was crushed to death in Macon on October 29, 1971, when his motorcycle skidded as he swerved to avoid an oncoming truck. His funeral was a media event in which the remaining band joined by other musicians from throughout the country staged a concert of his music behind the casket.

Oakley, who admired and sought to emulate Duane, never got over his depression and died in an almost identical motorcycle accident within three blocks of the first a little over a year later on November 11, 1972.

The band regrouped under Gregg and in late 1971 finished the album it had begun with Duane, *Eat a Peach,* which went to Platinum and yielded three chart singles, "Ain't Wasting Time No More," "Melissa," and "One Way Out." Chuck Leavell, a superb musician who later toured with the Rolling Stones and at that time had played with the American Eagles and Sundown, was recruited to replace Duane, and bassist Lamar Williams from the Deep South Spiritual Singers was tapped to take Oakley's place.

Even without its two foremost talents, the group found its greatest popularity with its Watkins Glen performance in July 1973 and the August release of its smash fifth album, *Brothers and Sisters,* which sold more than two million copies and brought a Number One single with Betts's "Ramblin' Man."

Gregg's marriage to Cher Bono, the birth of their son, Elijah Blue, and the divorce all made national headlines. The two did a joint album, *Two the Hard Way,* in 1977. These

Gregg Allman

things, plus the continuing dispute over the band's direction between Leavell who wanted to go jazzier and Betts who insisted on more country in their sound, resulted in the group's disintegration in late 1975.

Although several albums of their works were subsequently released, they did not get back together until 1979 when Gregg, Dickey, Butch, and Jaimoe reconstituted the band with the additions of guitarist Dan Tobler and bassist David Goldflies for an album and tour.

Gregg formed his own Gregg Allman Band in 1983, and in 1987 he had a Top Thirty album, *I'm No Angel.*

In 1982 Duane was inducted to the Georgia Music Hall of Fame with Gregg and his mother accepting the award. The Allman Brothers Band was inducted into the Rock and Roll Hall of Fame in 1996.

The reorganized band, with the addition of Warren Haines, won a Grammy for Best Instrumental with "Jessica" in 1996.

BILL ANDERSON

Perhaps the truest measure of success of country music superstar Whispering Bill Anderson of Avondale Estates, Georgia, is that *Billboard* magazine ranks him alongside his boyhood idol, Hank Williams, as one of the "True All-Time Greatest Country Music Songwriters." And, if that is not enough, add that, with fifty, he holds more BMI awards than any other composer and that he was elected to the Country Music Songwriters Hall of Fame before the age of forty.

The great irony of the career of James William Anderson II is that, while he did not grow up in poverty like many of his country music contemporaries, he probably is best known for his classic song about poverty, "Po' Folks," which gave the name to his band, one of the finest in the business, and the chain of restaurants with which his name is associated.

Born November 1, 1937, in Columbia, South Carolina, he was reared in Griffin and Decatur, Georgia, was torn between emulating Williams in music and Stan Musial in baseball, and gave up the latter to humor his mother's wish that he go to college. While studying journalism at the University of Georgia, he first covered sports for a Decatur weekly and the Atlanta dailies and then became a disc jockey, commuting from Athens to nearby Commerce, where he performed on an afternoon show with a rubber duck called "Josh" and started writing and recording songs he tried to sell through the mail-order house of TNT Records of San Antonio, Texas.

One of the songs was "City Lights," which he penned while sitting one night on the roof of the tallest building in Commerce, the three-story Andrew Jackson Hotel, and which TNT dismissed by pressing only five hundred copies and sending them to Anderson for personal distribution. He sent copies to fellow deejays and when Ray Price caught it on his car radio, he pronounced it "the best song I ever heard" and scrapped a recording he had scheduled for the following week in favor of it.

"City Lights" became the Number One song of 1955, earned a Gold record, and became an all-time country hit that decided Anderson on a musical career, which he launched disastrously with a roadtrip with Roger Miller that ended with their car breaking down in Arizona and their having to hock their record player to get back home. But, after finishing work on his degree in 1959, he headed to Nashville where that year another of his compositions, "That's What It's Like to Be Lonesome," made the Top Ten and he signed a contract with Decca (now MCA) Records.

In 1960 he made top chart levels with "Tips of My Fingers," which he recorded himself. The next year he wrote "Happy Birthday to Me," for Hank Locklin and did "Walk Out Backward" and the smash "Po' Folks" for himself, followed by a crossover hit "Mama Sang a Song" in 1962. But in 1963 he had his greatest year with "Still," which made it to the top in both the country and pop charts, brought him a Gold record, was named *Variety* magazine's Number One Song of the Year and won him recognition as both Male Vocalist and Top Country Songwriter of the Year, titles he would subsequently repeat four times in both categories. He had a second hit that year in "8 by 10" and scored his first international success when both were covered in England by Ken Dodd.

Most of his recordings of the sixties were of his own songs, among which were the hits, "I've Enjoyed As Much of This As I Can Stand," "I Love You Drops," "I Get the Fever," "Wild Weekend," "My Life," and "But You Know I Love You." He took Alex Zanetis's "Me" to the top in 1964. Other Anderson works were recorded by Porter Wagoner, Faron Young, Charlie Louvin, and Jean Shepherd.

He and Jan Howard won the first of his two Duet of the Year awards with their "For Loving You" in 1967, the second coming in the next decade for his work with Mary Lou Turner, "That's What Makes Me Love You" and "Sometimes." In 1970 he had a change-of-pace hit with "Where Have All the Heroes Gone" and charted Number Two with "Quits" and "The Corner of My Life."

In all he has more than five hundred songs to his credit, of which fifty-two have been single hits. He has done thirty-seven albums, received fifteen music trade paper awards, and been a regular on the Grand Ole Opry since 1961.

Anderson was third only to Porter Wagoner and the Wilburn Brothers in having a syndicated country music television show, and his *The Bill Anderson Show* was seen for nine years in more than one hundred cities coast-to-coast. He was the first country artist to host a network game show, doing ABC-TV's *The Better Sex*, has appeared in the ABC soap opera *One Life to Live*; is a frequent guest star on top variety, game, and talk shows, is host of the nationally syndicated television program *Backstage at the Grand Ole Opry*; and is a featured star of the Nashville Network. He has done five movies, composed and performed the title song for a sixth, and

Bill Anderson

narrated a seventh. He is an entrepreneur not only in the restaurant but also the music publishing business. His touring show logs one hundred thousand miles and more than a hundred days of performances throughout the country each year.

His classmate Billy Dilworth, who also is one of the ranking country deejays of the nation, calls the personable and soft-spoken Anderson "country music with style and class." Anderson, who objects to being called a "button-down hillbilly," denies being "goody-goody," and maintains that what he does is "just simply country music." He has avoided songs with certain overtones, having gone so far as to get Cal Smith to record his hit song, "The Lord Knows I'm Drinking," Conway Twitty "I've Never Been to Heaven," and Porter Wagoner "Cold Hard Facts of Life." He is amused at the reactions to his breathy singing style that flocks of admiring women find sexy.

He attributes the success of his songs to "empathy," which he defines as "the ability to identify with other people—put yourself in another man's place, feel what he feels, think what he thinks."

He continues to write both songs and prose. He cowrote Vince Gill's hit "Another Bridge to Cross, Another Bridge to Burn," an autobiography, *Whispering Bill,* and the hilarious *I Hope You're Living as High on the Hog as the Pig You Turned Out to Be.*

He also recorded on Curb Records an updated version of "Deck of Cards" during the Persian Gulf War.

Always at ease and smooth as silk, he hosts TNN's *Backstage at the Grand Ole Opry* and numerous Georgia Music Hall of Fame awards dinners. He was inducted into the Georgia Music Hall of Fame in 1985.

Bill Anderson, Little Richard, and Zell Miller

TONY ARATA

When Tony Arata writes a song, he does not have to peddle it. With the track record his compositions have established, he has the *creme de la creme* of country music superstars lined up begging to record it.

Take "The Dance" from Garth Brooks's album *Garth Brooks* in 1990. It went to Number One for three weeks in *Billboard* and *Radio & Records*. It was named Song of the Year by the Academy of Country Music and was nominated for Song of the Year by the Country Music Association in 1991. According to *Radio & Records*, it was the most-performed song of 1990.

In 1994 his "Dreaming with My Eyes Open" by Clay Walker and "I'm Holding My Own" by Lee Roy Parnell both hit Number One on the charts; and, in 1995, his "Here I Am" was a Number One single for Patty Loveless from her Country Music Association Album of the Year, *When Fallen Angels Fly*.

A list of his big songs is like a litany from the top of the ratings. Here is a partial reading: "Part of Me" by Suzy Boggus; "Same Old Story," "Face to Face," and "Kickin' and Screamin'" by Garth Brooks; "Man in the Mirror" and five other songs over three albums by Jim Glaser; "I Hear a Call" by Emmylou Harris; "Handful of Dust" and "Everybody's Equal" by Patty Loveless; "Slower" by Dan Seals; and "Same Old Story" by Tanya Tucker.

He cowrote "The Change" for Garth Brooks with Wayne Tester, "Someday I will Lead the Parade" for Patty Loveless, and "I Used to Worry" for Delbert McClinton with Scott Miller.

Born in Savannah in 1957, Arata graduated in journalism from Georgia Southern University and broke the family tradition of becoming school teachers, which had attracted his brother and sisters to the classroom, by moving to Nashville a decade ago to follow the calling of songwriting. His wife, Jaymi, received her masters degree from Georgia Southern and worked for Hyatt Hotels in Savannah and the Envoy Corporation in Nashville before becoming a full-time mother to their two daughters, Kate born in 1992 and Allison born in 1994.

Arata is a staff writer for Forerunner Music of Nashville, which has a copublishing agreement with Little Tybee Music, which he owns himself.

He is a member of the board of directors of the Nashville Songwriters Association International and is active in the affairs and programs of the American Society of Composers, Authors and Publishers, the National Academy of Recording Arts and Sciences, and the Country Music Association.

His father, Howard, resides on Tybee Island, and his wife's parents live on Wilmington Island.

CHET ATKINS

The musical mind boggles at the thought of what might have been the consequences to the future of country music had not a severe, chronic asthmatic condition forced Chester Burton Atkins to leave his stepfather's hardscrabble farm in the Clinch Mountain foothills near Luttrell in East Tennessee to live and grow up with his divorced music-teacher father in Mountain City, Georgia, in 1935 at the age of eleven.

Possibly, the lad the world now knows and admires as Chet Atkins, the incomparable virtuoso of the electric guitar and unexcelled impresario of homegrown musical talent, would not have grown up to become the "father" of what now is known as "The Nashville Sound," which transformed Nashville, Tennessee, into Music City, USA.

Chet Atkins was the discoverer and/or molding genius behind the development of such musical superstars as Dolly Parton, Willie Nelson, Waylon Jennings, Floyd Cramer, Jim Reeves, Hank Locklin, Don Gibson, Skeeter Davis, Connie Smith, Dottie West, Jerry Reed, Porter Wagoner, Charley Pride, and George Hamilton IV.

Thus the state of Georgia can claim as much credit for giving country music one of its all-time great artists and leaders as can the state that birthed him and reaped the greatest rewards of his talent and vision. His Georgia heritage has been enshrined in musical history for all to know with his induction into the Georgia Music Hall of Fame.

Atkins would have earned his place in the record books as the winner of more Country Music Association awards than any other performer if for no other reason than proving that country musicians can play more than three-chord hillbilly songs. In fact, his sophisticated and polished approach to the medium brought perfection to the unique finger-picking style of guitar performances initiated by his idol, Merle Travis, in which the melody is played by the fingers or a pick held by the fingers and the accompanying base line is added with the thumb.

Classy excellence was so much a hallmark of his brand of country music that he was fired by radio station KWTO in Springfield, Missouri, where he played in the late 1940s and was given the nickname of "Chet" by his friend, booking agent Si Simon, because his music was "not hillbilly enough." It was a pivotal turning point in his career because Simon sent some transcriptions of his playing to RCA Victor producer Steve Sholes who signed him to the contract that ultimately led to his heading the recording studio RCA opened in Nashville and, in 1968, becoming a RCA vice president.

But back to the beginning of the life that culminated in his impact upon modern American music and culture. Despite the long hours and hard work he had to put in on the farm in East Tennessee, Atkins showed a natural bent for music by mastering the ukelele at an early age and, by nine, becoming sufficiently proficient on the guitar and the fiddle to play at Saturday night hoedowns, roadhouses, and tourist camps. He traded his stepfather two rifles (some sources state an old pistol) for a guitar to begin his largely self-taught journey into music.

When his father brought him to Georgia, his guitar-playing helped him overcome teasing about his hillbilly accent and earned him not only the attention of the girls but also the gratitude of his male compatriots for providing cover for their school rest room craps games. While they gambled in the toilet, Atkins would play outside; and, when he began singing, it was his signal to them that the principal or some faculty was coming. That boyhood experience in the rest room gave him the idea in his later career for creating the first recording echo chamber.

As a teenager, he got a job with the National Youth Administration and saved his money to buy an electric guitar, like the one his older stepbrother Jimmy played with the Les Paul Trio. Because there was no electricity in Mountain City, he accompanied his father to Columbus in order to play wherever he could find an available electrical outlet. That led to a job playing on Parson Jack's popular radio show on station WRBL.

When his father left for a war job in Cincinnati and young Atkins was turned down by the draft because of his asthma, he went to Tennessee and landed a performing job on the Archie Campbell/Bill Carlisle Show on radio station WNOX in Knoxville. Three years later he was being heard coast-to-coast from radio station WLW in Cincinnati, followed by stints with Red Foley in Nashville and the disastrous (but fortunately brief) detour as a radio performer in Missouri.

He made his first recording for RCA in 1947 and recorded his first significant hit, "The Galloping Guitars," in Atlanta in 1949. In 1947 he returned to Knoxville to play with Homer Haynes and Jethro Burns, the latter of whom subsequently became his father-in-law. His best known personal composition is the classic 1953 "Country Gentlemen."

Chet Atkins

In 1950 he joined Mother Maybell and the Carter Sisters and accompanied them to the Grand Ole Opry. That was also when he began recording sessions with scores of major and minor artists, notably Hank Williams's "I'll Never Get Out of This World Alive" and the Carlisles' "No Help Wanted."

When he came to Nashville with RCA, customers were tired of fiddle and steel, and country record sales were in a nose dive. That was when he, and to lesser extents Owen Bradley of Decca and Don Law of Columbia, came up with the Nashville Sound and started making records with guitars, pianos, horns, vocal choruses, and new and unusual instrumental and vocal sounds.

Atkins scored successes with Jim Reeves's "Four Walls" and Don Gibson's double-sided smash hits, "Oh Lonesome Me" and "I Can't Stop Loving You." He mixed flamenco, country, pop, and rock and really made his mark and perfected his new sound by adapting the approach songwriter Don Robertson took in bending piano notes like a steel guitar on his demo of "Please Help Me, I'm Falling" and teaching it to Floyd Cramer. Two smash recordings resulted—Hank Locklin's "Falling" and Cramer's "Last Date." He followed up with Boots Randolph's Top Ten "Yakety Sax" and his own guitar version, "Yakety Axe."

Then he signed Parton, Reed, Jennings, and Nelson; gave the world its first black country singer in Pride; did various RCA pop sessions in Nashville with Perry Como and other mainstream headliners; won Grammys with albums he cut with his two greatest idols and inspirations, Merle Travis and Les Paul; and performed and recorded with the Boston Pops.

He was the youngest performer ever inducted into the Country Music Hall of Fame, won thirteen Grammys between 1967 and 1993, received the first Country Music Association Instrumentalist of the Year award in 1967 and eight more since, and has had a street named for him in Nashville's Music Row.

He resigned from RCA in displeasure over the corporate direction of record-making in 1981 and signed with Columbia the next year. He beat the "Big C" of colon cancer in 1973 and, hale and hearty in his seventies, remains a guitar picker at heart, modestly oblivious to the fact that he, perhaps more than any other one individual, is responsible for changing the face of country music as we know it today.

He was inducted into the Georgia Music Hall of Fame in 1995.

ATLANTA RHYTHM SECTION

The Atlanta Rhythm Section was composed of six of the most talented young musicians of their or any other time; they have been molded and merchandised by the genius of songwriter/producer Buddy Buie.

Though some critics have viewed them as no more than a Southern boogie band "with class," they have credentials to prove they collectively can produce the magic their publicity promises of making audiences feel a part of their music. As proof of their magic they performed at the White House and have had the cheering ovation of more than sixty-one thousand fans who packed their celebrated Champagne Jam in 1978.

The New York Times calls the group, which was based at Doraville, Georgia, "the best the South has to offer," but an English critic came closer to their true ranking in pronouncing them "the quintessential American band."

The Atlanta Rhythm Section was not so much the product of creation as evolution, and if it could be said to have had any starting point, that probably would have to be fixed as the time of the migration of Dennis Yost and the Classics IV from Jacksonville to Atlanta because it was from that group that guitarist J. R. Cobb and keyboardist Dean Daugherty came and the Cobb-Buie songwriting team developed.

With Barry Bailey on the lead guitar, Paul Goddard on the bass, and Robert Nix on the drums, they first sat as a group in 1970 to backup Roy Orbison in a recording session; with the addition of lead vocalist Ronnie Hammond, a recording engineer who could also play guitar, keyboard, and drums, they established themselves as Atlanta's best and most demanded studio backup group. At the same time, Buie and engineer Rodney Mills, said to be "one of rock and roll's great natural resources," were developing Studio One as one of the nation's finest recording facilities.

Unlike other contemporary groups, ARS shunned gimmicks, antics, and flashy costuming to emphasize collective and individual talents in the development of a hybrid brand of rock 'n' roll, embracing as much British rock as traditional Southern rhythm and blues and incorporating melodic strains missing in the music of other Southern bands.

There was a strong emphasis on songs, particularly those written by Cobb and Buie, as Buddy searched for "the perfect sound." These efforts,

*Atlanta Rhythm Section
with Governor Carter, Buddy Buie, and J. R. Cobb*

however, tended to keep them in the studio and to give them a faceless image, and it was not until they "took to the streets" with a series of concerts that their work began to be recognized and their albums to sell well.

Although the Cobb-Buie team had written a number of smash successes for the Classics IV, beginning with "Spooky" in 1968, the Atlanta Rhythm Section did not achieve a hit until its sixth album, *A Rock and Roll Alternative*. From this, their top single, "So Into You," skyrocketed to the top and gave the group its first Gold record in 1977. That fall they attracted fifty thousand fans to their Dog Day Rock Fest at Grant Field and, with the help of promoter Alex Cooley, topped that with their record Champagne Jam the following year. Also in 1978 Chip Carter invited them to entertain at the birthday party given his father at the White House; the president commented that they had much in common in that his and their critics said they "didn't have a chance when they started."

The tag "Champagne Jam" stuck and has been applied to ARS music since. In 1979 they had another pair of singles, "Do It or Die" and a revival of "Spookey," and issued a double album of their earlier work, including the minor hit "Doraville," written by Buie, Bailey, and Nix in

1974. In 1980 their tenth album, *The Boys from Doraville*, created a stir with "Cocaine Charlie," "Rough at the Edges," and "Next Year's Rock 'n' Roll" and featured the group's new drummer, Roy Yeager.

Three of the band's six members are from Georgia. Barry Bailey grew up in Decatur and started playing guitar on a twenty-dollar Sears Silverstone when he was twelve. Paul Goddard's musical career started in Rome, Georgia, where he beat the vents of the kitchen stove to get different tunes at the age of four until his parents upgraded him to a ukelele. And Ronnie Hammond is from Macon, where he played drums, guitar, and keyboards for the Celtics. Cobb and Nix got their starts with Dennis Yost in Jacksonville, and Daugherty came from Alabama by way of the Roy Orbison organization.

The catalyst of the organization was Buie, who not only gave the band its song-oriented melodic style but also produced its quality recordings in his Studio One. He insisted that none of the ARS songs run over four minutes, a restraint not characteristic of other rock groups of any section. As a songwriter he had more than twenty chart records in the sixties; in addition to the Rhythm Section, he also has worked with stars such as Tommy Roe and Bobby Goldsboro. He said he is "unashamed" of his love of commercial music and was in New York City writing it when Atlanta music entrepreneur Bill Lowery lured him south with the publication of "Party Girl." Atlanta and Georgia have been his home ever since.

DALLAS AUSTIN

Dallas Austin does not have to file a claim for his place among the most influential and successful songwriter/producers of the 1990s. The twenty-four-year-old recording prodigy from Columbus, Georgia, has turned out the hit records to prove that he already is there.

His credits for 1995 alone speak for themselves. He is the man who gave the world TLC's "Creep," Madonna's "Secret," and Monica's "Don't Take It Personal (Just One of Dem Days)." He has also been a principal figure in the production of Michael Jackson's "HIStory." And, if those are not convincing enough, he started off 1996 with sophomore albums for Joi and Usher, remixing singles for Michael and Janet Jackson and Georgia's R.E.M., and working with Fishbone, the legendary black rock-and-roll band, on their offerings for Austin's new label, Rowdy.

Austin moved from Columbus to Atlanta in 1986 after learning first the guitar and then the keyboards under the tutelage of Jimmy Nolan, who plays lead guitar for James Brown. Although he never has had formal lessons, he has played in school marching and talent-show bands with much older performers and smilingly admits that he "can do a little something on everything."

He produced his first song in 1989, a moderately successful single, "Hey Mr. DJ," for Joyce Irby, a former member of Klymaxx, and followed that up by scoring his first Gold single with "I Will Always Love You" for Troop. Things really took off for him when he wrote and produced a majority of ABC's (Another Bad Creation) double-Platinum album, *Callin' at the Playground Ya Know*, which brought forth two Top Ten pop singles in "Iesha" and "Playground."

He wrote and produced most of the Boyz II Men debut album, *Cooleyhigh-harmony*, which with eight million in sales worldwide became the best-selling album in R&B history and earned him *Billboard*'s Top Pop Producer of 1991 designation before his twenty-first birthday.

He went from that high to producing and writing the majority of the tracks for TLC's first album, *Ooooooohh . . . On the TLC Tip*, which sold more than three million copies, with two of his songs from it becoming Top Ten pop singles and turned that group into headliners and winners at the 1996 Grammy awards show.

Besides creative work done by his production company, Dallas Austin Recording Projects (DARP, Inc.), he has established and owns several subsidiary companies that operate under its umbrella. DARP Studios is regarded as the premiere recording facility in Atlanta and has turned out recordings for such diverse artists as George Clinton, Jazzy Jeff and the Fresh Prince, Madonna, Nine Inch Nails, TLC, and Too Short. DARP producers, embracing Arnold Hennings, Tim Kelley and Bob Robinson, Debra Killings, PME, Spearhead X, and Colin Wolfe, are working with, among others, Boyz II Men, the Barrio Boyz, Color Me Badd, De La Soul, Dr. Dre, Johnny Gill, Hi-Five, Madonna, Erick Sermon, Shanice, Silk, Tracie Spencer, and Too Short.

And last, but not least, is his Rowdy Records, a joint venture with Arista, which released fourteen-year-old Monica's debut album, *Miss Thang*, and is producing solo albums by Jamal and Mr. Malik, both formerly of the rap duo Illegal, which won the Best Rap Single award of 1993 from *Billboard*.

"I got all this by writing songs," the humble and down-to-earth Austin says, emphasizing that his goal is to be able to "write songs like Babyface," and adding, "I don't value the money as much as my heart and respect."

WENDY BAGWELL AND THE SUNLITERS

Wendy Bagwell is an ex-marine with a flair for telling funny stories and writing and arranging captivating music. With his group the Sunliters, he has made gospel singing fun the world over and has collected a string of impressive awards to prove it.

Wendy, a successful businessman whose home is Smyrna, Georgia, has tickled the funny bones of people all around the globe with his hilarious accounts of his childhood escapades and the experiences of the other Sunliters and himself in their international travels. His recording, "Here Come the Rattlesnakes," not only became a Gold record but also earned him a special award from the Gospel Music Association and selection as Comedian of the Year by *Record World.* He attributes the success of his comedy to the fact that, while other entertainers have experiences similar to those he relates, "They just have more sense than to get on stage and tell about them."

Jerri Morrison and Jan Buckner, the two female Sunliters, have been acclaimed for their unique blending harmony, and "Little Jan," as she is called by the group, has received the Female Vocalist of the Year award of the Gospel Music Association. She plays the piano, harp, bass guitar, and other instruments and works with Wendy in writing and arranging all of the group's music. Jerri is a one-woman rhythm section with her tambourine, casabel, and other percussion instruments and is called "Leather Lungs" by Wendy, who credits her powerful voice for what he calls the fact that "hardly nobody knows I can't sing." The five men who complete the band play seven different instruments among themselves.

Attesting to the group's popularity abroad is its choice by the U.S. State Department to sponsor it on an extended tour of Europe and the presentation to it of the Showmanship Award of the United States Government. In addition to the numerous awards the Sunliters have received from the Academy of Recording Arts and Sciences, they also hold the Pioneer Award of the Southern Gospel Music Association and the Marvin Norcross Award presented by *Singing News* and considered the highest honor that can be bestowed on any person or group in the gospel music industry.

In 1990, the group was inducted into the Georgia Music Hall of Fame. And they have not slowed down yet. The concerts, hits, and honors keep coming, including *Voice* magazine's Diamond Fan Award in 1992 and 1993, Number One song in *Cash Box* for "Walk around Me Jesus," and a Grammy in 1995.

Wendy Bagwell and the Sunliters

RAZZY BAILEY

No country music star ever hit bottom harder or bounced to the top more spectacularly than Razzy Bailey, the poor kid who grew up in Big Snapper Creek, Alabama. He paid his dues in the honky-tonks of Georgia and Florida and now retires to the farm he bought near LaGrange to reflect upon the events of a checkered life that proves that truth is both stranger and more colorful than fiction.

Born on Valentine's Day in 1939 and named for his father, Erastus, a cotton mill laborer, sometime truck driver, and amateur picker and songwriter, Razzy grew up without the comforts of indoor plumbing and electricity. He learned to play the guitar on an instrument "with a neck so warped it looked more like a bow and arrow" and to sing the blues from the black fieldhands with whom he worked. He took a leadership role in the Future Farmers of America so that he could play in the LaFayette, Alabama, chapter's band, which he helped to win second place in state competition.

From the time he put all his savings at the age of ten into making a dimestore recording, his undeviating goal was to make it as a writer, singer, and recorder of songs. His first job after graduating from high school was with a band playing a club between Columbus and LaGrange, Georgia, which was shut down four months later when the highway was closed.

He married his high school sweetheart, Sandra Pressley, at the age of nineteen and took a succession of daytime jobs as butcher, soft-drink delivery truck driver, and insurance and furniture salesman to support his growing family and to subsidize his nighttime playing in whatever locales he could find a slot, including an Atlanta strip joint. The closest he came to success was when he persuaded Atlanta music publisher Bill Lowery to have Joe South, Billy Joe Royal, and Freddy Weller record "9,999,999 Tears," a song he wrote (which would become a hit a decade later) only to have it flop.

The longest musical engagement he had during this period was a trio he formed and appropriately named Daily Bread, which became the house band for a club in Naples, Florida, for six months. He did some recordings, mostly on minor labels, and came to the attention of Joe Mascolo (who later would remember him when he moved to RCA) when he cut "Stolen

Brenda Lee, Zell Miller, Freddy Weller, and Razzy Bailey

Moments," "Dancing on Brimstone," "I Hate Hate," and "Peanut Butter" for MGM, none of which went anywhere at the time.

He moved to Macon in 1976 where he signed a contract with Phil Walden's Capricorn Records. His drinking, he admits, had become excessive, and his wife took their children and left him. The Razzy Bailey story could have ended right there had he not turned in desperation to psychic June Mahoney of Cassadaga, Florida, who inspired him to listen to his "inner guts." She advised him to seek his release from Walden and predicted one of his songs would become a hit if he would go back to Nashville and try pitching them again. Shortly thereafter, Mascolo recommended Bailey's material to Dickie Lee, whose rerecordings of "9,999,999 Tears" and "Peanut Butter" made the first a Number One hit and carried the second to top chart levels. This opened the long-closed doors, and RCA started to issue some of his singles in 1978.

"What Time Do You Have to Be Back in Heaven" charted in August and lasted to the end of the year. In 1979 he had successes with "Tonight

She's Going to Love Me," "If Love Had a Face," and "I Ain't Got No Business Doing Business Today."

Between 1980 and 1983 he had eight straight Top Ten smashes and five Number One singles: "Loving Up a Storm," "I Keep Coming Back," "Friends," "Midnight Hauler," and "She Left Love All over Me." As his name and sound became known, his way with translating heartaches and everyday experiences into songs with which the working public could identify made a him a success. His work won him awards as New Male Vocalist of the Year from the Academy of Country Music and *Record World* and *Cash Box* magazines. He has appeared on *Hee Haw, Austin City Limits,* and the *Mike Douglas Show,* and has raised the prospect of doing movies, which is the next dimension he wishes to add to his career.

Many persons, hearing him for the first time, are surprised to learn that he is white, and even Charlie Pride has commented upon the remarkable way in which Razzy has captured the bluesy sound, saying, "You can get away with singing like a black; I can't." Bailey says his singing style and musical sound were not developed consciously but rather are the products of an upbringing in which he was "influenced a lot by black farm workers" with whom he toiled as a lad in "the most authenic context for rural blues in the country, the Alabama fields." The result is what the critics call "a rich, butterscotch sound" in which "a tremulous, almost rhythm and blues lushness sticks to his voice."

Perhaps his greatest pleasure and satisfaction comes from the fact that he and his father, from whom he learned his soulful licks on the guitar and banjo, teamed up as coauthors on several records.

JOHN BERRY

John Berry has been described by *Country Music* magazine's Bob Allen as "Nashville's mid-1990s answer to Pavarotti."

It is an apt summation of the big, burly country-pop power balladeer whose booming, mellifluous, almost operatic, baritone can command the hushed and rapt attention of the most boisterous nightclub audience. He is a serious musician who writes his own songs, initially recorded and produced his own albums, directs his own band, and does things both musicwise and careerwise in "my way" to a degree that would leave even a Sinatra in the shade.

Although his career was sidelined by surgery for a colloid brain cyst the very same week in 1993 that his Grammy-nominated single, "Your Love Amazes Me," first hit Number One on the charts, he never has lost sight of his goals or faltered in his determination to decide and direct his own musical destiny.

Born in Aiken, South Carolina, he grew up in Atlanta where, unlike many of his contemporaries, he was influenced less by country music than by such diverse performers as John Denver, Jackson Browne, and silky-voiced soul groups such as the Stylistics of Philadelphia. He began writing his own songs as a youngster, but joined but one band because, as he put it: "I decided early on that I wasn't going to throw the fate of my career in with other musicians who didn't know what they wanted to do with their lives, because I knew what I wanted to do."

He really did not get started toward his goals until in 1985, when in his mid-twenties, he decided to move from Atlanta, where the best he had been able to do was $100-a-week from a part-time gig at a music store, to Athens, where he quickly began earning $600-a-week or more from his music alone.

His first Athens venue was in a restaurant called Wrappers, where he became so popular with the college crowd that the owners converted it into a nightclub. From there he became a fixture in various clubs around the University of Georgia.

When he was not playing the clubs, he was busy in the recording studio he established in his new home, working sometimes nonstop for twenty-four hours a day. He did five albums, for which he wrote all the songs, and then did two more—*Things Are Not the Same* and *Saddle the Wind*—in professional studios with financing from his own pocket and the help of friends. The *Wind* album was released in 1990 and sold more than twelve thousand copies locally and paid for itself within a few months.

During his second week in Athens, he met his future wife, Robin, in a nightclub, but it took him two years to persuade her to go out with him. Eventually, she not only married him but also became a popular singer with his band and a coperformer in the Christmas Show he produces yearly for his church, the Green Acres Baptist Church of Athens.

In 1992 John and Robin decided that, while they never would leave their home on a farm near Athens, they would begin making regular trips to do industry showcases in Nashville. Although they had trouble getting anybody who was somebody in the recording business to come, they did succeed in attracting Herky Williams, an A&R executive at that time with Liberty Records, who had heard about Berry from his sister who became a fan while attending the University of Georgia.

Williams was so impressed that he insisted that his boss, Jimmy Bowen, the head of Liberty Records, attend one of Berry's future showcases. Bowen's reaction was so favorable that, afterwards, he walked up to Berry and said, "Let's make some records."

The result was the hit single, "Your Love Amazes Me," which garnered a Grammy nomination and headlined the Platinum-selling Liberty, now Capitol, debut album, *John Berry*.

Berry began barnstorming the country in the same methodical way he planned and carried out the Nashville showcases, but he began having continuous headaches, which culminated in his "blanking out" in a performance in Philadelphia. He managed to do one subsequent show in Washington, D.C., before catching a flight home—which he does not remember—to be with Robin who had gone into labor with their second child. A nurse at the hospital took one look at him and ordered him to the emergency room, which called in a neurosurgeon.

A CAT scan revealed the cyst and, fortunately, after initially considering a craniotomy, which would have involved taking off the top of his skull, his doctors decided to try a new laser-camera technique through which the cyst would be drained through holes drilled into each side of the skull. Major anesthesia could not be used when the surgical cage and clamps were bolted to his skull; Berry described the resulting experience as "unbelievable!"

"Something like that does give you a new perspective," he relates. "I don't seem to be as possessed about things as I was before. It takes a while, but there's a lot of growth that comes out of something like that. . . . Not that I'd recommend it to anyone."

Berry resumed performing within a month of the surgery and now has a tour bus in which his entire family, including his third child born since the operation, can accompany him. He also garnered Country Music Association nominations for the Horizon Award, which goes to the top newcomer, and the Top Male Vocalist award, which recognizes veteran performers.

"Music is a very serious thing to me. I've never done just fun music," he elaborates in describing the past, present, and future of his career.

"I've finally found, musically speaking, what I do best and what I need to be doing; that is, songs that really say something and which, technically and emotionally, challenge me with their range.

"I'm also planning on spending a whole lot more time writing. I just feel like I have a whole lot of things I want to say; and this sure seems like the right time to try and say them."

NORMAN BLAKE

Few but the most ardent purists among the devotees of bluegrass, folk, and traditional music will recognize the name of Norman Blake.

But almost any music lover will know to whose work you refer if you mention that of the dynamic and stunning lead guitarist on Bob Dylan's "Nashville Skyline Rag" and Joan Baez's "The Night They Drove Old Dixie Down."

Small wonder then that this talented artist who was born in Chattanooga, Tennessee, in 1938 and grew up in Rising Fawn, Georgia, and Trenton, North Carolina, has been named by *Guitar Player* magazine as the nation's fourth "Best Country Guitarist" behind Roy Clark, Merle Travis, and Jerry Reed.

His virtuosity in acoustic music and his mastery of the old-time style not only on the guitar but also on the mandolin, dobro, fiddle, and autoharp has made him in great demand both as a backup musician and as a solo performer.

His Rising Fawn string ensemble, composed of himself on those instruments, his wife Nancy on cello and single-row accordian, and James Bryan with a fiddle mastered under the tutelage of Bill Monroe, has turned out some of the most versatile and successful acoustic albums of the last twenty years.

Since dropping out of high school to play mandolin for the Dixie Drifters, he has made guest appearances on the Grand Ole Opry; cut an acclaimed bluegrass album titled *12 Sheets of Bluegrass*; played with John Hartford, Vasser Clements, and Tut Taylor who has called him "one of the finest guitar pickers alive"; and toured as a backup musician with June Carter. This led to a stint as a regular on the *Johnny Cash Television Show*. He was also featured with the Nitty Gritty Dirt Band on its monster album, *Will the Circle Be Unbroken*. He was a guitarist and dobroist on Bob Dylan's *Nashville Skyline* album and toured and recorded with John Harford.

Blake particularly loves to play traditional Appalachian music and mourns the demise of bluegrass popularity. Although much of his work follows the style of Doc Watson, he does not conform to any category of traditional, bluegrass, or progressive music but combines elements of all and uses a thumb and a finger pick to mix in bass runs and Carter Family-style leads on the guitar.

He is a guitar picker's guitar picker, a back porch down-home singer who adds authenticity to country music. His personal musical preference is railroad songs such as his classic "Last Train from Poor Valley."

Norman Blake

HAMILTON FREDERICK BOHANNON

One of the most innovative and creative of contemporary American musicians is Hamilton Frederick Bohannon, the former music teacher from Newnan, Georgia. Known professionally by just his last name, he had a hit laden career spanning three decades.

For five years, he was the house conductor for Motown Records and led his twenty-seven-piece band, Bohannon and the Motown Sound, in backing the recordings of such stars as Diana Ross and the Supremes, Gladys Knight and the Pips, Martha Reeves and the Vandellas, the Spinners, the Four Tops, the Temptations, the Miracles, Marvin Gaye, and Smokey Robinson.

A graduate of Atlanta's Clark College in music education, Bohannon left the classroom to perform in a Georgia band with guitarist Jimi Hendrix. He came to the attention of Stevie Wonder, who made him his drummer from 1965 through 1967 and paved the way for him to become musical head of the Motown operation. In that capacity he established "The Beat" as his musical trademark and became identified by both his soulful manner of conversing with the band and the ever-present flower in his lapel.

He wrote, arranged, directed, produced, and published music for drums and played drums for all of the compositions on all of the nine Motown albums he recorded. He became the first artist since the Beatles to have two top records on the singles charts in the same week. His 1978 album, *Summertown Grove*, is considered a classic combination of jazz and disco tunes. Such notables as Grammy-winning arranger Jerry Hey, Michael Henderson, Wah-Wah Watson, and Ray Parker, Jr., were members of his band.

He severed his connection with Motown when it moved to the West Coast; he then signed with Mercury Records to do five popular albums, including his biggest hit, *Let's Start the Dance,* in the seventies. He founded his own Phase II Records, Ltd., and in 1983 joined Charles Fach, who left Mercury to establish Compleat Records, in a joint recording venture of their two companies to issue another Bohannon album and single under the title of "Make Your Body Move," which he wrote, arranged, and directed in collaboration with Ray Parker, Jr.

During the Phase II years he also did "You're the One," "April, My Love," "Thoughts and Wishes," and the soulful "Take the Country to N.Y. City" with fellow Georgian Jean Carne.

He stopped touring in 1980 and devoted himself to the publishing business and to spending time with his family. In 1989, he recorded an album for MCA, *Here Comes Bohannon*, but his time in the 1990s has mostly been spent licensing his music through his Bohannon Ponteverde Music. Some artists who have utilized his work include Ed O. G. and de Bulldogs, Young MC, Bell Bro DeVoe, and 1993 Grammy winner, Digoble Planets, whose Platinum album *Reaching* featured two Bohannon compositions. He also wrote the music for the movie *Encino Man* and television's *Entertainment Tonight*. In 1996, he was planning to record for Kaper Records and also work with his son on an album.

Hamilton Frederick Bohannon

TONI BRAXTON

Trendy *People* magazine listed her among the most beautiful women in the world and called her mesmerizing voice "unique enough to make her the model to match in years to come." Mass audience *Time* magazine declared her "destined for pop diva-dom." The staid and stuffy *New York Times* pronounced her "rich, throaty, alto [and] torchy lovelorn style a throwback to an earlier era." With so broad a spectrum of the media in agreement as to the excellence and promise of Toni Braxton, the talented and charismatic young singer and pianist from Severn, Maryland, there could be no doubt, as *Ebony* magazine put it, that she "has arrived, . . . [and] you can bet she'll be around for a long time."

The crown jewel in the stable of recording stars being groomed and promoted by Atlanta's soaring new recording enterprise, LaFace Records, and its ambitious, visionary, and energetic coowners, Antonio "L. A." Reid and Kenny "Babyface" Edmonds, Braxton went into musical orbit with her first effort, two chart-topping singles taken from LaFace's multiPlatinum-plus soundtrack from the Eddie Murphy movie *Boomerang* in 1992. The first was her duet with her boss, Babyface, "Give U My Heart," and the second was her solo hit, "Love Should Have Brought You Home."

Most stars make movie soundtracks after they become known, but with Braxton it was the opposite, a fact that gave her a great advantage in providing a margin of sufficient time to put together her debut album bearing her name, *Toni Braxton*, which was in keeping with the LaFace policy of creating quality music. Accordingly, it has sold more than seven million copies; won three Grammy, three American Music, and two Soul Train awards, as well as producing two Number One Gold singles, "Another Sad Love Song" and "Breathe Again." She also was nominated for a fourth Grammy in 1996 for Best Female R&B Vocal for her "Baby, Brandy, I Belong to You."

The phenomenal album was planned and crafted so carefully that its songs were a dazzling—often described as "breathtaking"—showcase of her range and prowess as a sensual, passionate, and vibrant young songstress who can touch every mood with consummate ease. She was able to switch from the hauntingly-soulful "Another Sad Love Song" to the sensual and jazzy "Seven Whole Days," both products of the pen of Babyface. She

Toni Braxton

proved she could groove with the best of them with the upbeat "I Belong to You."

She ran the gamut of emotions of tenderness with "You Mean the World to Me," joy with "Spending My Time," melancholy with "Breathe Again," pain with "Best Friends," and sexuality with "Candlelight." She says she endeavored to do an album that "expresses who I am—a typical young woman who's been through some of life's experiences."

Braxton says she has been singing since she could walk and got a lot of practice singing with her four younger sisters in their church choir.

During high school she entered every local talent show she could find, sneaked to "watch" *Soul Train* when her parents were not around, mastered the piano, and began writing her own songs. She says she was influenced by the "Eighties Music" of Whitney Houston, Chaka Kahn, Quincy Jones, and Stevie Wonder. She was studying to be a teacher at Bowie State University when she was discovered by the LaFace organization.

She has made appearances on all major television talent outlets—the *Today Show, Good Morning America,* the *Tonight Show,* and *Entertainment Tonight.* The videos she made for her hit singles have been in heavy rotation on VH1, MTV, BET, and the Box.

Now known in the trade as "The First Lady of LaFace," she says she always can fall back on being a teacher if her music career should fizzle.

"I just want people to love and appreciate the music because I sing it from my soul," she says. "Just having the chance to make a living as a singer is incredible to me."

BRICK

Three young black men who formed a rock group called Hellaphanalia while studying at Atlanta's Morris Brown College were the nucleus of a musical group that came to be called Brick, which became one of the most popular and successful acts in the funk-rock scene since 1975. The group of five incredibly talented, college-trained musicians translated the positive feelings they had in common about their Southern heritage into a hybrid musical style combining soul, disco, and jazz they called "Dazz."

The Morris Brown originals in what became the multitalented quintet were: lead guitarist Regi Hargis-Hickman, who was born in Austin, Texas, and came to Atlanta to live with his grandparents, Bishop and Mrs. E. L. Hickman; bass guitarist and spokesman Ray Ransom, who is the son of a high school principal in Waycross, Georgia, and who was president of the Morris Brown Marching Band; and keyboardist Donald Nevins, of Macon, Georgia, who later left to pursue his own musical goals in New York City.

Their ranks were expanded to include brass and reed man Jimmy Brown of Savannah, Georgia, with whom Ransom also played in an Atlanta group called Dawn's Early Light, and drummer Eddie Irons, the son of a professor father and attorney mother who moved to Atlanta from Tallahassee, Florida. Irons met Hargis-Hickman and Nevins after leaving nearby Morehouse College to follow a solo musical career. All excellent singers, aspiring writers, and multiple-instrument performers, they practiced at Eddie's house after forming as a group. They adopted the name Brick after Regi's inspiration while watching Eddie's father put in a brick pond. They agreed with Regi that the term "had nothing but positive connotations . . . something solid, hard, durable."

According to Ransom, the group was unanimous in the determination to achieve a dynamic band sound that would be both artistic and funky, yet have depth and use, but not surrender to, "high-tech sounds." He said they set out to capture "a Southern feel or mood . . . a bluesy, jazzy sort of thing" that would not go "against the grain of what Brick is: five guys who live in Georgia among the trees, birds, and crickets." The result was a team effort that transformed them into a tight, exuberant group of eminent musicians specializing in soul-disco-funk material and featuring fluid and mellifluous vocals over commandingly funky rhythm tracks.

Brick issued its first single, "Musicmatic," independently in late 1975; it made *Billboard's* soul singles chart and brought the group a contract with Bang (later Bang/CBS) Records. Its first album, *Good High,* issued the next year and dedicated to Atlanta as "The Next Great Music City," went to Gold as did the featured single, "Dazz," and brought the group's musically-coined style to national attention.

Their second album, *Brick,* was released in 1977 and certified Platinum in March of 1978, the presentation being made by Georgia Governor George Busbee. It featured three hit singles, "Dusic," which became a Gold record, "Ain't Gonna Hurt Nobody," and "We Don't Wanna Sit Down, We Wanna Get Down."

A third album, *Stoneheart,* in 1979 was highlighted by the hit single "Raise Your Hands" and a cut entitled "Marching Band," in which the group was joined by eleven of the nation's foremost college band percussionists. In 1980, their *Waiting on You* album produced two single hits: "Push, Push," and "All the Way." In 1981, Motown's Ray Parker, Jr., produced the *Summer Heat* LP in Los Angeles with its "Sweat 'Til You Get Wet" hit single and the unique "Seaside Vibes," in which the group turned a Hargis-Hickman original tune into a demonstration of its sound virtuosity by duplicating the sounds of the beach, from the roller skaters to the waves crashing on the shore.

In 1982, their *After 5* album was recorded at Monarch Studios in Alpharetta, Georgia, and was produced jointly by Brick and Phil Benton. It featured female vocalists Donna McElroy and Donna DeWitt.

In 1979 Brick was the star of the Atlanta Jazz Festival; *Atlanta Journal* critic Scott Cain said the 50,000 fans found their music "irresistible."

Brick

ALICIA BRIDGES

Singer and songwriter Alicia Bridges says music has "been the moving force in my life for as long as I can remember," and it was her total dedication to it that caused her to say "the hell with" a career behind a computer terminal in Charlotte, North Carolina. She came to Atlanta where she came to the attention of music publisher Bill Lowery and scored a smash hit with her first recording of one of her own songs, "I Love the Nightlife."

Alicia's single-minded pursuit of a musical career had its beginning at the age of ten on a cotton farm near Lawndale, North Carolina, when she asked her father to teach her how to play his four-string guitar. When she won a talent contest sponsored by a Shelby, North Carolina, radio station two years later and was denied the prize of performing on a local radio show because of her age, she convinced the rival station, WADA, to put her on if she could sell enough advertising to sponsor her own program—and she did. She dropped out of college where she was studying physical education to work first in a bank and then in advertising for Sears; but, in her words: "One day I said the hell with it. I didn't want to end up behind some computer terminal. I wanted to sing." She got a job singing first at a Holiday Inn and then at a strip joint in Charlotte before relocating to sing in clubs in Atlanta, where she met her current writing partner, Susan Hutcheson.

Her work came to Lowery's attention, and he signed her to a contract with his organization and carried her and Susan to Studio One in Doraville, where they recorded their hit. Since that time Alicia has concentrated on her writing. She also has had a leadership role in the Georgia Music Festival staged yearly as part of Georgia Music Week sponsored by the Music Industry Committee of the Georgia Senate.

Although her original interest in music was aroused by the rock 'n' roll of Elvis Presley, whose "Don't Leave Me Now" was the song with which she won her first talent contest, Alicia now considers herself a true rhythm and blues singer in the mode of Tina Turner, Aretha Franklin, Gladys Knight, and Patti Labell.

She says listening to black singers such as Dinah Washington, Lena Horne, and Ertha Kitt helped her develop her own unique vocal delivery encompassing blues and rock, and that she also was influenced by white rock artists such as David Bowie, Mick Jagger, and Janis Joplin. With the exception of Joplin, however, she feels most white female vocalists are "phony." As she puts it:

"There's this clean, all-American thing that comes across in the music of most white female vocalists, . . . and I don't believe that innocence is actually there. If you're going to sing about love, emotion, the blues, or you've hurt me so much, then let's get down to it and sing about it."

Alicia's singing style is physical as well as vocal. As she describes it: "I jump around a lot when I'm performing. Sometimes I get on my knees and beat on the floor with my fist. I really get carried away."

Alicia Bridges

JAMES BROWN

Recording company puffery generally can be taken with many grains of salt, but Polydor Records did not overstate the case in its publicity release that stated that James Brown "makes Horatio Alger look like an underachiever."

The success story of this superstar who started in show business at the age of eight by singing and dancing for nickels tossed by soldiers whose shoes he shined in front of the Augusta, Georgia, radio station he vowed one day to own (and did), is as spectacular as the wardrobe of five hundred suits, three hundred pairs of shoes, and the fleet of six custom-made limousines he owns.

The career of the raucous rhythm and blues performer whose vocals, contortionistic acrobatics, and percussive, polyrhythmic musical beat brought him the title of "Soul Brother Number One" in the 1960s and 1970s almost got sidetracked before it started when conviction for car theft and breaking and entering put him in an Alto, Georgia, reform school for three years as a teenager.

But the reform took root in the heart of the black street kid who had known nothing but a life of deprivation and hustling from the time of his birth (stated variously by biographers to have been in 1928 in Pulaski, Tennessee, and by Brown to have been in 1933 in Macon, Georgia). On leaving confinement, he vowed to become a big-league baseball pitcher, an ambition scotched by a leg injury he sustained playing semi-pro ball.

He also turned to the church. He sang in a Baptist choir; taught himself to play drums, bass, piano, and organ; and formed a gospel group called the Swannees, which was to become his famous Flames. At the studios of the same WRDW that later was to become Brown's, they cut a demonstration record that attracted the attention of Syd Nathan of King Records, who signed them to a contract with his subsidiary label, Federal Records. Their first release for this company in 1956 was "Please, Please, Please," written by Brown and John Terry; it reached Number Six on the R&B charts and became the first of more than twenty Brown records to be million sellers. It was followed by "Try Me," which made Number One in 1958. But it was mostly through his pioneering of road tours for black artists and the tortuous crisscrossing of the nation for one-night stands that

Brown established the reputation of being "the hardest working man in show business" and built the growing national audience that put his classic album *The James Brown Show Live at the Apollo* on the *Billboard* album charts for sixty-six weeks beginning in 1963.

He engaged in a bitter legal struggle with Nathan over artistic control of his work. He formed his own production company and merchandised a package of his songs, including one of his biggest hits with whites, "Out of Sight," through Mercury's subsidiary, Smash. Brown went back to King Records with his having "full control" and made history with the international hit "Papa's Got a Brand New Bag," which sold two million copies, won him a Grammy for Best Rhythm and Blues Record of the Year, and set the wave of the future for R&B.

Striving to develop a sound distinctive from that of their contemporaries, Brown and the Flames injected grittiness, hysteria, and Latin cross-rhythms at the same time Ray Charles was tempering rawness with sweetness. Brown and the Flames inexorably pulled rhythm and blues into the mix of lowdown, funky blues and the high-flying emotional gospel of sanctified black churches. This combination became the trademark of mainstream contemporary black pop of the 1970s and the primary forerunner of the Jamaican reggae and Nigerian Afro-beat styles of the 1980s.

Their heavy shuffle beat treated every instrument as a drum and subordinated everything to Brown's semi-improvised, evangelistic, unconventional gospel-and-blues lyrics that shrieked with raw-throated emotion and were punctuated by acrobatic gyrations climaxing in his famed "collapse" routine in which he feigned fainting. He was covered by colorful capes and was helped offstage only to return in new, more flamboyant costumes to repeat the process three times.

When critics panned him and his works as "repetitive," writer Robert Palmer said that their comments were as banal as "attacking Africans for being overly fond of drumming." Brown never achieved a large white following, and only six of his singles ever made *Billboard's* Top Ten, the highest being Number Three "I Got You (I Feel Good)" in 1965; but in his own rhythm-and-blues category he has placed seventeen singles in first place and a total of fifty in the Top Ten, to say nothing of his many hit albums and his concert work that earned him as much as $12,500 a night in the mid-sixties when he could fill a large hall by himself, something no other R&B performer could do. His "collapse" was featured in the 1965 film *The T.A.M.I. Show,* and he did soundtracks for two movies of the 1970s, *Black Caesar* and *Slaughter's Big Rip-Off.* He became the first black man to win *Cash Box* magazine's Male Vocalist award, which came in 1979.

Other of his Number One R&B hits in addition to "I Got You" include "It's a Man's Man's Man's World" in 1966; "Say It Loud—I'm Black And I'm Proud" in 1968; "Give It Up or Turnit a Loose" and "Mother Popcorn (Part 1)" in 1969; "Super Bad" in 1970; "Hot Pants" and "Make It Funky" in 1971; "Talking Loud and Saying Nothing" and "Get on the Good Foot" in 1972; and "The Payback (Part I)," "My Thang," and "Papa Don't Take No Mess" in 1974. He sweetened his sound with strings and vocal groups in the last of the 1970s, but the disco fad prompted him to go for a harsher and more aggressive approach. His audience tired of that, however, and his first disco-oriented release, "The Payback" on Polydor, went to Gold in 1974. His highest single placement since that time was "Get Up Offa That Thing," which reached Number Four in 1976.

James Brown and Zell Miller

During the 1960s Brown also became involved in politics as an exponent of black capitalism; he supported the presidential candidacy of Vice President Hubert Humphrey, entertained troops in Vietnam and

James Brown

Korea, and toured Africa to cite his own success as an entrepreneur in the record production, music publishing, and radio business (always taking pleasure in noting that the three stations he owned included Augusta's WRDW where his career started).

Then he devoted much of his time to encouraging young people to get an education and to avoid the perils of crime and drugs and donated ten percent of the proceeds of his concerts to black charities and ghetto causes. He received the commendation of President Lyndon Johnson for his multihour television appearances in Boston and Washington urging restoring of peace and an end to violence in the riots that followed the assassination of Dr. Martin Luther King, Jr. A similar performance during the Augusta race riots also was credited with minimizing the violence and damage of that outbreak.

Following Brown's comeback concert at Irving Plaza in New York City in 1980, critic Kurt Loder observed that although Brown's voice "may be muted . . . the legend—make no mistake—lives."

After a dry spell from the charts, he hit the Top Ten again in 1986 with "Living in America."

In 1983, Brown was inducted into the Georgia Music Hall of Fame and was also one of the first members of the new Rock 'n' Roll Hall of Fame in Cleveland.

T. GRAHAM BROWN

They do not have a sheik in the town of Arabi, which is a "wide place in the road" on U.S. Highway 41 south of Cordele in southwest Georgia. But that watermelon-growing farming community did produce a one-of-a-kind entertainer affectionately known as "His T-ness."

That is the appellation bestowed upon T. Graham Brown by his friends and fans when they could not come up with a single term that would adequately describe this farmboy, soul shouter, Southern rocker, blues man, and flamboyant performer of everything from beach music and soulful ballads to Southern boogie and rhythm and blues.

He started out as Anthony Graham Brown who wanted a career as a pitcher or center fielder in professional baseball, but got detoured while sitting on the bench at the University of Georgia to earning $150-a-week as the Tony-half of the Dirk and Tony duo playing beach music at the Holiday Inn in downtown Athens.

He changed his performing name to T. Graham Brown to distinguish himself from his previous musical identity in 1976 after Dirk refused to go along with his desire to expand into a full band and widen the horizons of the kind of music they played.

With a band he called REO Diamond, he switched from the cool, reserved beach-style music to a wild-and-wooly brand of country. In what he now calls his "David Allen Coe period," he changed his image to one of long hair, an earring, a tattoo, and a big, black cowboy hat and started touring the Southeast.

"We drank a lot of Jack and busted guitars on the stage," he recalls. "But we packed 'em in."

When he and his musical compatriots tired of full-bore country and rock music, they turned to blues and soul. With the addition of horns and the expansion of their traveling company to nine, they called themselves T. Graham Brown and Rack of Spam and resumed roaming the Southeast to perform.

The best term with which anyone has been able to come up to place Brown's music in a generic category is "Heart & Soul"—a delineation that comes close to describing music that cuts through all styles and goes straight to the heart and soul of the listener. In his plain-speaking way,

Brown uses the word "mongrel" to describe himself when he came to Nashville in his red 1959 Chevrolet station wagon in 1982 with a "sack full of songs" and a determination to carve out his own stylistic niche in country music.

He denies that he had any grand plan for succeeding, but he does concede that the synthesis of so many influences into his own, individualistic style gave him the potential to become an artist with wide appeal. As he puts it: "I had just come out of a stone R&B band. I had the rock and roll/country band before that, doing pretty much everything that Hank, Jr., does now, and then I had fronted a soul band. So I basically came to town a mongrel. I was just going to see what happened."

His wife, Sheila, backed him all the way and took two jobs to support them so he could "hang out" on Music Row and get to know people. He would sing during happy hours and do a lot of hard drinking. He met Harlan Howard and Terry Choate, the latter hiring him to do some demos at Tree International and subsequently getting him signed by Capitol/EMI America when he became head of A&R for that label.

His debut single was one of the songs he had demoed, "Drowning in Memories," which went to Number Thirty-nine. He followed it up with "I Tell It Like It Used to Be" and "I Wish That I Could Hurt That Way Again," which made the Top Ten and Top Three respectively. In early 1986 he had back-to-back Number One singles with "Hell and High Water," which he cowrote, and "Don't Go to Strangers."

That was the year he quit drinking and was picked by Kenny Rogers to be his opening act, a gig that lasted for two years. In 1987 he turned out a second album, *Brilliant Conversationalist*, which concentrated on rock and blues and yielded three hits: "She Couldn't Love Me Anymore," "The Last Resort," and the title cut, which also turned into a popular video. Those successes led to promotional tours of Germany and England where, in the former, he covered the Otis Redding classic, "Sittin' on the Dock of the Bay," and, in the latter, Capitol issued his "Rock It, Billy." His resulting popularity in Germany led to the inclusion of his "Later Train" on the soundtrack of the German movie *Zabou*.

The same year he expanded his career into acting, appearing in two movies—*Greased Lightning* with Richard Pryor and *The Curse*, in which he appeared as a redneck hotel clerk with David Keith and John Schneider.

In 1988 his third album, *Come As You Were*, took a turn back to country music and went to Number Ten. It featured the smash Number One hit, "Darlene," the Number Five cut of "The Last Resort," and the

T. Graham Brown

popular R&B/soul rendition of "Never Say Never." He also did another David Keith movie, *Heartbreak Hotel*, in which he played righthand man to Keith's Elvis and his band, the Hardtops, portrayed Elvis's band.

But his biggest production of that year was the birth of his son, George Anthony, whom he calls "Acme."

His defining year, by any yardstick, has to be 1990 when he co-produced his fourth album, *Bumper to Bumper*, with legendary Muscle Shoals producer/pianist Barry Beckett. It showcased the full range of his "Heart & Soul" music highlighted by six of his own songs running the full range of young to failed love and dealing with relationships that might have and could never have been realized. His "If You Could Only See Me" and his duet with Tanya Tucker, "Don't Go Out," both hit the Top Ten, and "Moonshadow Road" closed out the year in the Top Twenty. Featuring a tight rhythm sound, punctuated by an occasional wailing sax and punchy horns, he delivered trademark "T-ness" on "Expecting Miracles," "I'm Sending One Up for You," "You Can't Make Her Love You," and "Eyes Wide Open."

His "We Tote the Note" was pure Southern boogie and "Blues of the Month Club" was quintessential B. B. King-style. "For Real" was a slow love ballad, and "Bring a Change" was a soul anthem. With the Otis Redding classic, "I've Been Loving You Too Long," he proved again that he is one white singer who can do full justice to the works of that Georgia legend.

In 1991 he released a fifth album, *You Can't Take It with You*, which featured the Top Forty cut of "With This Ring."

With all of his other accomplishments, the breadth of this performer's career would be incomplete without mentioning his work in doing television commercials, which dates from his early years in Nashville. He did spots for Coca-Cola, Kraft, and McDonalds, but the one most remembered is the one he did for Taco Bell in which he not only sang but also portrayed himself dropping his guitar and literally making "a run for the border."

Everyone who likes good, strong music can find something in the music of "His T-ness" to like.

BOUDLEAUX AND FELICE BRYANT

When Hank Penny talked him into switching from classical violinist with the Atlanta Civic Symphony to swinging country fiddler with his Radio Cowboys on station WSB in 1938, Bouleaux Bryant used a four-letter term to categorize that kind of music. But after almost four decades of achieving fame and fortune in writing more than six thousand country songs, the four letters he should have used are "G-O-L-D."

Everything Boudleaux and his wife, Felice, touched turned to gold since their marriage in 1945. Called the Rogers and Hammerstein of Nashville, Tennessee, they were the undisputed champions of country songwriting. The words and music they turned out have sold more than one quarter of a billion records and tapes ranging from all the twenty-seven hits recorded by the Everly Brothers to the internationally renowned country classic, "Rocky Top."

Their songs have been recorded not only in every style but also by every significant artist and group since the early fifties, ranging from Eddy Arnold to Bob Dylan, the Carter Family to Lawrence Welk, Dean Martin and Elvis Presley and the Boston Pops Orchestra to the Grateful Dead. As the first professional songwriters who were not also performers to move to Nashville, they probably contributed more successful songs to the mainstream of music coming out of Music City than any other songwriter or team of songwriters.

Born February 13, 1920, in Shellman, Georgia, Boudleaux was named for the French soldier who saved his lawyer-father's life in France in World War I. He grew up in Moultrie, Georgia, in a musical family that had its own band and paid its way to the 1934 Chicago World's Fair by performing on tours along the way. He was given a violin for his fifth Christmas and was sufficiently classically trained to join the Atlanta Symphony at the age of eighteen, but his association with Penny and his innovative country music ideas switched him from "longhair" to "hillbilly" and set him on the course that gave the world some of its most memorable songs.

He met his Italian singer-dancer-elevator-operator wife while playing with a jazz group in Milwaukee. He brought her home to Moultrie, and they were playing clubs in that area when they sold their first song, "Country-Boy," to the Acuff-Rose organization in Nashville, which made

Boudleaux Bryant

a hit of it with Little Jimmie Dickens.

They moved to Nashville to become $45-a-week song pluggers, and it has been rare indeed when one of their songs has not been in the charts since. They had the foresight to specify in their contract that all copyrights would revert to them after ten years, and their own firm, the House of Bryant, manages the royalties. In recent years they launched performing and recording careers of their own with several albums already released with particular success in Europe.

In 1953 they began a highly successful relationship with Carl Smith by writing his Top Ten hit, "Hey Joe," a song that gave Frankie Laine a million seller in the pop field. Eddy Arnold had hits with their "I've Been Thinking" and "Richest Man" in 1955. In 1957 they contracted to do some songs for the two singing sons of Boudleaux's barber, Ike Everly. They produced the string hits beginning with "Bye, Bye Love" and continued with "Wake Up Little Susie," "All I Have to Do Is Dream," "Bird Dog" and "Devoted to You." The Everly Brothers sold more than fifteen million recordings of Bryant songs but did not have a major hit after a contract dispute ended the relationship.

Although both wrote words and music, usually Boudleaux did the score and Felice supplied the lyrics. Their phenomenal string of hits included "Raining in My Heart" by Buddy Holly, "Blue Boy" by Jim Reeves, "Let's Think about Loving" by Bob Luman, "Mexico" by Bob Moore, "My Last Date" by Skeeter Davis, "Baltimore" by Sonny James, "We Could" by Charlie Pride, "Take Me As I Am" by Mark White, "Come Live with Me" by Roy Clark, "Sweet Deceiver" and "Penny Arcade" by Christy Lane, and "Hey Joe, Hey Moe" by Joe Stampley and Moe Bandy (an updating of their first hit, "Hey Joe").

"Rocky Top," which was written jointly in about ten minutes while they were taking a break from writing songs for an old folk album for Archie Campbell, was first done by Buck Owens and later by virtually every major country artist. Carly Simon and James Taylor made the Everlys' "Devoted to You" a major hit for a second time in 1978. *Billboard* magazine in 1974 made a list of more than four hundred artists who recorded Bryant songs.

Before Boudleaux died in 1987, he and Felice lived in Gatlinburg, Tennessee. Since his death, Felice has continued to write. In 1986 they were inducted into the National Songwriters Hall of Fame and in 1991 they received the ultimate acclaim when they were inducted into the Country Music Hall of Fame.

PEABO BRYSON

Peabo Bryson calls himself a "romantic ballad singer" and denies that he wants or tries to be a sex symbol. But the slender, handsome black farm boy from Mauldin, South Carolina, who lives in a palatial mansion near Atlanta's airport, has made himself a millionaire by turning on female audiences with his songs about love and passion. Dressed all in white with his shirt opened to his naval and his suit adorned with a red handkerchief, Peabo does indeed look like a sex symbol.

He hit recording gold with his second album, *Reaching for the Sky*, in 1977 and has topped success with success since as a solo performer and in duet with such female stars as Natalie Cole, Roberta Flack, and Melissa Manchester.

The oldest child on a farm family deserted by his father, Peabo began farm work at the age of seven to help support his grandmother, mother, and siblings. His mother taught him to love music, and when only twelve he won a local talent contest in 1963 singing a song by his idol, Sam Cooke.

At fourteen he left home to join a singing group, and two years later was touring the world and recording first on the Custom and then the Bang labels with Mose Dillard and the Tex-Town Display. Impressed by Peabo's songwriting, Bang's Eddie Brisco gave him a contract. His first single "Disco Queen," Peabo regarded as "awful"; however, his first album, *Peabo*, issued 1976, hit the charts and Peabo hit the road.

After Peabo had several concerts with Natalie Cole, Capitol Records vice president Larkin Arnold signed him with that label where his premier album, *Reaching for the Sky*, earned him a Gold record and, by his own estimate, "a couple of million dollars." His follow-up, *Crosswinds*, with its hit single, "I'm So into You," duplicated that success and put him at the top of the soul charts. Then came his *Best of Friends* duet album with Natalie Cole, which set the pattern for the resurgence of duet songs, particularly those featuring Peabo.

In 1980 Peabo released the solo album, *Paradise*, which resulted in a nationwide summer tour with Roberta Flack and their highly successful double duet album, *Live and More*, as well as his doing the male lead vocal in Melissa Manchester's pop hit, "Lovers After All."

In 1981, he directed the production of an album compiling and reissuing all of his tracks recorded before his contract with Capitol, and this album, *Turn the Hands of Time*, also went to the top of the charts. Since that time he has devoted himself largely to concerts that always attract sell-out female audiences who often drown out opening acts with cries of "Bring on Peabo!"

Always the showman, Peabo enhances his all-white costuming by opening his concerts amid wisps of white smoke while singing the title track from his *Crosswinds* album. He establishes a cozy, almost hypnotic, rapport with his audience from the beginning and features in succession his suggestive "I'm So into You," his keyboard performance of his caring tribute to women, "She's a Woman," and his powerfully moving "Feel the Fire," and climaxes with the lazy sensuality of "Don't Touch Me."

Chicago Sun-Times critic Patricia Smith wrote in 1979 a review about his impact: "When the lights came up and the double-breasted knight was gone, everyone sat smiling in their seats for a minute. The good feeling he left was not easy to shake."

In 1984 he joined Elektra Records and recorded four albums; then moved back to Capitol in 1989 before going to Columbia in 1990. Along the way he had hit duets with Natalie Cole "What You Won't Do for Love," with Regina Bell "Without You," and Roberta Flack "Tonight I Celebrate My Love (For You)."

And, of course, fans of the daytime soap opera *One Life to Live* can hear him singing the theme song every weekday.

BUDDY BUIE

Buddy Buie dedicated himself to the search for "the perfect sound" when he teamed up with Bobby Goldsboro, his hometown buddy from Dothan, Alabama, while they were students at Auburn University in 1961. While he continues that unrelenting quest more than three decades later, critics agree he may never come closer than he has with the music of the Atlanta Rhythm Section or the records he produces at his Studio One in Doraville, Georgia, which is regarded by musicians as one of the nation's finest recording facilities.

Buddy's name never has become a household word because his megatalents as manager, producer, and songwriter have kept him in the background, while the artists he directs and the songs he writes, arranges, and records make the musical headlines. He produced such stars as Billy Joe Royal, Tommy Roe, B. J. Thomas, and Roy Orbison, and had more than twenty chart records in the 1960s. He managed Bobby Goldsboro until he became a superstar.

Buie and guitarist J. R. Cobb formed the songwriting team that made Dennis Yost and the Classics IV the television and recording sensation of the 1960s with such hits as "Spooky," "Stormy," "Traces," and "Everyday with You Girl."

Buie established his own recording company in 1970, which grew into Studio One. His facilities attracted some of the finest musicians of the world, including Cobb and Yost, and the quality of their studio sessions prompted him to mold them into a band that he dubbed the Atlanta Rhythm Section and that, by 1973, became a major act pronounced by critics as "the quintessential American band."

It was Buie who insisted that ARS shun gimmicks and flashy costumes, limit recordings to no more than four minutes, and concentrate instead on music that, under his guidance, evolved into a hybrid brand of British rock, traditional Southern rhythm and blues, and melody lines missing in other Southern bands of the decade. In five years they produced hits with Buie songs like "Doraville," "So into You," "Imaginary Lovers," "Champagne Jam," "Georgia Rhythm," and many others to which the classification "Champagne Jam" stuck and continues to apply. Their successes ranged from an invitation to play the Carter White House to packing sixty-one thousand fans into Georgia Tech's Grant Field for the unequalled and still-talked-about Champagne Jam of 1978. ARS popularity and demand continued unabated into the decade of the 1990s.

In 1978 Buddy formed a management partnership with Arnie Geller called the Buie-Geller Organization. They established BGO Records, which made it big right off with more hits from the Atlanta Rhythm Section and the discovery of Alicia Bridges, whose monster single, "I Love the Nightlife," was an industry sensation. Buddy also produced Stillwater's first album, which yielded the Top Forty hit, "Mindbender."

In September 1984, Buddy had the honor of being inducted into the Georgia Music Hall of Fame. He and his cowriters continue to be actively involved in contemporary country music with recordings by Travis Tritt and Wynonna Judd. "Rock Bottom," a Buie-Cobb song, went to the top of the charts in 1994, and Gloria Estefan put the classic "Traces" on her newest album.

Perhaps the one word best describing Buie's talents is "catalyst." He has demonstrated an unequalled ability to bring together individual talents and mold them into even-greater collective entities. He insists upon quality in all that he does, and his enduring and unending passion is to achieve the "perfect sound." Those who know him are willing to bet that, if anyone ever finds it, Buddy Buie will be he.

Buddy Buie and Jimmy Carter

JEAN CARN

Jazz singer Jean Carn is a big star in Washington, Philadelphia, New York, Chicago, and Los Angeles, but she deliberately has kept a low profile in her hometown of Atlanta in order to be able to rear her children in virtual anonymity.

Born Sarah Perkins, she was active in chorus, band, and orchestra at Washington High School and sang opera at Morris Brown College while performing in local nightclubs. After marrying keyboardist Doug Carn, she moved to California, where they recorded three albums for the Black Jazz label and she sang with Earth, Wind, and Fire on two of their albums. After her divorce she was signed to a solo contract by Kenny Gamble and Leon Hull of Philadelphia International and became a part of the "Philadelphia Sound," which included Teddy Pendergrass and the Ojays.

Recording with jazz drummer Norman Conners, she has broadened her repertoire to a more commercial blend of rhythm and blues, pop, disco, and jazz styles, and her Philadelphia International albums have included such hits as "Start the Fire" and "My Love Don't Come Easy." Contending "You can boogie and become enlightened at the same time," she also has concentrated on message songs such as those emphasizing the plight of black males on her album *Shortage of Good Men*.

Jean Carn

Joseph A. (Cotton) Carrier

For more than half a century Cotton Carrier was an influential presence on the music scene of Georgia. From the time he came to Georgia from Kentucky in 1941 to be master of ceremonies of the WSB Barn Dance to his service as general professional manager of the Lowery Group of music publishing companies, he was a major contributor to the development not only of modern country music but also of popular music in general as we know it today.

Born to a banjo-playing father and an organ-playing mother on a farm near Arthur, Kentucky, Carrier decided by the time he was sixteen that he had rather be known as "Cotton" than to pick the stuff and that singing and playing the mandolin, guitar, and fiddle "beat working on the farm." He and some other boys his age formed a hometown hillbilly band that played at a local service station. He became confident enough in his musical ability to hitchhike around the country making a living through guest appearances on local radio stations. He later landed a permanent spot with a hillbilly group called Goober and His Kentuckians and was working as their fiddler for station WPAD in Paducah, Kentucky, when he was hired by WSB to come to Atlanta to be fiddler and master of ceremonies of its popular new Barn Dance.

Cotton became widely known through those Saturday night appearances on stages throughout the Atlanta area and worked with such popular Georgia performers as the Hoot Owl Hollow Girls, Boots Woodall, Pete Cassell, Harpo Kidwell, the Swanee River Boys, Chick Stripling, Hank Penny, James and Martha Carson, and the pretty accordionist Jane Logan, whom he soon made Mrs. Cotton Carrier. In addition he appeared on WSB's early morning Dixie Farm and Home Hour, mid-morning Cracker Barrel Program, and the noontime Georgia Jubilee. Virtually every night, he and a group of WSB musicians would journey to some outlying town to do a show at a school auditorium or movie theater. He also formed his own band, the Plantation Gang, which was one of the last groups to appear on the WSB Barn Dance before it went out of existence in 1950. At one time or another the Gang featured such well-known Georgia musicians as Kink Embry, Dean Bence, Church Franklin, Lee Roy Blanchard, Arlie Wade, Willis Hogsed, and Calvin

Bragg. As country music turned more to records than live performances, he also became a disc jockey and had his own popular Columbia Record Roundup on WSB every Saturday night at 11:30 P.M. and for a few years in the early 1950s the *Cotton Carrier Show.*

The advent of television found Cotton equal to the challenge, singing with Boots Woodall and the TV Wranglers on WAGA-TV of Atlanta. He also branched out into booking, bringing out-of-town talent to the Sports Arena and other Atlanta stages, and was responsible for Elvis Presley's first Atlanta appearance on December 2, 1955—a performance for which he and three backup musicians received a total of three hundred dollars and about which Cotton later said he was not "overly impressed." He did, however, find Elvis a sincere and polite young man who "sang his heart out."

Cotton also wrote songs. His first hit was recorded in 1953, the year the Weavers made it big with a version of "On Top of Old Smoky," in which the lines of the song were alternately recited and sung. The Smith Brothers, a popular Atlanta gospel quartet, asked him to write a song in that same format for them. He produced with the smash, "I Have But One Goal," which was the first hit of Bill Lowery's fledgling music publishing firm that subsequently grew into the Lowery Group.

When country music and musicians began gravitating to Nashville, Tennessee, in the decade of the 1960s, Cotton elected to stay in Atlanta, a city with which he had fallen in love. Bill Lowery invited him to join his organization as a record promoter, and the two of them developed into the team that has since produced a steady stream of blockbuster hits that have scored in all categories of the charts. He was general professional manager with the Lowery Group until his death July 18, 1994.

Joseph A. (Cotton) Carrier

JAMES AND MARTHA CARSON

Few remember them today because they made their last recording together in 1950 and divorced in 1951, but during the 1940s James and Martha Carson were the sweethearts of country music when they started as "James and Martha" the mandolin-guitar gospel-singing duet on the WSB Barn Dance in Atlanta.

Their recordings made James's composition, "Man of Galilee," a gospel hit; "The Sweetest Gift, a Mother's Smile," a bluegrass standard; and "He Will Set Your Fields on Fire," a gospel classic. They rank only behind the Louvins and the Blue Sky Boys as one of the greatest country duets of the early years. Martha went on to greater fame as a solo performer on the Grand Ole Opry and in posh supperclubs like that of the Waldorf Astoria in New York City and as the writer of "Satisfied" and more than one hundred other songs of the gospel genre.

Both were natives of Kentucky. He was born James William Roberts on February 18, 1918, near Richmond, the son of Fiddling Doc Roberts. She was born Irene Amburgey on May 19, 1921, at Neon, one of the singing Amburgey sisters. They met while performing on the WLAP Lexington Morning Roundup. He followed her as she and her sisters became first the Coon Creek Girls on the CBS Renfro Valley Barndance and then the Hoot Owl Holler Girls on the WSB Barn Dance in Atlanta.

Hank Penney got around WSB's rule against married performers by changing Robert's last name to Carson, taking Irene's performing name of "Marthie," and billing them as "James and Martha–The Barn Dance Sweethearts." They were an instant and enduring success for ten years and made a number of recordings for RCA, White Church, and Capitol labels while in Atlanta, including Hank Williams's "I'm Going to Sing, Sing, Sing," Albert Brumley's "I'll Fly Away," and James's "Budded on Earth to Bloom in Heaven."

James moved on to join Wilma Lee and Stoney Cooper's Clinch Mountain Clan, the Masters Family, and Cas Walker. Martha recorded with her sisters as the Amber Sisters and then pursued a career as a single gospel and country singer who produced, in addition to "Satisfied," such hits as "I'm Gonna Walk and Talk with My Lord," "Let the Light Shine on Me," "Lazarus," "Ole Blind Barnabus," "It Takes a Lot of Lovin'," and

"I Can't Stand Up Alone." Both have remarried and have two children each. Martha lives in Nashville, Tennessee, and James in Lexington, Kentucky.

Martha Carson

FIDDLIN' JOHN CARSON

The music of Fiddlin' John Carson from Fannin County, Georgia, was the first of what we know today as country music to be broadcast by radio and recorded for the phonograph.

He and his daughter Rosa Lee, who was known as Moonshine Kate, were the first stars despite the fact that little of the fame and none of the fortunes produced in the country music industry ever were theirs.

When he walked into the "studios" of the brand new radio station WSB started by *The Atlanta Journal*, Carson, fifty-four years old, had won the Georgia Fiddlin' Championship seven times and had a colorful reputation as a traveling performer who made a living playing and "passing the hat" when he was not working in the cotton mill, painting houses, or making moonshine.

When he announced that he would "like to have a try at the newfangled contraption," Lambdin Kay obliged him. His only pay being a snort of the engineer's whiskey, Carson performed "Little Old Log Cabin in the Lane." There being no FCC or radio logs kept at that time, the date generally is fixed at September 9, 1922. Some who disagree with this date insist that it came within the first week of the station's signing on the air on March 16, 1922, but probably it was on Carson's birthday of March 23. They point out that Carson always came back to WSB to perform on his birthdays well into the 1940s.

At any rate, it was before anyone else, and he returned soon thereafter with Ed Kincaid and Bill Badgett, two of his "cronies" as his early informal band was called, and played "Sally Goodin" and "Alabama Gals." According to *The Atlanta Journal* of September 21, 1922, he came back again with Rosa Lee and his wife Jennie Nora, who was a "straw beater" to do a repeat of "Little Old Log Cabin." That performance brought him invitations to be a guest performer at the WSB radio booth at the Southeastern Fair in October and regularly in the studios thereafter.

The *Journal* reported that Carson's fame spread "to every corner of the United States where WSB is heard." His popularity inspired Polk Brockman, an Atlanta furniture dealer who had been successful in developing and merchandising "race" records for the black market for Okeh Records, to persuade Okeh president Ralph Peer to bring his recording equipment to Atlanta to record Fiddlin' John.

On June 14, 1923, in a vacant building on Nassau Street in Atlanta, Georgia, Carson cut two sides, "Little Old Log Cabin" and "The Old Hen Cackled and the Rooster's Going to Crow." Peer pronounced them "pluperfect awful" but agreed to press five hundred on a blank label for Brockman's personal use.

With Fiddlin' John hawking them from the stage of the next fiddlers' convention, Brockman promptly sold every disc. Peer immediately rushed into a major pressing on the Okeh label and invited Carson to New York to record twelve more sides.

This venture gave Okeh the cream of Carson's repertoire including the above two and "Billy in the Low Ground," "Sally Goodin," "Fare You Well, Old Joe Clark," "Nancy Rowland," "Kicking Mule," "When You and I Were Young, Maggie," "Casey Jones," "The Farmer is the Man That Feeds Them All," "You Will Never Miss Your Mother Until She's Gone," "Be Kind to a Man When He Is Down," "Papa's Billy Goat," and "Tom Watson Special." The next year he and Rosa Lee recorded his classic and personal favorite, "Little Mary Phagan," which he wrote in commemoration of the infamous murder-lynching case.

Carson's grandson and namesake, John Carson, who was an All-American football player at the University of Georgia, has a list of more than one hundred and fifty songs written by Fiddlin' John, and his recordings for both Okeh and RCA number more than three hundred. Only nine of those were ever copyrighted because neither John nor Rosa Lee could read music and had to rely on others to transcribe their works, mostly WSB staff pianist Irene Spain, who later said she was embarrassed by some of the "ugly words" of Carson's lyrics.

He got into several copyright disputes with Okeh Records, with Gid and Gordon Tanner, and particularly with Irene's stepfather, the blind, hymn-singing preacher Andy Jenkins, when both of them claimed to be the author of the hit ballad "Floyd Collins." Carson sold all his copyrights for a pittance shortly before he died.

From the age of three, Rosa Lee performed with her father, first as a buck dancer and then later as a guitar and banjo player. She adopted the name Moonshine Kate at the suggestion of the record company after she and Fiddlin' John recorded the popular "Corn Liquor Still in Georgia." The youngest of Carson's ten children, she was quiet, shy, and totally opposite to the "brassy wench" she played on stage and in recordings. Of all the talented and shifting performers who made up Carson's bands—first the Cronies and at the height of his recording popularity, the Virginia Reelers—she was his favorite, and it was to her that he left the treasured violin reputedly made by the son of Stradivari; at the age of ten, Fiddlin' John Carson had inherited it from his father.

Carson and his daughter apparently started the tradition of country stars endorsing and performing for political personalities. They entertained audiences for Tom Watson in his 1920 U.S. Senate campaign, for Gene Talmadge in all his campaigns, and for Herman Talmadge in his first campaign for governor. Herman Talmadge rewarded him with a job as elevator operator and the title of Elevator Commissioner in the State Capitol, a title he held to his death.

Rosa Lee married her childhood sweetheart, Wayne Johnson, and they retired after respective careers with the city of Atlanta and in business to live on Lake Seminole near Donalsonville in Southwest Georgia. Reminiscing about her father, she said he never objected to being called a "hillbilly" rather than "country."

Reports dispute whether Fiddlin' John was paid for each record he sold or was on salary from the record companies with which he worked, but either way he realized very little of the wealth he earned for the companies or the promoters of his appearances throughout the United States. He died almost penniless at the age of eighty-one in Atlanta on December 1, 1949.

Moonshine Kate and Fiddlin' John Carson

RAY CHARLES

It was the unspoken consensus of the Georgia General Assembly, when it voted in 1979 to make the Hoagy Carmichael-Charles Gorrell tune "Georgia on My Mind" the official state song, that its first performance as such would be by Ray Charles, the black musician born in Albany, Georgia.

He had sung that song in every concert he had played since first recording it, but Ray Charles probably had contributed as much to the integration of American society through his pioneering in the erasing of racial boundaries in music as any civil rights leader through confrontations and demonstrations.

He readily accepted the invitation to sing and on March 7, 1979, received a thundering ovation when he officially introduced Georgians to their new state song in a performance at the State Capitol. Ray Charles, along with Bill Lowery, was inducted into the Georgia Music Hall of Fame in 1979, the hall of fame's first year. This honor came almost a quarter of a century after he recorded his first great hit song, "I Got a Woman," in the studios of Atlanta's radio station WGST.

It had been a long, hard road of struggle and success, tragedy and triumph for Charles, who was born Ray Charles Robinson on September 23, 1930, the son of an automobile mechanic who died when Ray was ten and of a strong-minded mother who took in washing and died when he was fifteen.

He was blinded by glaucoma when he was six after the family moved to Greenville, Florida. Two of his most vivid sighted memories are of the horror of seeing his younger brother drown in one of his mother's washtubs and of the pleasure of learning his first piano chords from Wylie Pittman. Pittman was a neighbor who ran a general store in which he kept a piano on which he played the "race" records of Big Boy Crudup, Tampa Red, Blind Boy Fuller, and Big Joe Turner and the swing recordings of Duke Ellington, Count Basie, and Benny Goodman. Drumming into his head that he was "blind, not stupid," Charles's mother insisted that he learn to do everything a sighted child would do, including chopping wood, and enrolled him in the St. Augustine School for the Deaf and Blind at the age of seven where he learned to read, write, and play music by braille as well as to make brooms and mops and to tool leather billfolds and belts.

He quickly decided he preferred music to crafts as a life's calling and mastered the piano, organ, alto clarinet, and trumpet to the point that, by his early teens, he was professionally proficient in music ranging from Chopin and Sibelius to Artie Shaw and Art Tatum. He refused to eat in grief over his mother's death, but after being force-fed by friends who convinced him his mother would want him to carry on, he lied about his age to get a union card and began playing in clubs around Florida until he saved $600, which he used to move as far away as he could get, Seattle, Washington, where at the age of seventeen he won a talent contest and formed a trio to play a regular gig at the Elks Club.

He dropped his last name to avoid confusion with that of the fighter Sugar Ray Robinson and established a reputation for himself as an emulator of the music of his idol Nat "King" Cole. It was during the teen period of his career that he became hooked on heroin, which turned into a twenty-year habit culminating in his arrest on federal drug charges in 1965 and a year-long period of enforced probation and hospitalization in which he kicked it for good.

Swingtime Records put him under contract in 1949, and he moved to Los Angeles, where he debuted with "Confession Blues," which, like a number of its successors, did little until he hit with a Top Ten rhythm and blues number "Baby, Let Me Hold Your Hand" in 1951. He went on the road with Lowell Fulson, put together a band for Ruth Brown, and played briefly for Moms Mabley before going to New Orleans in 1953. There he joined up with bluesman Eddie Jones, who was known as Guitar Slim, an unsophisticated primitive for whom Ray arranged and then backed on his million-selling blues classic, "The Things That I Used to Do," for Specialty Records, which started him on the development of the musical identity that was to bring him subsequent success. Atlantic Records, which bought his contract in 1952, recorded him in New York that year on the boogie-woogie classic "Mess Around," the novelty number "It Should've Been Me," and the blues tunes "Losing Hand," "Funny," and Fulson's "Sinner's Prayer." The next year Atlantic Records went to New Orleans to do a series of Ray Charles originals, including the single "Don't You Know" and a moving version of Guitar Slim's "Feelin' Sad."

But they were preludes to the 1955 recording in Atlanta of "I Got a Woman" in which Charles broke into his new style of gospel-based piano topped by the exuberance and earthiness of his full-throated raspy baritone punctuated with falsetto shrieks. This attracted the attention of both black and white audiences and brought the protest of blues singer Big Bill

Ray Charles

Bronzey who took him to task for blending gospel and blues and declared "He's crying sanctified."

From that time on his name was constantly on the R&B and pop charts, and he had such acclaimed singles as "Blackjack," "Come Back," "Fool for You," "Greenbacks," "This Little Girl of Mine," "Drown in My Own Tears," "Hallelujah, I Love You So," "Lonely Avenue," "Mary Ann," "What Would I Do without You," "Right Time" and "What'd I Say," which critics agree was one of the most sensual and explosive singles of the modern pop-rock era.

He did two standing-room-only concerts at Carnegie Hall in 1963 and became popular in concerts and appearances at theaters, clubs, and jazz festivals throughout the nation. He won the first of his ten Grammys also in 1963 for the song "Busted" as the Best Rhythm and Blues Recording of the Year. His albums were consistent best-sellers throughout the late 1950s and 1960s, including *Yes, Indeed* and *At Newport* in 1958; *What'd I Say* in 1959; *In Person* in 1960; *Dedicated to You* and *Genius + Soul = Jazz* in 1961; *Modern Sounds, The Ray Charles Story*, and *Greatest Hits* in 1962; *Great Ray Charles* and *Recipe for Soul* in 1963, and *Sweet and Sour Tears* in 1964.

The gospel genesis of "I Got a Woman" started Charles on an evolution of assimilation of parts of all music forms from blues, gospel, and funk to pop standards and jazz into what was to become his own unique brand of soul. The Raelettes, the backup group of five females, became his choir, and a seventeen-piece band added orchestral fullness as he embarked upon tempering rawness with sweetness at the same time that James Brown was going in the other direction by injecting grittiness and hysteria.

Charles completed the dimension and added further to the criticism of the purists when he moved over into country and western when he shifted his contract to ABC-Paramount. Then he came out in 1962 with the three big hits "You Don't Know Me," "You Are My Sunshine," and "I Can't Stop Loving You," the latter of which went to Number One, earned Gold and Platinum records, and ultimately sold more than three million copies. It was also during this period that "Georgia on My Mind" was first recorded and released and became a standard of all Charles's concert programs.

From then on country and western songs were a regular part of his repertoire, and none of his albums was released thereafter without one of these songs. To those who complained, he responded that he listened to the Grand Ole Opry as a child and loved country music because "It's kind of like the blues" and the "lyrics are so plain . . . even a four-year-old can understand what you're singing."

By adding his own interpretations and stylings to the various forms of music, Charles, in effect, made it acceptable for black people to sing country and western music and white people to appreciate soul; thus he paved the way for black country singers like Charley Pride and white soul singers like Joe Cocker.

Charles always avoided racial controversy and once told Dr. Martin Luther King, Jr., he would give concerts and raise money for him but would not march or go to jail for him. He notes he was singing protest songs like "You're in for a Big Surprise" long before "black is beautiful songs came along."

His singles hits of the 1960s and 1970s included "Sticks and Stones," "Hit the Road, Jack," "Them That's Got," "Ruby," "I've Got News for You," "Mint Julep," "Busted," "Don't Set Me Free," "No One," "Your Cheating Heart," "Take These Chains from My Heart," "Crying' Time," "Together Again," "Let's Get Stoned" (which went to Number One), "Here We Go Again," "Don't Change on Me" and "Feel So Bad." An excellent example of his many multi-style albums was *True to Life*, which included soul/country versions of the songs "The Jealous Kind" and "I Can See Clearly Now." At the end of the decade he left ABC and reaffiliated with Atlantic.

He has appeared as guest on every television program of consequence, including Public Broadcasting System's acclaimed country music show, *Austin City Limits*. A millionaire, he also established his own music publishing firm and issued records under his own labels, Tangerine and Crossover; he purchased two jet planes to get himself and his company to an average of three hundred concert appearances each year. He bought a $300,000 home overlooking the Pacific Ocean he cannot see, where he lives with his second wife and three sons (he also has a grown daughter by an earlier marriage).

In addition to his ten Grammys, he has five consecutive awards as Top Male Vocalist in the International Jazz Critics' Poll conducted by *Down Beat* magazine and a Bronze Medallion from the Government of France, a country where his concerts always attract SRO audiences.

Perhaps no modern singer and his success have been more analyzed than Charles and his phenomenal accomplishment of having sold more than two hundred million records embracing all media except classical. Georgia historian Bernice McCullar said his music draws people because of "the pain, the misery, often the despair that comes through," and the foremost jazz critic Whitney Balliett maintains that Charles is "revered by every class, color and creed, perhaps because he touches the listeners' emotions with his voice."

While agreeing that he has "known sheer agony" and has been through "quite a bit of poverty and all kinds of hassles," Charles thinks of himself "as a musician who enjoys all kinds of music," but admits that he does "try to bring out my soul so people can understand what I am." He says he does not choose his songs because of their categories but on the basis of whether he likes them and feels there are ways he "can enhance . . . put

Ray Charles

myself" into them. He quite often turns down songs he "doesn't feel," pointing out he declined an offer of $25,000 and half the rights to do the title song of the movie *Walk on the Wild Side* because it "didn't feel right to him."

Always comfortable with country music, he and Willie Nelson had a Number One hit, "Seven Spanish Angels," in 1985. The following year President Ronald Reagan presented him the distinguished Kennedy Center Award Medallion on a nationally televised program in Washington, D.C.

He laughs at the jokes about and parodies of his image and playing style—eyes hidden by dark glasses, stomping of the feet, and rocking back and forth with the rhythm of his music— and he turns aside the assessment of Frank Sinatra that he is "the only genius in our profession" by saying "Art Tatum—he was a genius. And Einstein. Not me." But he adds that he does intend to "keep singing until the people tell me it's time for me to go out to pasture."

J. R. COBB

J. R. Cobb is known by his initials; but, based upon his ability and success in writing and performing songs of all styles—country, pop, and rock—it would have been appropriate for his middle name to have been "Versatility."

Born in Birmingham, Alabama, and schooled in Jacksonville, Florida, Cobb came to Atlanta at the age of twenty-one and teamed up with Bubby Buie to become one of the greatest songwriting teams of the current era. Their very first song, "I Take It Back," was a hit produced by Georgian Chips Moman and recorded by Sandy Posey. They turned out compositions that ranged from the beautiful "Traces of Love" to Travis Tritt's hard country rock "Homesick." He and Buie also were joined by members of the Atlanta Rhythm Section in producing the songs the Section took to the top: "Champagne Jam," "Georgia Rhythm," and "Do It or Die."

The first million-seller of the Cobb-Buie team was "Spooky," an instrumental hit by Georgians Mike Sharpo of Atlanta and Harry Middlebrooks of Thomaston; and, after Cobb added the lyrics, it became the giant hit that today is at the three-million mark in sales. This was followed by the equally recognizable "Stormy," "Everyday with You Girl," and "Most of All," which was recorded by B. J. Thomas. Their latest effort is Wynonna's "Rockbottom."

Cobb also teamed up with Ray Whitley to write the beach favorite, "Be Young, Be Foolish, Be Happy," recorded first by the Tams and then revived and made a hit the second-time-around by English song stylist Sonia. Most of the tunes Cobb has turned out, singly or in tandem with others, have either become standards or are on their way to being such in the future.

This multitalented individual also tours with the Highwaymen—Johnny Cash, Waylon Jennings, Kris Kristofferson, and Willie Nelson—as a background singer and acoustic guitar player, but he always has stated that what he enjoys most is writing songs.

Cobb was inducted into the Georgia Music Hall of Fame in 1993.

ALBERT COLEMAN

Cosmopolitan is the only word adequate to describe the breadth of the musical genius and the scope of the personal experience of Albert Coleman. The originator and conductor of the Atlanta Pops Orchestra, he has given more than five decades of his life to the single-minded pursuit of his goal to make beautiful music available without cost for the appreciation and edification of the masses.

Coleman is a true Renaissance man of music; his life's story is worthy of a Boris Pasternak novel. Although his baton has directed many of the finest symphony orchestras of the world and his electic musical accomplishments span the spectrum from classics to country, the acclaim he has received has far exceeded the meager financial rewards his great talents have earned.

Coleman was born Alfred Emil Emmanuel Crosner in 1911 in Paris, France, the son of a French musician named René and a beautiful Italian bareback horse rider named Carolina, who performed together on the vaudeville stages of South America and in the circus rings of Europe. He was taught the violin by his father, performed with the troupe from the age of five, and escaped with his parents from Russia in the wake of the Bolshevik Revolution in 1917 by riding on the top of a train across Siberia to China.

He grew up among Russian exiles in Shanghai, where he mastered the Russian, Chinese, and English languages, in addition to his native French, and came under the tutelage of the conductor of the Shanghai Symphony Orchestra, in which he played the violin. He was sent back to France to study violin and conducting at the Paris Conservatory; but when his father died in Saigon, French Indochina, when Albert was fourteen, he formed a dance orchestra, in which he played drums, saxophone, and violin, to supplement his mother's income as a language teacher.

His engagements took them throughout the Orient, and at the age of twenty-one, he was guest conductor of the Sydney, Australia, Symphony Orchestra. At the age of twenty-two, he became music conductor for the A. B. Marcus Show, a Ziegfeld-type touring company with which he worked for the next twelve years. He toured in the Far East and around the world, including a visit to Atlanta, where he was playing at the Roxy

Theatre in 1939 when the premiere of *Gone with the Wind* was held down the street at Loew's Grand Theater. His performances took him to Australia, New Zealand, Fiji, Hawaii, the Philippines, China, Japan, Hong Kong, Java, Borneo, the Malay States, Burma, India, and South Africa.

He and his mother escaped from Singapore in advance of the Japanese invasion in 1941 and went first to Mexico and then to Canada, where he met his first wife, ballerina Gwnnyth Moore. They were married in Atlanta, where he accepted a position as music director of radio station WSB in 1945, a post he held for three years. When he became an American citizen in Atlanta on January 28, 1948, he petitioned at the time for his name to be changed to Albert Coleman. He has made his home there since, and his daughter and son were born there.

He conducted four programs a day on WSB, including a very popular midnight show on which he played the violin while other staffers played the organ and read poetry; as part of the station's promotional activities, he established a community orchestra and held the first of Atlanta's pop concerts at Emory University in 1945.

The next year he gave a similar concert at Fort McClellan, Alabama. In 1947 under his baton began the yearly summer series of free public pop concerts that continued until 1976 with the joint financial sponsorship of the city of Atlanta, the Atlanta Federation of Musicians, and the Fox Theater, until the concerts moved outdoors to Chastain Park. Coleman's music organization, which at its zenith was composed of fifty-five musicians and a chorus of thirty voices, took the name Atlanta Pops Orchestra, drew SRO audiences at the Fox and crowds up to ten thousand at Chastain, and attracted as many as two hundred audition requests a year from aspiring young Georgia musicians. The free programs enjoyed the support of Atlanta mayors William B. Hartsfield, Ivan Allen, Jr., and Sam Massell, but were discontinued on a series basis when Mayor Maynard Jackson withdrew the city's six thousand dollar-a-year subsidy in favor of increased support for the Atlanta Symphony Orchestra in 1976. This action resulted in strained relations between Coleman and ASO conductor Robert Shaw, which often spilled over into print. The orchestra continues to perform for conventions like that of the National Conference of State Legislatures in 1981 and for July 4th and Georgia Music Week concerts at Stone Mountain Park.

Because the pops concerts were not planned to be money makers, Coleman never received more than minimum compensation for his services and found it necessary to book talent, work as a radio disc jockey, conduct hotel and nightclub orchestras, play as session and backup musician in Atlanta and Nashville recording studios, and make appearances as guest conductor for more than sixty symphony orchestras around the nation, ranging from Almogordo to Wichita. He conducted orchestras for Atlanta's Theater under the Stars; for the Southern, Civic, and Ruth Mitchell Ballets of Atlanta; for two Southeastern tours by Henry Mancini; for Chet Atkins's European tour; for the WSB-TV Twenty-fifth Anniversary Silver Gala; and for television specials for Kraft, Bob Hope, and Ed Sullivan. He recorded for RCA, including the *Music City Pops* album in 1971, which was highly praised for its combination of country music and the big band sound. In 1983, he and Atlanta music publisher Bill Lowery issued a country album that was nominated for a Grammy titled *Just Hooked on Country*. It was patterned after the smash *Hooked on Classics* album done by the Royal Philharmonic Orchestra.

Although now in his eighties Coleman has made no concession to age. His French accent is as thick as ever. He is active in the promotion of Georgia's growing music industry and reassembles his Pops Orchestra whenever he can obtain funding for the performance of his acclaimed versions of music, running the gamut from rock to Rachmaninoff. He was inducted into the Georgia Music Hall of Fame in 1983.

Albert Coleman, Bill Lowery, and Zell Miller

COLLECTIVE SOUL

Unorthodox probably would be the best way to describe the approach taken by singer/guitarist/songwriter Ed Roland and drummer Shane Evans to break their quintet, Collective Soul, based in Stockbridge, Georgia, out of the obscurity of the pack and into international fame and recognition.

After five years of assembling and playing with various line-ups of what the band finally would become, in a desperate, last-ditch attempt to get his material heard, Roland put together what essentially was a demo of his own efforts as a songwriter and released it under the title, *Hints, Allegations, and Things Left Unsaid*, and threw it to the wind to see what would happen.

Well, happen things did. One of the demo tracks, "Shine," exploded regionally in Georgia, eventually registering RIAA Gold success and spending eight weeks atop the AOR charts, tying the record set fifteen years earlier by Pink Floyd's "Another Brick in the Wall." It brought the band a contract with Atlantic Recording Corporation, an opening slot on the Aerosmith tour, an appearance at Woodstock '94, a performance by Ed on *The Late Show with David Letterman*, and Platinum status for the cut, first in Canada and then in the United States.

"We were very shocked," Roland said in retrospect. "I was hoping to sell ten to twenty thousand records, just enough to be able to make a real Collective Soul album."

Since albums, as a general rule, spawn rather than follow performing success, this cart-before-the-horse experience for Collective Soul brought the group its first official album, appropriately titled *Collective Soul*. It is described as a "bracing" collection of twelve songs, written mostly by Roland, ranging from the "muscular riffing" of the opening track, "Simple," to the "gospel-tinged ballad" that closes the collection, "Reunion." Four of the final titles were written by Roland while he and his associates were whittling the original thirty-five songs being considered down to the chosen dozen.

Like *Hints* before it, the official album was produced by Roland with Matt Serletic and, with the exception of the track "Gel," which had been completed before the album sessions began and already was a rock radio hit, mixing was handled by recording industry veteran Bob Clearmountain, whom the band had met at Woodstock '94.

"Gel" was different because it was produced for the soundtrack of the movie, *The Jerky Boys*. It is a tune that provided a heaving, rhythmic guitar frame for Roland's searching lyrics in a hard-edged context. Asked what it is all about, Roland replied:

"This song is about the coming together of mankind for this movie about these guys making prank phone calls."

The other performer in the final make-up of the band is Roland's brother, guitarist Dean Roland, the two of them having grown up in a strict household under the discipline of a minister-father and never having heard any rock 'n' rollers except Elvis Presley and Jerry Lee Lewis before they were eighteen years old.

Ed studied guitar for a year at Boston's Berklee School of Music before returning home to begin working at an Atlanta area recording studio. He and Evans pursued their dream of a performing band with a recording contract for five years before making it come true with their roundabout strategy.

Once Collective Soul had arrived, it was invited to be the opening act for Van Halen for two months, followed by a nationwide headlining tour on its own. Ed said he and his brother and their fellow band members "won't take it for granted. . . . We still have a lot of growing to do."

Collective Soul

CONFEDERATE RAILROAD

When the Nashville division of Atlantic Records launched its search for that label's answer to the Pirates of the Mississippi, Kentucky Headhunters, Little Texas, Diamond Rio, Highway 101, and the other bands that began dominating the country music scene in the early 1990s, Georgia's Danny Shirley and his Confederate Railroad had just the sound Atlantic wanted.

Lead singer Shirley, drummer Mark Dufruese, keyboardist Chris McDaniel, lead guitarist Michael Lamb, bassist Wayne Secrest, and steel guitarist Gates Nichols had been perfecting their brand of rough and rowdy Southern rock/country hybrid music for ten years as a working band. They had paid their dues as the opening act and touring band with David Allen Coe, had played with Johnny Paycheck, had opened for Lynyrd Skynyrd, and had made a regional name for themselves in the clubs around Augusta. Shirley also had often performed at Miss Kitty's near Atlanta where he shared club dates with another then-unknown Georgia talent, Travis Tritt.

Atlantic executives made the decision to promote the band as a group, instead of Shirley as a headliner backed by the band. It was a most fortunate casting because Confederate Railroad hit the tracks running, striking paydirt with its debut single, "She Took It Like a Man," a catchy story of a jilted lover who refused to take rejection quietly, which was accompanied by a hilarious video featuring then head football coach Jerry Glanville of the Atlanta Falcons and which topped all the other band videos at the time. The Nashville Network put it into the Video PM Show's Hall of Fame.

By the time their self-titled album was issued in 1992, Confederate Railroad was on the road and on the way. The album spawned six singles, including three that made the Top Ten—"Jesus and Mama (Would Always Love Me)," "Trashy Women," and "Queen of Memphis." Shirley and his cohorts had to argue loud and hard for the inclusion of "Jesus and Mama" because the powers-that-be at Atlantic thought their fans might not like its comparison to the rougher honky-tonk image of such cuts as "Trashy Women" and "Time Off for Bad Behavior."

While "She Took It Like a Man" was a satirical rock tune with a shuffle beat, "Jesus and Mama" was a bitter sweet ballad of loyalty and faith overcoming despair written by Dean Hicks and Danny Mayo, who earlier had written hits for the Oak Ridge Boys and Alabama.

Railroad's faith in their product was vindicated when "Jesus and Mama" shot to the top of the charts and gave them the second hit of their Atlantic career.

Coach Glanville and his Falcons so liked the reaction they received from their first Railroad video, they volunteered to perform in a second one for "Queen of Memphis."

In 1994 Atlantic released Railroad's second album, *Notorious.*

Confederate Railroad

ARTHUR CONLEY

There is no telling how far Arthur Conley, a soul singer born in Atlanta, Georgia, on January 4, 1946, might have gone had his manager, the late Otis Redding, not perished in a plane crash just as Conley's career was taking off.

Conley became Redding's protege in 1967 after Redding heard one of his demonstration records and told his own manager, Phil Walden, that he was "the most dynamic young talent I've ever heard." He recorded him on his own Jotis label and produced the single, "Sweet Soul Music," which was distributed by Atlantic Records and became a Gold record. The fact that it went to the top of the charts in England, Holland, the Philippines, and Puerto Rico brought him an enthusiastic European tour.

Later that year Redding produced him back on the charts with two more singles, "Shake, Rattle, and Roll" and "Whole Lotta Woman." His career began to lose momentum with Redding's tragic death, although he did have lesser hits with "Funky Street," "People Sure Act Funny," "Dora's Love Soul Shack" in 1968, his version of the Beatles' "Ob-La-Di, Ob-La-Da" in 1969, and "God Bless" in 1970.

JOHNNY DARRELL

Music stars who were discovered in drugstores have nothing on country music singer and songwriter Johnny Darrell of Marietta, Georgia. He was discovered by United Artists producer Kelso Herstin while Darrell was working as manager of the Holiday Inn just off Music Row in Nashville.

His career as a recording artist was launched with the first of many successful versions of Curley Putnam's classic, "Green, Green Grass of Home," on the Cartwheel label.

While his successes have not been as spectacular as those of some of his contemporaries who expanded the Nashville Sound in the mid-sixties, Darrell proved his ear for hit songs with messages by also being the first to record "Ruby, Don't Take Your Love to Town" (which he had to fight to do because of its controversial subject matter), "The Son of Hickory Holler's Tramp," "With Pen in Hand," and others that were later turned into hits by bigger names.

His talent was early recognized by Kris Kristofferson himself who produced him on six sides for Monument Records in 1972 after he recorded ten albums for United Artists between 1965 and 1969. He also worked on the West Coast with Clarence White of the Byrds, Rusty Young of Poco, Mike Potts of Bread, and other leaders in the fusion of country, pop, and rock styles of the time.

Darrell, who was born in Muscadine, Alabama, grew up in Marietta and Atlanta. He recorded two highly acclaimed albums for Capricorn Records of Macon, *Water Glass Full of Whisky* and *Rice Colored Gin*. Critics praise his voice as one "which transcends country, pop and rock . . . [and] carries the full emotions of the songs as they were written."

MAC DAVIS

Despite the fact that his adoring stepfather, the late Georgia Public Service Commissioner Bill Kimbrough, set him up with a job with the State Board of Probation on the top floor of the State Capitol, Mac Davis could not stay away from the swimming pool at Emory University where he banged on the bongo drums and twanged on his guitar to attract girls. In so doing, he perfected the free-wheeling, crossover rock-pop-country musical style that made him one of the most popular and successful songwriters and performers from the late 1960s to the present.

Davis writes songs and makes jokes about the Texas roots dating from his birth in Lubbock on January 21, 1941, but it was in Georgia that he honed his easy-going "good-ole-boy" manner into the sharp talents of the all-around entertainer who has achieved stardom as the writer and singer of hit songs, the host of his own and special television programs, a headliner at Las Vegas, and an actor in major movies.

From growing up as a choirboy whose idols were Elvis Presley and Buddy Holly, he forsook government employment for a rock group he and his Emory buddies formed called the Zots. They made a reputation for hot licks in the Atlanta area teen hangouts of Misty Waters and Knotty Pines. He was seventeen when he sold his first song, "The Phantom Strikes Again." He later received $2.42 in recording royalties.

He gave up rock 'n' roll in 1961 to take a job as Atlanta regional manager for Vee Jay Records and moved to a similar position with Liberty (now United Artists) Records in 1965. Later he was promoted to head Metric Music, its musical publishing operation in Hollywood. There he began to tout the backlog of songs he had written over the years. He scored in 1967–1968 when Lou Rawls and Glen Campbell made the charts with "You're Good to Me" and "Within My Memory" respectively. Elvis Presley recorded his "A Little Less Conversation" in 1968, which prompted Colonel Tom Parker to rub his curly locks "for luck" and Davis to write some new songs for him.

He gave Presley three hits in 1969–1970—"In the Ghetto," "Memories" and "Don't Cry, Darling"—and wrote music for Elvis's first television special and two of his movies. He then penned "Friend, Lover, Woman, and Wife" and "Daddy's Little Man" for O. C. Smith, "Watching

Scotty Grow" for Bobby Goldsboro, and "Something's Burning" for Kenny Rogers and the First Edition.

His career skyrocketed in the early 1970s when he signed with Columbia and scored with successive Gold Records of "Baby, Don't Get Hooked on Me," "I Believe in Music" (which became a pop standard recorded by more than fifty different artists), "Stop and Smell the Roses," and "One Hell of a Woman." He made a series of best-selling albums around those singles and most of his pop hits also made the country lists.

He had his own television show on NBC, made guest appearances on all the major talk and variety programs from Johnny Carson down, and became a regular headliner in Las Vegas. He was named Country Music

Mac Davis

Association Entertainer of the year, hosting the CMA annual awards telecast for two consecutive years, and received the People's Choice award for Favorite Male Entertainer.

He was still putting hits in the country charts when his pops successes slowed; they included "I Still Love You," "Forever Lovers," and "Picking Up Pieces of My Life." The latter was an autobiographical song, as was "Watching Scotty Grow," which was written about his son.

He began doing a number of highly rated television specials in the mid-seventies and late in the decade moved to Casablanca Records, which put him back in the Top Ten in 1980 with the single "It's Hard to Be Humble," and earned him a Gold record for the album by the same name. Later in the 1980s he added two more top singles "Let's Keep It This Way," and "Texas in My Rear View Mirror," his own composition. Next came singles successes with "Hooked on Music" and "You're My Bestest Friend" and a top-selling album, *Midnight Crazy*. To date he has done three well-received movies: *North Dallas Forty, Cheaper to Keep Her,* and *The Sting II.*

Critics dispute his classification, and, while most tend to put him in the country and western category, he contends one "can't put a label on my music" because it contains "a little bit of everything." He thinks his music appeals more to pop audiences old as well as young. Of all his work, he prefers to do nightclub acts where he can improvise songs from titles suggested by members of his audience.

In the 1990s he appeared on Broadway as Will Rogers in *The Will Rogers Follies* and was a cowriter with Dolly Parton on her hit "White Limozeen."

MATTIWILDA DOBBS

Mattiwilda Dobbs, the product of one of the most distinguished and respected black families of Georgia and the nation, often is credited with doing for blacks in opera what Jackie Robinson did for them in professional baseball.

The daughter of John Wesley Dobbs, the wealthy black entrepreneur who was the acknowledged head of black society in segregated Atlanta and one of the early leaders and officers in the National Association for the Advancement of Colored People, Mattiwilda graduated from Spelman College and studied voice for four years in New York. There her talent won for her the John Hay Whitney Fellowship to study in Paris. She went on to triumph in the prestigious Geneva Competition, which resulted in an audition at La Scala in Milan, Italy, and the role of Elvia in Rossini's *Italian Woman in Algiers*. This brought her glowing reviews. She was acclaimed throughout Europe prior to returning to the United States for an American debut in San Francisco in 1955, one year after the school desegregation decision of the U.S. Supreme Court, and subsequently she became one of the first black persons to sing with the Metropolitan Opera in New York City.

Her voice received the highest critical praise wherever she performed, and her concert tours took her throughout the world, including Sweden, where she met her husband, Swedish government official Bengt Janzon. She made Sweden her home for eighteen years following their marriage. She returned home for a second time in 1975 to hold a successive series of voice professorships at Spelman, the University of Illinois in Urbana, the University of Georgia, and since 1977 at Howard University in Washington, D.C.

Although her main professional activity now is teaching rather than performing, she continues to give four to five concerts a year and to regard Atlanta as her home. In November of 1983 she received the J. Weldon Johnson Award at the annual NAACP Freedom Fund Dinner in Atlanta in recognition of her thirty-five years of stellar achievements in the arts and her contributions to eliminating racial barriers and opening doors for talented black singers in the field of opera.

She has five sisters, all of whom are renowned college professors; she credits all their success to the encouragement of her late father.

"My father said he was a believer in women's liberation because he had six daughters," she told *The Atlanta Journal* in one of her rare interviews. "Even though he wanted us to get married, he wanted us to have our own careers."

She also professes great pride in the accomplishments of her nephew, Maynard Jackson, who served two terms as mayor of Atlanta and was the first black to be elected to such an office in a major Southern city.

Dobbs was elected to the board of directors of the Metropolitan Opera in 1989.

Mattiwilda Dobbs

Dr. Thomas Andrew Dorsey

Dr. Thomas Andrew Dorsey, who grew up in Georgia, began his musical career known as Georgia Tom playing barrelhouse piano in one of Al Capone's Chicago speakeasies and leading Ma Rainey's jazz band. He was still going strong at the age of eighty-three after being "whipped into shape to do the Lord's will" and becoming the world-renowned "Father of Gospel Music." He lived to see the greatest of the more than one thousand gospel songs he wrote, "Precious Lord, Take My Hand," translated into thirty-five languages and sung to ovations from Paris to Sierre Leone. His life is immortalized in the highly acclaimed 1982 musical documentary film, *Say Amen, Somebody*, and his achievements are appropriately recognized by his induction into the Georgia Music, Nashville Songwriters Association, and Gospel Music Association Halls of Fame, and by the establishment of the Thomas A. Dorsey Archives containing his collected works and memorabilia by Fisk University of Nashville, Tennessee, which conferred upon him the honorary degree of doctor of music.

Dorsey learned his religion from his Baptist minister father and the piano from his music teacher mother in Villa Rica, Georgia, where he was born July 1, 1899, and came under the influence of local blues pianists when the Dorseys moved to Atlanta in 1910. He and his family relocated to Chicago during World War I where they joined the Pilgrim Baptist Church. There he studied at the Chicago College of Composition and Arranging and became an agent for Paramount Records. He wrote his first religious song, "If I Don't Get There," in 1921, for which the term "gospel music" was coined to describe it when published in *The Gospel Pearls* by the National Baptist Convention. But his musical interests were more secular at the time, and, after working in Capone's establishment, he graduated to playing the piano, composing and arranging for Les Hite's Whispering Seranaders, and playing along with Fred Pollack as a sideman with Will Walker's Syncopators. With Pollack, he formed his own Wildcat's Jazz Band to back Gertrude Nix Pridgett "Ma" Rainey, who recorded his "Broken Hearted Blues" and "Broken Soul Blues" for Paramount. He was a dominant influence in shaping the style and career of slide guitarist Hudson "Tampa Red" Whittaker, with whom he recorded the best-selling blues hit "Tight Like That" in 1928. Ultimately, Dorsey wrote more than four hundred and sixty rhythm and blues and jazz songs.

A two-year illness beginning in 1925 brought him back to the faith of his father after a minister convinced him "the Lord has work for you" and that he would "be healthy and happy and live for a long time" if he did it. He worked simultaneously in the fields of gospel music and jazz for several more years and had another hit recording with the "hokum" record, "Terrible Operation Blues," done with Jane Lucas in 1930. He was one of the few to welcome Mahalia Jackson to Chicago from New Orleans in 1929 and joined with fellow composer Theodore R. Frye to form the Dorsey Trio, the first group to call itself "gospel singers." In 1931 he and Frye organized the first black church gospel choir in Chicago at Ebernezer Baptist Church, which, as Mahalia later recalled, brought objections from "colored ministers . . . [who] didn't like the hand-clapping and the stomping and . . . said we were bringing jazz into the church and it wasn't dignified."

Dr. Thomas Andrew Dorsey

But the Dorsey style of combining Baptist lyrics with sanctified beat, which previously had been limited to black holiness congregations, caught on, and in 1932 he was appointed choral director of his own Pilgrim Baptist Church, a post he continued to hold as well as that of assistant pastor to which he was named after his subsequent ordination. Discouraged by his own efforts to publish and sell his songs through the old method of peddled "song sheets" and dissatisfied with the treatment given composers of "race" music by the music publishing industry, Dorsey became the first independent publisher of black gospel music with the establishment of the Dorsey House of Music in Chicago in 1932. He also founded and became president of the National Convention of Gospel Choirs and Choruses, and because his own light voice was not suited for the gospel sound, he established the pattern for instrumental accompaniment of gospel songs previously done a capella by hiring Chicago singer Rebecca Tolbert to sing his songs as he played them on the piano, setting the style for such well-known gospel pianists as Roberta Martin, Evelyn Gay, Curtis Dublin, and Herbert Pickard. Additionally, he was the originator of black music concerts, the first being his "Battle of Song" between Roberta and Sally Martin (not related) in Chicago in 1936.

He wrote his classic and most famous song, "Precious Lord," in the grief following the death of his first wife in childbirth in 1932. It since has been recorded by such diverse artists as Mahalia Jackson, Tennessee Ernie Ford, Roy Rogers and Dale Evans, and Elvis Presley, and was the favorite gospel song of both Dr. Martin Luther King, Jr., who asked that it be sung at the rally he led the night before his assassination, and of President Lyndon B. Johnson who requested that it be sung at his funeral. Almost equally well known is his "Peace in the Valley," which he wrote for Mahalia Jackson in 1937 after becoming her pianist in 1935 (a relationship that continued until 1946), which was made into a million-seller country hit by Red Foley and covered by the Jordanaires. Carmen Lombardo made his "My Desire" famous; Morton Downey was successful with his "When I've Done My Best"; Sister Rosetta Tharpe recorded his "Rock Me"; Brother Joe May did his "Search Me, Lord"; the Five Blind Boys popularized his "Our Father"; and others who recorded and sang his works include the Ward Singers, the Roberta Martin Singers, Dwight "Gatemouth" Moore, Sam Cooke, Jimmy Witherspoon, and the Reverend James Cleveland.

Others among the more famous of his hundreds of gospel songs are "If You Ever Needed the Lord Before," "Life Can Be Beautiful," "Let Us Sing

Together," "I'm Going to Live the Life I Sing About," "In the Scheme of Things," "Watching and Waiting," "I'll Tell It Wherever I Go," "Say a Little Prayer for Me," "How about You," "If You See My Savior," "If I Could Hear My Mother Pray," "I Will Put My Trust in the Lord," "The Lord Has Laid His Hands on Me," "Stand by Me" and "We Will Meet Him in the Sweet By and By." He recorded a few of his songs in the early 1930s, but they mostly were done by others. It was not until 1980 that he did his first album as a solo performer, *The Maestro Sings His Masterpieces.* He so dominated the field, however, that during the 1940s and 1950s all gospel songs were referred to as "Dorseys."

One must differentiate between spirituals, which are handed-down religious folk songs, and gospel songs, which are contemporary religious music composed in the style set by Dorsey. While he was an admirer of the hymns done by Dr. Charles A. Tindley of Philadelphia, whom he called his "Idol," Dorsey was the first to combine the sensitivity of black audience demands and reactions; the sincerity and religiosity of Tindley's style; his own autobiographical religious experiences; and compelling rhythms, riffs, and vocal stylings out of the R&B and jazz genres into songs that went back to the roots of black religion and culture. He was the first to organize and sophisticate the "call and response" technique of singing introduced into this country by African slaves and to employ the "closed" harmonic sound of black singing that presents all notes of chords in condensed, high sounds. He also established the differentiations among "slow," "without rhythm," and "fast" gospel songs—classic examples being his slow "Peace in the Valley," his fast "If You Ever Need the Lord Before," and his without rhythm, "Precious Lord, Take My Hand." It was a source of wry amusement to him that many of his "slow" and "without rhythm" songs have become so anglicized that they are used as opening "hymns" at Ku Klux Klan rallies and other segregated, racist functions.

Dorsey's biographer, Ruth Smith, called him a "Twentieth Century David," explaining that "As David sang and played in the courts of Saul, the king, so does Dorsey sing and play before the ministers and their congregations that they might be relieved of the evil that God has suffered to befall them because of their waywardness."

In October 1979, he was the first black elected to the Nashville Songwriters Association's International Hall of Fame. In December 1980 Operation Push highlighted its Jubilee Celebration with the presentation to him of its Push Par Excellent award. In September 1981 his native Georgia honored him with election to the Georgia Music Hall of Fame; in March

1982 he was the first black elected to the Gospel Music Association's Living Hall of Fame; in August 1982 the Thomas A. Dorsey Archives were opened at Fisk University where his collection joined those of W. C. Handy, George Gershwin, and the Jubilee Singers; in September 1982 he was inducted into the New York City Songwriters Hall of Fame; and in October 1982 the world premiere was held of George Nierenberg's film about him and his gospel-music contemporaries, *Say Amen, Somebody*, as part of the New York Film Festival.

In the early 1980s he formed the Dorsey Gospel Team with educator Dr. Clayton Hannah and music arranger Gregory Cooper to tour the nation to present programs of his works, saying "You've got to do something to live," and to present his rebuttal to then-current interpretations of his songs that he said have "junked them up." Summing up his life, he said all his work has been "from God, for God, and for his people."

PETE DRAKE

To put food in the mouths of his wife and six children, Roddis Franklin "Pete" Drake, the son of a Georgia Baptist minister who gave up an Atlanta bread route for the recording studios of Nashville, literally taught the pedal steel guitar to talk.

Pete Drake, more than any other individual, created a resurgence of use of that instrument in both country and pop music to the extent that he played in thirty-eight of the recording sessions of forty-eight BMI award-winning songs for 1966, and probably was more in demand as a backup musician than any artist of his time.

Not only did he have a Gold record for his own 1964 hit, "Forever," but he also backed an astounding list of hits for others ranging from Tammy Wynette's "Stand by Your Man" to Bob Dylan's "Lay, Lady, Lay" to albums for Beatles' George Harrison and Ringo Starr.

His Stop Records, Pete's Place Recording Studio, and Window Music Publishing Company were among the busiest in the Music City.

Born in Augusta on October 8, 1932, and reared in Atlanta, Pete bought his first steel guitar from a pawnshop for $33 and taught himself to play it in the style of Jerry Byrd while still in his teens. He built his own pedal steel guitar and formed his first band, Sons of the South, composed of the incredible fledgling talents of himself, Jack Greene, Dory Kershaw, Roger Miller, Jerry Reed, and Joe South.

Moving to Nashville on the encouragement of Egyptian Ballroom owner Kathleen Jackson, he responded to rebuffs from recording artists who wanted "string sections" by developing techniques for duplication of all string sounds on the steel guitar, making himself "the cheapest string section in Nashville." He backed Roy Druskey's hit, "I Don't Believe You Love Me Anymore," and followed it with George Hamilton IV's smash "Before This Day Ends."

Then following through on an idea born when watching some old Alvino Rey films, he developed a mouth device that permitted him to speak words through the amplified strings of the steel guitar. Its debut created a sensation at the Grand Ole Opry, for which he subsequently wrote and recorded its theme "For Pete's Sake." His albums were big successes and he employed the technique for the hits of Roger Miller, "Lock, Stock, and

Teardrops," and Jim Reeves, "I've Enjoyed As Much of This As I Can Stand." His work won for him the *Cash Box* Instrumentalist of the Year award in 1964 and *Record World's* Fastest Climbing Instrumentalist of the Year and Number Two Most Programmed Instrumentalist of the Year awards in 1964 and 1969 respectively.

Both Bob Dylan and Joan Baez asked for him to work on the three albums they each recorded in Nashville, including Dylan's *Nashville Skyline* and Baez's *David's Album*. Ringo Starr came to Nashville to do his *Beaucoups of Blues* album with him, and George Harrison invited him to England to do his *All Things Must Pass* album with him there.

He also did backup work for the hits of Lynn Anderson with "Rose Garden," Charlie Rich with "Behind Closed Doors," and Johnny Rodriguez with "Pass Me By." He recorded a classic series of albums with Grand Ole Opry veterans such as Ernest Tubb, Charlie Louvin, and Jan Howard.

The list of stars with whom he worked sounds like a who's who of pop and country ranging from Elvis Presley, Buffy Sainte Marie, and Perry Como to George Jones, Marty Robbins, and Bill Anderson. But he was proudest of creating the popular new sound of the steel guitar, which he called "the most soulful of all instruments" and warned "if you don't want to get hurt, don't listen to it."

He was inducted into the International Steel Guitar Hall of Fame in 1987 and died the following year from respiratory problems.

Pete Drake

DIXIE DREGS

It looked as if the musical dreams of classmates Steve Morse and Andy West were dashed for good when Steve was expelled from Richmond Academy in Augusta, Georgia, in the early 1970s for refusing to cut his long hair, but then Morse met two more talented musicians in Rod Morgenstein and Allen Sloan when he went to the University of Miami. Along with West, they formed the Dixie Dregs Band in 1972 and broke out of the pack of bands flourishing in that decade with a no-vocals, all-instrumental sound—similar to that of the Mahavishnu Orchestra—that defied labeling and has been described variously as progressive jazz, rock, country, and even classical music.

Guitarist Morse and bassist West had called their original high school group Dixie Grit, but they changed the "Grit" to "Dregs" when they reorganized since they were all that was left. Morgenstein became the new drummer, Sloan the electric violinist, and Steve Davidowski the keyboardist doubling on alto and soprano saxophone. They were playing in a nightclub in Macon, Georgia, in 1977 when Phil Walden of Capricorn Records, the man who made the Allman Brothers Band famous, caught their act and signed them to a contract. At the same time Twiggs Lyndon, who had worked with Little Richard, Otis Redding, and the Allmans, signed on as their road manager.

The Dregs produced their first album for Capricorn, *Free Fall*, in March 1977 and followed it quickly with a second, *What If*, which produced the hit single "Taking It off the Top." This brought the invitation for them to star on the closing night of the Montreux International Jazz Festival in Switzerland on July 23, 1978. Immediately thereafter Capricorn released a double live album *Hotels, Motels, and Road Shows* featuring the Dregs.

T. Lavitz succeeded Davidowski as keyboardist, and the band enjoyed great popularity on the nightclub and concert circuits. The group recorded its fourth and most successful album, *Dregs of the Earth*, for Arista in 1980, and was nominated for a Grammy as Best Instrumental Group in 1981.

ROY DRUSKY

Roy Frank Drusky's boyhood dream was to be a professional baseball player and he once had a tryout with the Cleveland Indians. But he soon realized that writing and singing songs was what he really wanted to do. He proceeded to put more than fifty hits on the charts between 1953 and 1977, including ten Number One records. He also went on to establish himself as one of the most popular stars of the Grand Ole Opry and is a director of the Opry Trust Fund.

Born June 22, 1930, in Atlanta, Drusky taught himself to pick a pawnshop guitar while serving in the Navy. After service, he played in clubs and worked as a disc jockey for a Decatur radio station and then worked at Channel 11 television in Atlanta. He moved to Minneapolis as a deejay and club performer and recorded his first hit "Such a Fool" for Starday Records in 1953. This initial success led to contracts with Columbia and Decca. His composition "Alone With You" was a hit for Faron Young. He joined the Opry in 1958.

He made the Top Ten in 1960 with "Another" and repeated the performance in 1961 with cowritten releases of "I Went Out of My Way" and "I'd Rather Loan You Out." In 1963 he had a hit with "Second Hand Rose." His first Number One record was a duet in 1965 with Priscilla Mitchell, "Yes, Mr. Peters." He was again in the upper charts in 1966 with "White Lightning Express" and "World is Round." He had three singles in the charts in 1967 and in the 1970s scored with "All My Hard Times," "Close to Home," and "Betty's Song."

Other Number One hits include "Three Hearts in A Tangle," "Long, Long Texas Road," "Jody and the Kid," and "Strangers."

He has done country music movies, toured extensively at home and abroad, issued more than thirty-five albums, won more than two dozen music awards, and established his own music publishing firm, Funny Farm Music.

Roy is a devout layman in the Seventh Day Adventist Church.

Roy Drusky

JERMAINE DUPRI

Just as Hank Aaron's home run record is expected to stand forever, so Jermaine Dupri's record-shattering achievement of having been the youngest professional music producer in history is likely to remain unexcelled.

He produced his first record in 1987 at the age of thirteen, landing a recording deal with Geffen Records for the female rap trio, Silk Tymes Leather; hit it big with the discovery of the precocious hip hop duo Kris Kross three years later; and convinced Sony Music/Columbia Records to offer him a label deal for his So So Def Recordings, Inc., at the age of nineteen in 1992.

At the ripe old age of twenty-three, he's an astute businessman sitting at the helm of his own recording empire, producing hit-after-hit records not only for Kris Kross but also for the likes of Da Brat, TLC, Xscape, Notorious B.I.G., and Mariah Carey.

This has come as no surprise to those who watched Dupri's development as a child prodigy and entrepreneur extraordinare since the day in 1982, at the age of nine, he talked his way onto the stage and danced with superdiva Diana Ross to the cheers of seventeen thousand fans at her Atlanta concert.

Of course, it did not hurt that his father, Michael Mauldin, was the coordinator of that Atlanta show; just as it has not been any obstacle to his recording career that his father now is the executive vice president of the BlackOut (Black Music) division of Columbia Records. But the record is clear, father or no father, that Dupri has the touch for making it big for himself and the talent he discovers and molds. He and his So So Def label are giving a new generation of music listeners the pleasure of hearing and supporting great new music.

Dupri discovered the co-called "Chrises"—Chris Kelly and Chris Smith—when they were twelve years old while they were shopping for sneakers at Atlanta's Greenbrier Mall. He was impressed by their youthful charisma and advanced sense of style and grooming; and, after a little conversation, the three of them began the mutually beneficial symbiotic relationship that has made all of them rich and famous and established Atlanta as the epicenter of hip hop.

It was he who gave Kris Kross its catchy name; dreamed up their backwards-jeans style of dress, which immediately caught on with pubescent and adolescent fans; wrote, arranged, and produced their multiPlatinum debut Ruffhouse album, *Totally Krossed Out,* and subsequent string of successes; and guided them from wide-eyed juvenile performers to sexy young males destined to be a recording and performing force for years to come.

When he got his own recording label, he racked up his second talent coup in signing the female quartet from his native College Park, Xscape, which soared to Number One with its debut single, "Just Kickin' It," and achieved Platinum status, as did both of their first two albums, *Hummin' Coming at 'Cha* and *Off the Hook.*

From there he nailed down his reputation of having the "Midas touch" with finding and recording on his label Da Brat, the first female rap artist to have a million-seller debut album with *Funkdafied,* as well as a Platinum single of the same title. He moved from there into the dance game with Playa Poncho and his hit, "Whatz Up, Whatz Up," and masterminded the return of rappers Whodini and the debuts of the new, sultry sound of NeeNa Lee and the lyrical excellence of Mr. Black. Another of his successful projects was the production in 1996 of the So So Def Bass All-Stars Compilation featuring the combined and coordinated talents of Player Poncho, Luke, Kilo, and other big and growing names from his talent stable.

KENNY "BABYFACE" EDMONDS

Take it from no less an authority than *Newsweek* magazine, singer/songwriter/producer Kenny "Babyface" Edmonds, co-owner with Antonio "L. A." Reid of Atlanta's soaring LaFace Records, "may be the most successful songwriter and producer in pop." *Rolling Stone* magazine goes a step further in its unqualified assessment that he "may well be the best singer/songwriter in the business." His statistics certainly seem to bear out such professional superlatives.

Over the past decade, Edmonds has had ninety-eight Top Ten R&B and Pop hits, thirty-seven Number One R&B hits, thirty-eight Top Ten pop hits, and ten Number One chart toppers that have produced record sales of more than twenty million singles and sixty-four million albums. These have won him four Grammy awards and six additional Grammy nominations for producing, writing, and performing since 1989, two of the nominations being shared with his partner, Reid. As an artist, two of his albums, *Tender Lover* and *For the Cool in You,* both went certified double-Platinum, and he was named one of *People* magazine's "Fifty Most Beautiful People of 1995."

He has written hit songs for an unbelievable who's who of current stars, including, in alphabetical order, Paula Abdul, Boyz II Men, Toni Braxton, Bobby Brown, Tevin Campbell, Mariah Carey, Sheena Easton, El DeBarge, Aretha Franklin, Johnny Gill, Whitney Houston, Michael Jackson, Gladys Knight, Madonna, TLC, Karyn White, and Vanessa Williams. At one time *Billboard's* Pop and R&B charts listed twelve songs that were written, produced, and/or sung by Edmonds.

He has credits for a veritable "cream-of-the-crop" list of soundtracks and/or featured songs for top movies of the 1990s, led by the phenomenal *Waiting to Exhale* and including *The Pagemaster, Poetic Justice, Boomerang, Ghostbusters II,* and *The Bodyguard.*

Two singles that he wrote and produced for Boyz II Men set and then shattered their own record—"End of the Road" became one of the biggest-selling singles of all time and surpassed Elvis Presley's "Heartbreak Hotel" in its thirteen-week stay on *Billboard's* Hot 100, and "I'll Make Love To You" broke that record with a fourteen-week stay at Number One and tied

Whitney Houston's "I Will Always Love You" as the longest-running Number One Hot 100 single ever.

Edmonds own single, "When Can I See You," from his *For the Cool in You* album, was a Top Five across-the-board hit on the Pop, R&B, and adult contemporary radio charts and achieved Gold status with sales of more than 500,000. That album also yielded three other Top Ten hits, including "For the Cool in You," "Never Keeping Secrets," and "And Our Feelings."

He co-headlined a tour with Boyz II Men, which prompted *USA Today* to opine that he "stole the show with a classy, crafty set," proving himself to be "a consummate performer . . . [and] the premier songwriter in the Pop/R&B world."

He serves as national spokesman and foremost fund-raiser for the Washington, D.C.-based Boarder Baby Project. He works out of the LaFace Records offices in Atlanta, and he and his wife, Tracey Edmonds, who is president of Yab Yum Records, reside in Beverly Hills, California.

Kenny "Babyface" Edmonds

WALTER FORBES

Walter Tillou Forbes always knew he would be expected to move into the management of the Forbes family textile and farming businesses, but he insisted upon following the siren song of his first love of music as a young man and made quite a name for himself in so doing.

He had his own band, the Lonesome Travelers, played on the Grand Ole Opry for ten years between 1960 and 1970, recorded two acclaimed bluegrass-style albums for Chet Atkins at RCA, and played the leading role in the Walt Disney television production, *The Nashville Coyote*, which was Disney's first venture into country music and the highest-rated Disney television feature of 1973. Of his performing efforts, Forbes acknowledges that they did not make much money but were a lot of fun and attracted a lot of attention.

Forbes came by his artistic bent naturally. He was the great, great nephew of Georgians Frank Stanton, who wrote "Mighty Like a Rose," and Lucy Stanton, who was a well-known artist of the impressionist era. His first musical memories are of hearing the banjo played at Grandfather's Athens YMCA camp at Georgia's Tallulah Falls and of listening to the John Allan Lomax collection of records, "Smoky Mountain Ballads," which included songs by the Monroe Brothers, Gid Tanner and the Skillet Lickers, Uncle Dave Macon, and the Carter Family, among others.

His first stage performance was with the Mickey Mouse Club in Chattanooga, Tennessee, in 1948. He played the mandolin in a high school band called the Dismembered Tennesseans at the McCallie School in Chattanooga during 1950–1953. He graduated to playing the guitar in the Golden Blues dance band at the Choate School in 1955–1956 and, while in service in 1957–1958, founded and played banjo and guitar in the Third Marine Division Poor Boys in Japan and Okinawa, an ensemble that was so good the Armed Forces sent it to perform at various military bases in the Far East.

Forbes played guitar and was the lead singer with the Lonesome Travelers in Chattanooga in 1958–1960; his fellow performers in that band were Norman Blake, Bob Johnson, and David Johnston. They appeared twice on NBC's the *Today Show* and began performing at the Grand Ole Opry in 1960 as Walter Forbes and the Lonesome Travelers while he was attending the University of Georgia. Chet Atkins liked them so much he produced two albums of their music, *Ballads and Bluegrass* in 1963 and *Folksong Festival* in 1964.

He met Jack Clement of Beaumont, Texas, in 1963, and the two of them, with Allan Reynolds and Dickie Lee, produced a number of musical and video efforts and developed the innovative concept of producing a stage show with a mixing board located in the audience. Although, as admitted, they did not make a lot of money, many of the ideas they explored and perfected have found their way into the mainstream of country music and video production.

Forbes went to work in the family business in 1965, but continued to play on the Grand Ole Opry until 1970. After he starred in the Disney television production in 1973, he and Clement recorded an album of songs from that movie for Disney, with Clement doing the talking blues narration over Forbes's singing and playing.

He found ways to use his music to sell thread and entertain customers, and he and Don Cassell, a salesman for Signal Thread Company, produced an album of original songs for Jack Music Publishing, *Tried and True*, a production for which Forbes played the mandolin, guitar, and dobro.

Forbes lives in Walker Country, Georgia, with his wife of thirty-five years, the former Katherine Sibley Bryan of Union Point, Georgia. They have three children and two grandsons, and he still owns and operates Malatchie Farms in Macon County.

Walter Forbes

THE FORESTER SISTERS

The Forester Sisters of Lookout Mountain, Georgia, are living proof that perky beauties with wholesome, well-scrubbed images can champion the causes of liberated women and make chauvinistic males like it.

That's what Kathy, June, Kim, and Christy Forester, who got their start singing in their church choir, did in their first hit with the Warner Brothers label in 1985 and have been doing with increasing frequency and popularity ever since.

That first recording, "(That's What You Do) When You're in Love," hit the Top Ten with its twist from a woman's point-of-view on the traditional cheating theme of country music. It was a stand-by-your-man song about forgiving a man who had cheated on his sweetheart but with the underlying implication that the woman had been doing some cheating of her own.

It was followed up by a single, "I Fell in Love Again Last Night," which went to Number One on the charts and led off a string of fifteen Top Ten singles, including five Number Ones. A year after the first of their feminist songs, they released their cut of "Lyin' in His Arms Again," which was a clever play on words by a spunky girl who cheated on her man in a clearly defined reversal of the gender of country's usual cheating role.

These and their other spirited, female-perspective songs were the product of producer Wendy Waldman, who had had a folk-rock singer/ songwriter career of her own in the 1970s. It was she who supplied them with one of their most moving early hits in 1988, "Letter Home," a simple narrative about a homecoming queen who foolishly married when she was too young and was deserted by the husband who left her to raise the children alone. The song lamented the impact of infidelity upon the woman left behind with the children, an aspect of cheating and family breakup that had seldom previously been explored by male-dominated country music.

But their most notable woman's song came in 1991 with their scornful, but humorous, diatribe against the opposite sex, "Men," which went over big with the following of young female boot-wearers the Foresters had attracted. After it came "I Got a Date" in 1992 and its popular video about a newly single mother going out on her first date after her divorce. It was cited by the critics as proof of Nashville's belated recognition of America's changing sexual and family demographics.

The Sisters also discovered brothers in the Bellamy Brothers with whom they did two hit duets before leaving Warner Brothers in 1993.

The Forester women were born to a father who was a farmer and a mother who was a millworker. All four were destined for school-teaching careers until they discovered their performing potential at clubs and parties in the Chattanooga, Tennessee, area.

After Kathy and June graduated from college and got their degrees, they decided to form a band, and Kim and Christy quit school in 1992 to join the older siblings. Since they lived just across the state line from Muscle Shoals, Alabama, they made their way there to do a demo that found its way into the hands of Jim Ed Norman and the executives at Warner Brothers. By the end of 1984 they had a contract and the following year hit it big with their first single.

From there, their sweet, soaring harmonies and lyrics with a contemporary bite took them to the top. Nashville and the entire country music world were unable to resist their sunny harmonies and golly-gosh-gee-whiz personalities. Women fans loved them and bought their records, and men found them too sweet, frothy, and wholesome to be threatening, their lyrics to the contrary notwithstanding.

Their up-tempo approach to their music and message left everybody who heard them feeling good, albeit for different reasons.

Before leaving Warner Brothers, they issued two albums: *Greatest Hits* and *Talkin' about Men*, the latter a concept album about the trouble men create for women.

WALLY FOWLER

The name of Wally Fowler, who was born near Rome, Georgia, in 1917 and grew up singing in a little country church in Bartow County, is not a household word; but those of some of the superstars he helped get their starts are, and any aficionado of gospel music can tell you that he was the father of the "All Night Gospel Sings" that have been packing auditoriums throughout the Southeast and much of the remaining eastern half of the United States since the 1950s.

A list of his firsts in the entertainment business is mind-boggling. He took on a young guitar picker by the name of Chet Atkins as his cohost on his Midday Merry-Go-Round program on radio station WNOX in Knoxville, Tennessee, for nine months in 1944 and 1945. He was the founder and original baritone for the Oak Ridge Quartet, now known as the fabulously successful Oak Ridge Boys, and worked with them on the "Prince Albert" portion of the Grand Ole Opry from 1946 through 1950. He introduced Hank Williams to general manager Hank Stone of the Grand Ole Opry. He founded Bullet Records and produced Francis Craig's smash hit, "Near You." He wrote Eddy Arnold's first million-selling song, "That's How Much I Love You"; the gospel classic "Wasted Years," which has been recorded by fifty-six gospel groups and individuals and which Elvis Presley was scheduled to revive at the time of his death; and, with Warren Roberts, "May the Lord Bless You Real Good," which was Dean Martin's hit song from his movie *Ada*. He gave the late Patsy Cline her first professional singing job on a program he produced in Virginia in the early 1950s, and he arranged Elvis's first audition with the Blackwood Quartet, which was where Elvis demonstrated for the first time how he could make women in an audience go wild. (His continuing friendship with Presley culminated in his writing two songs, "A New Star in Heaven" and "He's Never Alone," which are featured on his album *Wally Fowler Sings a Tribute to Elvis Presley*, along with his recorded recollections of his first meeting with Elvis. The album has been described as the "one sincere Elvis tribute.")

Although the first singing group he formed, the Georgia Clodhoppers, specialized in bluegrass music, Fowler's first and greatest love was gospel singing. In that field his name is best known. He sang with the legendary

V. O. Stamps over station KRLD in Dallas, Texas, before staging the first of his "All Night Gospel Sing" concerts in 1946 at the Ryman auditorium in Nashville. It packed the 3,400 maximum seating capacity of that hall and started Fowler on a seventeen-year career of producing such concerts monthly in the major Southeastern cities of Atlanta, Memphis, Birmingham, and Nashville, and later into the major centers of the North, Midwest, and Southwest. His shows consistently proved they could outdraw any other kind of entertainment, including wrestling and circuses, and were the subject of a number of national magazine articles, including one done by Furman Bisher for *The Saturday Evening Post* entitled "They Put Rhythm in Religion." Fowler also engaged in litigation with his brother and sister-in-law over his rights to the name "The Original Wally Fowler Gospel and Spiritual All-Night Singing Concert."

Fowler went on to realize his lifelong ambition of having his own recording label with the establishment of his Dove Records International, Inc., which specialized in the recording and publication of gospel music, his own and others.

He died of a massive heart attack while on a fishing trip in June 1994.

JESSE FULLER

Jesse Fuller never knew the exact date (March 21) of his birth in 1896 in Jonesboro, Georgia, because he was "given away" by his mother. But he had music in his soul that began coming out when he made his own mouthbow and guitar at the age of seven while living near Macedonia, Georgia. His musical inclination persisted through many menial jobs ranging from working in a Brunswick, Georgia, chair factory to stretching canvas for a circus. It culminated in his becoming an acclaimed folk-blues artist in California where he invented a unique instrument he called a "fotdella." He wrote "San Francisco Bay Blues," which became popular when it was recorded by Peter, Paul, and Mary. Fuller also saw his song performed at numerous folk festivals and by such legendary rock groups as the Rolling Stones and the Animals before he died in Oakland in 1976.

Fuller was "discovered" shining shoes near the gate of United Artists by Douglas Fairbanks, Sr., who got him bit parts in several movies, but he forsook Hollywood for Oakland where he worked in construction by day and came to the attention of jazz and folk artists in San Francisco through his musical dates at night. He opened another shoeshine stand that became a hangout for folk music fans in Berkeley. He became a close friend of folk-singer Barbara Dane with whom he performed. He also invented his "fotdella," which was a one-man band rig featuring piano strings and cymbals or washboard played by right and left foot pedals respectively, harmonica and kazoo held by harness and six- or twelve-string guitars. He was the uninvited hit of the 1959 Monterey Jazz Festival, which publicly brought him invitations to similar festivals throughout the United States and to England in 1966 to star with the Stones and the Animals.

Although it was written in 1954, "San Francisco Bay Blues" did not become known until it was recorded by Peter, Paul, and Mary. It then kindled an interest in Fuller's music that resulted in nine albums being issued between 1958 and 1967 by Prestige, GT, Arhoolie, and Fantasy Records, of which only the latter's *Brother Lowdown* remains commercially available.

Despite all the hardship and heartache of his life, Fuller never became bitter or despairing, and his music was always upbeat and featured messages of hope and beauty.

TERRI GIBBS

When success happened for Terri Gibbs, the blind country soul singer from Grovetown, Georgia, whose smokey, bluesy, velvet-throated voice has been described as the deepest alto in music, it came with the impact of the opening of the flood gates of a high dam. But in perspective, it was far less the Cinderella story it has been called than the culmination of years of stubborn dreaming and struggling dues-paying, the miracle of which is that it happened at all.

Not even Jimmy the Greek would quote odds on a country artist's first single being released on a major label, becoming a Top Ten smash, achieving crossover success, putting her on the Grand Ole Opry, and winning for her more than a dozen of the industry's top nominations and awards. But that is the way it was with Terri's "Somebody's Knockin'" in 1981.

It all seemed like a lot of magic except to those who knew her years of study, practice, hard work, and effort, and the disappointment, persistence, hope, and plain luck that made it more than just the aspirations of a girl born sightless on June 15, 1954, who could play tunes she heard on the piano from the age of three.

Gibbs's unique singing and playing style, which evokes surprise from initial listeners that she is a white woman, developed from a childhood of playing the piano instead of playing with dolls. She listened to a mix, from the harmonies of the Everly Brothers, to Loretta Lynn, Patti Page, and Pat Boone, from the soul of Aretha Franklin and Isaac Hayes to the rhythm and blues of Ray Charles to the rock of Elvis Presley and Janis Joplin. It is almost a shocking experience to see her for the first time rhythmically rocking on the piano bench in almost the same way as Ray Charles, whom she never will see, and singing with the same bluesy touch as he.

Gibbs's first public performances were of gospel songs in church and winning high school talent contests. At seventeen she opened an Augusta performance by Bill Anderson and at eighteen met Chet Atkins who invited her to send him a tape and then helped her come to Nashville to do a demo that somehow was lost until it came to the attention of Nashville songwriter/producer Ed Penney five years later.

During the interim she played keyboard and sang backup for a local band called Sound Dimension and then formed her own group that

Terri Gibbs

performed to local acclaim at Augusta's Steak and Ale Restaurant, singing fifty songs in three sets nightly for five years.

When Penney found the tape, it did not have her address; but luckily, one of the many other demos she subsequently made and sent to everyone in Nashville reached him shortly thereafter. Thus, the contact was made that resulted in her *Somebody's Knockin'* album and single of the same title being issued by MCA to almost instantaneous popularity.

In April of 1981 she received the Top New Female Vocalist award of the Academy of Country Music. In June she was nominated Most Promising Female Artist of the Year by *Music City News. Record World* magazine named her Most Promising Female Vocalist of Adult Contemporary Music and ranked her third as Top New Female Vocalist in Pop Music and in the ten Top Adult Contemporary Female Vocalists and in October gave her its Top New Female Vocalist of the Year in Country

Music award. In September the Atlanta Songwriters Association gave her the Georgia Recording Artist of the Year award, which was followed shortly by an invitation to appear on the Grand Ole Opry. In October the Country Music Association nominated her for Female Vocalist and Single of the Year and presented her with its New Horizon award as the top new talent of the year. That same month *Cash Box* magazine named her New Female Vocalist of the Year in Country Music, and she was presented the Grammy award for New Female Vocalist in Los Angeles.

She followed her initial success with a second album, *I'm a Lady*, from which singles were issued both of the title song and the old Tony Bennett hit, "I Wanna Be Around." Single releases also were made of "Rich Man" from her first album and of "Wishing Well," which was written by David Hensley and herself. She since has formed her own music publishing company, changed the emphasis on her career from concerts to music writing, and purchased a white antebellum home in Augusta where she lives and works with her pet chickens named after her favorite singers.

EMORY GORDY, JR.

Ask any fan of recorded music who Emory Gordy, Jr., is, and the response probably will be a blank stare. But play them a few recordings featuring his trademark melodic twists and driving, ball-of-fire bass style, and their fingers will start snapping and their toes commence to tapping as they recognize the unique rhythmic and hypnotic style this virtuoso bassist has brought to the music of many of the greatest performers of the past three decades—stars ranging from Elvis Presley to Neil Diamond, Emmylou Harris to Patty Loveless, and Mac Davis to Billy Joel.

It is a good thing that Gordy is self-deprecating to a fault, because in his incomparable musical career he has played on the road and in the studio with, as he puts is, "just about everybody who's somebody and a lot of people who aren't." He has laid down prize-winning, record-setting tracks for Debbie Reynolds, Liberace, Vince Gill, Razzy Bailey, the Bellamy Brothers, Jimmy Buffet, Roy Orbison, Rufus Thomas, Steve Earle, Dan Fogelberg, and many others. He played with Harris's incomparable Hot Band when it was at its hottest, his sensitive bass propelling such evergreen hits as "Two More Bottles of Wine," "C'est La Vie," and "Together Again," and he provided the sparkplugs for the classic "Ain't Living Long Like This" by Rodney Crowell and the acclaimed "Seven Year Ache" by Crowell's then-spouse, Rosanne Cash. He toured the United States, Australia, and Europe with John Denver, substituted for Otis Redding's guitarist at the Apollo, and fulfilled a long-held wish to produce an album for his idol, the legendary Bill Monroe.

Born in Atlanta on Christmas Day, 1944, Gordy proved himself a genuine musical prodigy by playing the piano at the age of four; mastering the trumpet at six; taking up the ukulele, banjo, guitar, and euphonium in high school; switching to the French horn to gain a slot with the Georgia State University Concert Band while majoring in mathematics academically; and further switching to the bass at the age of eighteen and deciding three years later that it would be his life's instrument of choice.

He met Joe South while playing at an Atlanta area sock hop in 1964 and credits him with teaching him "everything that I now know in the studio." South introduced him to Atlanta recording kingpin Bill Lowery, and that led to his recording with Razzy Bailey, Mac Davis, Freddy Weller, and Tommy Roe, and touring as a band leader with Lou Christy, Rufus Thomas, and the Tams.

Except for the chance to play with Redding, his move to New York in 1965 was both ill-fated and short-lived, but his subsequent move to Los Angeles in 1970 at the behest of drummer Dennis St. John, a longtime friend from Atlanta, proved more fortunate with the opportunities it brought to work with Reynolds and Liberace. It also led to his touring with Diamond, playing the guitar, mandolin, bass, vibes, percussion, and nine instruments in all, and producing the smash album, *Hot August Night,* which established Gordy as a much-in-demand sideman.

That culminated in a call in 1973 for him to sit in as a substitute bassist for a Presley recording session, a week's work that led to the hits "Separate Ways" and "Burning Love" and brought acknowledgement from Presley that Gordy's were the most prominent bass lines that Presley had had on any of his hits. Eventually, Gordy took over the live bass chair for all of Presley's recording sessions.

He was chosen to play bass for Gram Parson's posthumously released 1974 album, *Grievous Angel,* and, although he does not remember it, was spotted by Emmylou Harris at the recording sessions. She asked him to be a charter member of her Hot Band when she started her meteoric rise in 1975, an assignment he continued until 1977, playing on Harris's hit albums *Luxury Liner,* the all-acoustic *Roses in the Snow,* and the Grammy-winning *Blue Kentucky Girl* of 1979. During the same period he did studio work for Tom Petty, the Bellamy Brothers, and Billy Joel, before getting the call from Rodney Crowell who knew him from their Hot Band days.

At the present he spends most of his time in the studio, still producing independent country hits like "Lonely Days, Lonely Nights" with Patty Loveless and "Oklahoma Border" with Vince Gill. He has found common ground with Texas songwriter Steve Earle and has benefitted from the merger of Earle's road-weary angst and hillbilly rock with his own rock and country sensibilities.

Gordy's discography reads like a Who's Who of American Music of the mid-1960s through the mid-1990s. But it represents achievements upon which he refuses to dwell or count Gold records, saying:

"If you try to keep up with that stuff, you're like the guy in the Bible who looks back and turns into a pillar of salt. If you take one second to contemplate or look back on it, the world has left you."

If there is any one achievement of which Gordy is singularly proud it would have to be said his discovery of an ingenious way to play both regular and tic-tac bass lines simultaneously on one instrument, a "double bass" effect that is technically hard to explain but easy to recognize on such hits as Emmylou Harris's "Together Again" and "One of These Days." He uses three favorite basses that he treasures like his life—a refinished 1960 Fender jazz bass that he acquired in 1974, a 1960 Precision that he laughingly says "comes with overhead drive and adjustable cams," and an eight-string Hagstrom modified to four strings that he uses for his country "tic-tac" sound.

Gordy was inducted into the Georgia Music Hall of Fame in 1992.

Emory Gordy, Jr.

VERN GOSDIN

It is a supreme bit of irony that a song entitled "Yesterday's Gone" made a forty-year-old dream to sing on the Grand Ole Opry come true for Vern Gosdin after he had all but given up on the ambition.

Born August 5, 1934, in Woodland, Alabama, Vern and his brother Rex, who lived in Hampton, Georgia, listened to the Opry on a battery radio on the family farm and dreamed of growing up to sing like the Louvin Brothers. In the early fifties they had their Gosdin Family Gospel Show on Birmingham Station WVOK, but Vern left to come to Atlanta to support himself by selling ice cream while seeking work as a country music artist.

In 1956 he went to Chicago to run a country music nightclub and in 1960 joined Rex in California in a bluegrass group, the Golden State Boys. He later switched to a group called the Hillmen whose leaders, Chris Hillman and Clarence White, recorded a song written by Vern, "Someone to Turn To," for the soundtrack of the movie *Easy Rider*. He and Rex did "Hangin' On" for the Bakersfield International label, and it rose to eighteen on the charts and brought them a contract with Capitol in 1967, for which they recorded "Til the End" by Vern's wife Cathy. However, divorce and disillusionment with the lack of progress on their career brought a breakup of the act, and Vern returned to Atlanta to open a glass and mirror business.

In 1976 producer Gary Paxton, whom Vern had known in Los Angeles, called and asked if he would be interested in reissuing "Hangin' On." Consequently, he went to Nashville, where he did "Yesterday's Gone" with Emmylou Harris singing the harmony instead. That song made the Top Twenty and resulted in an album that resurrected "Til the End"; this recording made it to the Top Five.

The publicity brought an invitation to the Opry and a succession of hits beginning with "Mother Country Music" in October 1977 and continuing with "It Started All Over Again" and "Break My Mind" in 1978. Early that year he and Rex got back together to record "Never My Love," which was a hit, and they resumed performing together for concert dates. In 1979 he charted with "You've Got Somebody, I've Got Somebody" and "Sarah's Eyes." He followed with the hit "Too Long Gone" in 1981, and he began 1983 with the Top Ten success of his own composition, "If You're Going To Do Me Wrong (Do It Right)."

He had his first Number One song in 1984 with "I Can Tell by the Way You Dance" on Compleat Records. He later signed with Columbia and had a huge hit "Chisled in Stone" and in 1987 had a Gold-certified album.

Rex Gosdin, one of Georgia's most talented songwriters and artists, died in 1983.

Vern Gosdin

AMY GRANT

Georgia-born Amy Grant is the acknowledged "First Lady of Contemporary Christian Music." She also has shattered the previously-sacrosanct misconceptions that a gospel singer cannot also be a hit-maker in secular pop music or perform both sacred and sexy songs on the same albums and programs.

She made her appearance at St. Joseph's Hospital in Augusta on November 25, 1960, the second daughter of Dr. Burton Grant of Nashville, Tennessee, to be born there while he was stationed at Fort Gordon. The Grant family returned to Tennessee after the father's tour of duty, but Amy always has remembered her Georgia origin and returns often to perform concerts in Augusta, Atlanta, and other Georgia cities.

The youngest of four children, Grant also proved herself a musical prodigy, signing her first record contract and releasing her debut album of sacred music at the age of fifteen. She joined Myrr/Word Records in 1979 and began her rise as one of the world's foremost Christian singers. Her breakthrough year was 1982 when she won the first two of her five Grammys and the first three of her seventeen Dove awards.

Those initial Grammys were for Best Female Gospel Performance with her album, *Age to Age*, and for Best Gospel Single for "Ageless Medley," which was spun off from that album. The Dove awards, which are presented by the Gospel Music Association, were for Artist of the Year, Contemporary Album of the Year, and Best Recorded Music Packaging of the Year.

That also was the year she married Gary Chapman, the man who was to become the cowriter of her music and the father of her three children—Matthew, Millie, and Sarah. Gary was a singer/songwriter who had a recording career of his own with RCA. With his input, her string of successes have included: winning third, fourth, and fifth Grammys in 1984, 1985, and 1987 for Best Female Gospel Performance for "Angels," a track from her album, *Straight Ahead*; for the single, "Unguarded"; and for the Gold track, "Lead Me On," from the album of the same name, which was her first largely secular album issued by her second label, A&M Records, with which she had signed in 1985 to issue non-religious songs.

She also received more Dove awards for Best Recorded Music Packaging for *A Christmas Album* in 1984; for Best Contemporary Album for "Straight Ahead" in 1985; for Artist of the Year in 1986; for Best Short Form Video in 1988; for Artist of the Year, Best Contemporary Album, and Best Short Form Video in 1989; for " 'Tis So Sweet to Trust in Jesus" in 1990; and for Artist of the Year and Song of the Year in 1992.

She went to Number One on the pop charts in 1991 with "Baby Baby," which was nominated for two Grammys; to Top Three with "Every Heartbeat" and to Top Ten with "That's What Love Is For"; and took "Good For Me" to Top Ten and "I Will Remember You" to the Top Twenty in 1992.

She was honored by the American Cancer Society for her humanitarian efforts with its prestigious John C. Tune award, named Young Tennessean of the Year by the Nashville Chamber of Commerce in 1992, and awarded the Pax Christi (The Peace of Christ) award by the Benedictine Order at St. John's University also in 1992.

Amy Grant

Since she joined the A&M label, Grant has projected a sexier image in both her choice of secular music and her performances. She has discovered that her fans accept her both as a contemporary Christian and a secular artist, and she has developed a mix of her songs in both categories for her sellout concerts. She has gone back to her acoustic-based roots in the styles of Carole King and James Taylor in her song styling, and she has accepted the fact that she is a straight-on singer and communicator and not a dancer or model in her concert performances.

Her first secular breakthrough album in 1991, *Heart in Motion,* went quadruple-Platinum with sales of more than four million copies; and her follow-up, *House of Love,* has been double-Platinum with more than two million in sales. She has had well-received singles with her duet with Vince Gill and a remake of Joni Mitchell's hit ecology ode, "The Big Yellow Taxi." Both her Christian and secular recording companies have acceded the mix and have encouraged her to "go get 'em" wherever she wants.

JACK GREENE

Whatever future success he may achieve, Jack Greene, who got his musical start in Atlanta, will have to work hard to top the year 1967. His recording of Dallas Fraizer's "There Goes My Everything" won him Country Music Association awards for Song, Single, Album, and Male Vocalist of the Year, a Grammy nomination, top awards of *Billboard, Cash Box* and *Record World* magazines and *Music City News*, and an invitation to join the Grand Ole Opry.

Born January 7, 1930, in Maryville, Tennessee, Greene started on the guitar when he was eight and came to Atlanta in the late 1940s to play guitar with the Cherokee Trio and guitar and drums with the Rhythm Ranch Boys. He did a stint in the army and in 1953 joined the Peachtree Cowboys on WSB-TV.

Ernest Tubb noticed his talents, and Greene joined Tubb's Texas Troubadours in 1962. His versatility as a drummer, guitarist, and backup and solo vocalist made him a valuable member.

Jack Greene

His unprecedented smash of "Everything" in 1967 was followed by "At the Time" and a second Grammy nomination for it in 1968. He and Jeanie Seely also did a series of duets that brought them Grammy nominations. He parted company with MCA after several successful albums and signed with a new label, Frontline, and returned to the charts with such singles as "Rock I'm Leaning On" and "Devil's Den." His band was once called Jolly Green Giants but is now known as the Renegades. He lives in Hendersonville, Tennessee.

CONNIE HAINES

Georgians old enough to recall their experiences during World War II seldom fail to be overwhelmed by bittersweet memories whenever they hear the strains and refrains of golden oldies like "What Is This Thing Called Love," "You Made Me Love You," "I'll Never Smile Again," "Let's Get Away from It All," and "Oh, Look at Me Now."

Music lovers among them also will be reminded that the defining voice they remember singing those evergreen ballads in one of the most trying periods in American history was that of lilting Georgia songbird Connie Haines of Savannah.

Haines had eleven Gold record hits during that period, and she went all around the world several times entertaining servicemen and women in the field and the wounded in military hospitals with her renditions of them. She was given many citations for her selfless contributions to bolstering American morale, often at great risk to herself.

Pushed into show business by an ambitious mother, she won her first talent contest in Chatham County, Georgia, when she was only five years old. At the age of fourteen, she was the youngest headliner ever to appear at New York's Roxy Theater.

At sixteen, Haines became a regular with the Harry James Orchestra and sang for that popular musical organization with Frank Sinatra. She later headlined with the Tommy Dorsey Orchestra for several years and with Frankie Laine for two years.

Her heyday was in the time when radio was king, and she was known throughout the medium as the "Queen of the Airways." She had a radio show of her own and appeared a number of times on the Bob Hope Show.

Haines moved from radio to stage and television, starring on Broadway in such all-time hits as *Westside Story*, *Finian's Rainbow*, and *Come Blow Your Horn*. She did television with all the greats of TV's pioneer days, including Red Skelton, Perry Como, Ed Sullivan, and Milton Berle.

She entertained four different presidents at the White House and received the Courageous award for work with the American Cancer Society from President Ronald Reagan in 1988.

She was inducted into the Georgia Music Hall of Fame in 1992.

Connie Haines

ISAAC HAYES

When Isaac Hayes was growing up in the mind-numbing poverty of a post-World War II cotton sharecropping farm north of Memphis, Tennessee, he blotted out the bitterness of his orphaned deprivation by making up songs in his head about birds and trees and indulging in his fantasies about growing up to be like his idols—Billy Eckstine and Nat "King" Cole.

But his wildest dreams never envisioned the actual realities of his music winning an Oscar, his starring in movies, his making it as the designer of fashion jeans, and his residing in Atlanta's wealthiest neighborhood near the mansion housing the governor of Georgia.

Reaching those pinnacles required two cycles of rags to riches, but the rollercoaster progressions from youthful fieldhand to flamboyant performer to despairing bankrupt to respected professional never dimmed Hayes's basic goal in life to do all he could to fill the need of both black and white youths for "that positive impulse to put them in the hopes that it will deter them from doing negative things in life."

While establishing his shining bald head, outrageous wardrobes, and luxurious cars as personal trademarks, he refused movie parts as pimps and drug dealers and devoted large amounts of his wealth to such worthy and largely unpublicized projects as building low-income housing projects and heading Atlanta's Empty Stocking Fund Drive.

Born August 20, 1943, near Covington, Tennessee, he was orphaned by the death of his mother and the desertion of his father before he was a year old and was reared by his sharecropping grandparents, who brought him up in the church and sought to instill in him the strength and determination to better himself. Because of fieldwork his formal schooling was sporadic at best, and he recalls he soothed himself by sitting on the porch, making up songs, singing aimlessly to the sky, and daydreaming about being like Cole and Eckstine. As he told *Zoo World* in a 1974 interview: "I used to sing about anything—the birds, the trees, work, cotton. It made me feel so good to close my eyes and be whatever I wanted to be. I knew someday, somehow I would get there." He sang in the church choir from the age of five and taught himself to play the church piano and organ by the time he was a teenager.

After moving to Memphis to pursue his musical dreams, he was working in a packinghouse when he got a job one night a week as sideman for saxophonist Floyd Newman, a staff band member at Stax Records. Newman introduced Isaac to its president, Jim Stewart, who auditioned and hired him in 1963 to take the place of Booker T, the staff pianist, while he took leave to work on his college degree. Hayes began doing arranging, teamed with David Porter in writing, and, with Porter and Booker T, became the nucleus of Stax's "Memphis Sound," backing Otis Redding on most of his recordings and working with Rufus and Carla Thomas.

Hayes's debut as a recording soloist came as the result of a drunken spree in 1967 during which he and a Stax vice president went to the studio and made a tape that, upon sober reflection, they thought good enough to be released as the LP *Presenting Isaac Hayes*. It did not make the charts, but it did lead to the 1969 album *Hot Buttered Soul*, which not only made the charts but also became Number One nationally and topped two million dollars in sales by the end of 1970.

Isaac had his first hit singles in August 1969 with "Walk on By" and "By the Time I Get to Phoenix" and followed them with albums that placed him with the Beatles and Rolling Stones as performers who were Platinum sellers. *Isaac Hayes Movement* was on the charts from mid 1970 until late summer 1971, *To Be Continued* during all of 1971, and *Black Moses* from late 1971 well into 1972; the soundtrack from the movie *Shaft* was a top challenger for Record of the Year in 1971. *In the Beginning* and *Live at the Sahara Tahoe* were album hits of 1972 and 1973. His single hits of the period were "Our Day Will Come!" and "I Stand Accused" in 1970; "Never Can Say Goodbye," "Theme from *Shaft*," and "The Look of Love" in 1971; and "Do Your Thing," "Let's Stay Together," "Theme from *The Man*," and "Ain't That Lovin' You" in 1972. His "Theme from *Shaft*" not only was Number One for both single and album in 1971 but also won Hayes the Oscar for the Best Song from a Motion Picture for that year.

The successes of the *Hot Buttered Soul* album and the "Walk on By" and "Phoenix" singles propelled him, reluctantly at first, into concerts, beginning with a gig in Detroit. He says he was "scared . . . butterflies from head to toe" until he got on and realized "my bald head really got them off," and from that point on he worked assiduously at developing the exotic image of his monkish appearance achieved through shaven head and dark glasses contrasting with glamorous costumes featuring multi-colored capes, leather shirts with fur cuffs, black tights, and gold necklaces.

He also starred in the movies *Three Tough Guys* and *Truck Turner* and was a millionaire and owned mansions in Memphis and Beverly Hills before he was thirty. But his extravagant lifestyle, coupled with three marriages that produced nine children and philanthropies that sometimes got out of hand, brought him to bankruptcy and near ruin in 1977.

He cut his losses, moved to Atlanta with his third wife, Mignon, and recouped his fortune by resuming his recording activities. He established the syndicated Top Twenty radio show "Black Music Countdown" in 130 national markets, starred in the movie *Escape from New York*, and designed, introduced, and produced the Isaac Hayes Originals designer jeans and tops for men and women, featuring the "Isacki" top adapted from the kimono-like tunic worn by karate specialists (of which he is one). He produced jazz albums with Donald Byrd and signed to star in and score films for H.I.S. Films International of Marietta, Georgia. After recouping his losses, he bought a mansion in Northwest Atlanta's wealthiest enclave, and there he devotes himself to charitable causes, runs ten miles a day, and hopes to achieve his further ambition of appearing in a soap opera. Although his costumes are more subdued, his trademarks continue to be the shaven head accentuated by beard and dark glasses.

He was inducted into the Georgia Music Hall of Fame in 1994.

Isaac Hayes

ROLAND HAYES

Roland Hayes, the son of slaves from Georgia, changed musical and civil rights history before Martin Luther King, Jr., was born with an incomparable tenor voice that stilled the harshest of hostile audiences.

He worked in Chattanooga, Tennessee, to pay for the educations of his siblings while he studied at night. He eventually attended Fisk University in Nashville, Tennessee, where he sang and toured with the Fisk Jubilee Singers. It was on one of those tours that he decided to stay in Boston to study voice. When he could find no one to sponsor him, he took his savings from his job as a page and rented the Boston Symphony Hall for a concert in 1917.

At that time musical critics claimed no black man could understand European classical music and that no one would pay to hear one try to sing it. He proved them wrong on both counts. The hall sold out, and the critics admitted they never had heard a voice like his before.

He was the first African-American to give such a recital in the United States, and he followed up that triumph with both concerts and studies in Europe. In England he was acclaimed and invited to give a command performance before the king and queen.

In Berlin, Germany, an angry audience taunted, hissed, and jeered him when he appeared on the stage. He stared the hecklers down in silence for ten minutes; when he began singing, they took their seats in an awed hush. The morning newspaper reported that "the public had expected a sensation, but found an artist."

Hayes rediscovered the Negro spiritual and incorporated it with moving effect into his concerts. One of his students and proteges, Dr. Rawn Spearman, told a class at the Roland Hayes division of music at Madison Park High School in Boston:

"Students will always ask me, 'What did you learn from Roland Hayes?' My answer was always, 'He taught me the sense of humility.' He never raised his voice in anger. He wasn't out there carrying the flag, . . . but he walked on the stage, and he selected those songs, especially the Negro spirituals, that I believe told his message."

He was born in 1887 in Curryville near Calhoun in Gordon County, Georgia, into a family of former slaves who also prided themselves as music makers. He said of his childhood that he "drank in all the music I heard," both African and American. He joined his six siblings in a promise to their mother that each would take turns working and putting the others through school after their tenant-farmer father died. He worked in a machine shop, and, when it came his turn to go to school, he elected to continue to work days and go to night school in order that the other family members would have what they needed.

Hayes's daughter, Afrika, said his use of spirituals represented a return to his heritage. He selected and arranged them in ways that celebrated both their musical beauty and emotional meaning. His audiences understood the seriousness with which he sang them and comprehended his message that the song were not to be taken lightly as so many had done before he sang them.

By 1928 Hayes was considered the highest paid singer in the world. He was regarded an idol and mentor by such African-American artists who followed in his footsteps as William Warfield, Leontyne Price, Paul Robeson, and his fellow Georgian Jessye Norman.

He gave a well-received farewell concert at New York's Carnegie Hall on his seventy-fifth birthday in 1962. He received eight honorary degrees, many awards and citations, and the NAACP's Spingarn Medal for the most outstanding achievement among blacks.

He died in Boston on January 1, 1977, at the age of eighty-nine, and his life was perhaps best summed up by the dean of critics, Heywood Broun, who wrote: "Roland Hayes sang of Jesus, and it seemed to me that this is what religion ought to be: a mood instead of a creed; an emotion rather than a doctrine; a miracle in the process of performance."

The New England Spiritual Ensemble and the Boston Symphony Orchestra honored his memory with performances at the New England Conservatory in Boston in February 1996.

Roland Hayes

FLETCHER HENDERSON

When music lovers think of "swing," they think of Benny Goodman, who generally is credited with being the "King of Swing." When they think of big bands, they call to mind the musical organizations led by Goodman, the Dorsey Brothers, Glenn Miller, Duke Ellington, and the other greats who are icons and household names in the music business.

But history records that the genius who fathered both "swing" and big bands was Fletcher Henderson of Cuthbert, Georgia, a scholar who went to New York to get a graduate degree in chemistry and turned to music to support himself. He became the leader of the band at the famous Roseland Ballroom on Broadway and the arranger of the major part of the "swing library" that made up most of the repetroire of the newly formed Benny Goodman Band.

The son of a rural black educator, Henderson's birth year is variously listed at 1897 or 1898. He thought he was destined for a career in science and majored in chemistry at Atlanta University. When he went to New York for graduate studies, he found it necessary to work to feed himself. He took a part-time job doing the one thing he knew how to do, play the piano. He worked for Black Swan, America's first black-owned-and-operated record and music publishing company. When he was offered a full-time position as house pianist and musical director for that organization, he forsook chemistry and never looked back.

The Jazz Masters, which Henderson assembled in 1921, toured with the Black Swan Troubadours troupe until 1923. He formed the nation's first "big band" with colleagues from Black Swan in 1923; by the next year, they were playing at Roseland and doing dates at the Savoy and Apollo, as well as performing for dances on college campuses far and wide. His was a "big band" before big bands were cool, and among the famous alumni his organization produced were Louis Armstrong, Coleman Hawkins, Benny Carter, Ben Webster, Chu Berry, and Roy Eldridge. He left the band in the hands of his younger brother, Horace, and Carter in 1928 and returned to arrange for it full-time in 1933. When it fell on hard times, he turned to the new Goodman band and arranged its great library of hits that are now musical standards for the world.

It was during this period that he is credited with orchestrating band music's transition from the unformed jazz of the "Jelly Roll" Morton era into the carefully scored ensemble playing that became known as "swing" when popularized by Goodman. He developed the technique of using the predominant saxophone as the lead instrument in carrying musical themes, with the brass supplying intervals of call-and-response in the choral manner of traditional black music and worship.

In result, it was Fletcher Henderson and his orchestra that gave birth to the big-band approach to jazz, which everyone now recognizes and refers to as "swing" in both its classic and western variations.

When other white musicians followed Goodman's lead in organizing big bands to play the new-type jazz/swing, virtually all of them, as Goodman had done before them, turned to African-American arrangers to give an authentic sound to their music. Their black counterparts—such as Duke Ellington, Count Basie, Erskine Hawkins, Andy Kirk, and Earl "Fatha" Hines—simply followed and improved upon the musical trail that Fletcher Henderson had blazed before them.

Fletcher Henderson was inducted into the Georgia Music Hall of Fame in 1989.

Fletcher Henderson

JAKE HESS

If there were a title of "Mr. Gospel Music," Jake Hess, native Alabaman and adopted Georgian, would win it hands down, probably by acclamation. Of the myriad honors he has earned in a lifetime of gospel singing, the one that comes closest to defining his unique place in gospel music is the Diamond Award for Living Legend presented to him in 1994 by *Gospel Voice* magazine.

A lead singer from the age of five, Hess probably has appeared more often on television then any other gospel singer and, beyond question, is acknowledged to be the most imitated gospel singer of today because of his unique style, word pronunciation, and hand gestures. There is no more convincing proof of his stature in gospel music than the fact that he and his group, the Imperials, were chosen by Elvis Presley to back him on gospel albums and that Hess was the soloist at Elvis's funeral. He also was a singer at the final rites for the legendary Hank Williams.

Born on Christmas Eve 1927 the seventh son and youngest of twelve children of W. S. and Lydia Hess in the Haleyville Area of Alabama, Hess started singing professionally in the early 1940s. He appeared successively with the John Daniel Quartet, the Sunny South Quartet, and the original Melody Masters. He then joined with Hovie Lister as one of the charter members and the lead singer of the Statesmen quartet in 1948 in Atlanta and appeared with them on the *Arthur Godfrey Show* and syndicated television shows sponsored by Nabisco and Westinghouse. He departed as a Statesman in 1963 to form the Imperials and try out his own innovative ideas in gospel music in Nashville, Tennessee.

Ill health forced him to leave the Imperials in 1967, and he went into business with Nashville television personality Eddie Hill, hosting twelve television shows weekly for eight years. Then he and his children, Becky and Chris, formed the Jake Hess Sound in 1975 and moved to California where he hosted ten weekly television shows in 1975. In 1980 he conceived the idea for the Masters V, the group with which he sang for seven years. In 1990 he hosted a syndicated television program, *Jake Hess and Friends*, which was taped in Nashville and aired on more than four hundred stations.

He sang weekly at the University Cathedral in Los Angeles from September 1990 until he joined with Bill Gaither and Hovie Lister to reorganize the Statesmen quartet. Continued health problems forced him into semiretirement in 1993, and he moved to Columbus, Georgia.

Hess was one of the founders of the National Quartet Convention, is a member of the board of directors of the Gospel Music Association, was inducted into the Gospel Music Hall of Fame in 1987, won the SESAC Lifetime Achievement award in 1988 and the Alabama Music Hall of Fame America's Music award in 1989, received the Marvin Norcross award from *Singing News* Magazine in 1993, and holds four Grammys.

He was inducted into the Alabama Music Hall of Fame in 1995.

Jake Hess

BERTIE HIGGINS

Like his great-great-grandfather, Johann Wolfgang von Goethe, Bertie Higgins is a crackerjack storyteller; but, unlike that illustrious ancestor, the Florida songwriter who now calls Atlanta home eschews the hellish for the romantic in choosing the themes for his tunes.

His smash hit "Key Largo," which marked him as one of the comers of the 1980s, has an autobiographical premise no less schmaltzy than "boy meets girl, boy loses girl" interlaced with a lot of nostalgia about Bogart, Becall, and islands in the sun. And, as if in keeping with that classic premise of the movies of the 1940s, the ultimate outcome of that song not only was to increase his fortune from the twenty-five cents he had in his jeans the day he and fellow Atlantian Sonny Limbo wrote it to more than a million dollars, but also to complete the "boy gets girl" cycle with his subsequent marriage to his girlfriend Beverly Ann Seilberg, about whom it was written.

It is not that Higgins, who was born fifty years ago and christened "Elbert" in the picturesque Greek sponge-fishing village of Tarpon Springs on the Florida Gulf Coast, could not tell some devilish tales of his own rivaling those of Dr. Faust, what with eighteen years of poverty and his struggle in trying to get someone to listen to his songs. He is both intellectual and romantic and loves to tell stories that combine questions about life and the fantasies everyone dreams about living and loving in a tropical paradise. His love songs treat the efforts of mature males to understand and deal with the female psyche; his fantasy songs deal with the beauty and sensuality of the tropics; and his story songs combine past failings with future hopes all interwoven with the philosophy of "live it up today, for tomorrow we may die." Because he is first and foremost a storyteller, he currently is concentrating on his overriding ambition to be a successful screenwriter. He already has sold a script to Twentieth Century Fox, "Through the Eye," about dope smuggling on a shrimp boat, and is working on a script for a remake of *Key Largo*.

All of the ingredients of Higgins's background and life are incongruous. Born of Portuguese, Irish, and German extraction and reared in a Greek community, he at one time supported himself as a sponge diver and began his career in show business as a ventriloquist; he won top prizes both in talent contests for performing and at arts and crafts fairs for his self-designed, homemade dummies.

After acquiring a set of battered drums, he dropped out of St. Petersburg Junior College to join Tommy Roe's band, the Roemans, backing Roe on his greatest hits and playing with the Roemans on their own hit "Universal Soldiers." He played throughout the world with Tom Jones, the Beach Boys, the Rolling Stones, and others. Tiring of travel, he ,returned to Florida to work at writing songs and to support himself by playing in nightclubs. Several recording deals fell through, however, and the closest he came to success was the successful recording of his "Waiting for the Rain" by Emma Hanna in Australia and Patricia Dahlquist in Canada and the use of several of his original compositions by the ABC television program *20/20*. During this period he also met and became a protege of the late actor Richard Boone, who tutored him in screenwriting.

He moved to Atlanta in 1980 and was sleeping in a bare apartment in Smyrna, Georgia, on a quilt given to him by his mother when he teamed up with Sonny Limbo, writer of Gladys Knight's superhit, "Midnight Train to Georgia." He had a quarter in his pocket when he and Sonny—after spending a night drinking beer and watching the Humphrey Bogart-Lauren Bacall movie *Key Largo* on cable television—wrote a song by the same title based on Bertie's broken romance. Limbo persuaded his friend Scott McClellan of Pyramid Studios in Lookout Mountain, Tennessee, to record a demo of it. Atlanta music publisher Bill Lowery, who had known Higgins from his days with the Roemans, liked it and, with the addition of some more Bogart-Bacall touches that he suggested, sold it to Atlanta entertainment attorney Joel Katz and his new Atlanta-based label Katz Family Records.

Higgins and Limbo also wrote "Casablanca," "Down at the Blue Moon," "White Line," "The Tropics," "Port O' Call" and "Just Another Day in Paradise," the latter becoming the title of the album containing them all.

"Key Largo," promoted by a personal tour of radio stations in the Southeast by Higgins, was released in late 1981; was Number One in Atlanta by Christmas; and by mid-1982 had reached Number One in Adult Contemporary and Number Eight in the Top Forty and the Top Fifty in Country. "Casablanca" simultaneously became a top hit in Japan. It not only made Higgins a lot of money but also earned for him the Atlanta Songwriters Association's Songwriter of the Year award.

In addition to working on his movie scripts in 1983, Higgins also toured with his band and issued a second album, *Pirates and Poets.* With a single, "When You Fall in Love," he expanded his efforts in the preservation of Florida wildlife, particularly the endangered pelican, and made plans for the realization of his further dreams of establishing his own recording complex and Bertie Higgins's Key Largo Restaurant and Bar in Tarpon Springs.

Bertie Higgins, Alan Jackson, Billy Joe Royal (on stage),
Jan Howard, Zell Miller, Joe South, Bill Anderson, and Doug Stone

LENA HORNE

There are few adults who do not know who Lena Horne is or have some opinion about this singer/dancer/actress. But despite how one feels about the high profile performer and early civil rights activist, those who have differing opinions about her agree on two points: (1) in her time, she has been one of the most beautiful women in the world, and (2) her recording of the Ted Koehler-Harold Arlen classic, "Stormy Weather," from the movie of the same title, is the greatest torch song of all times.

Born in Brooklyn, New York, on June 30, 1917, her parents divorced when she was three, and she was bounced among various relatives for her upbringing. For a while she lived with her Uncle Frank who was dean of students at what was then Fort Valley Junior Industrial Institute and now is known as Fort Valley State College in Georgia. Then she moved to Atlanta to be with her grandmother, Cora Calhoun Horne, and her newspaper-editor grandfather on West Hunter street.

Grandmother Horne had a formidable influence on Lena's early life. She was a leader in the Urban League, the Women's Suffrage Movement, and the NAACP, enrolling Leana as a member of the latter organization when she was two years old. She helped a young Paul Robeson finance his college education and was a confidant of controversial black sociologist and separatist W. E. B. DuBois when he was young "Willie." She was also a well-known figure at Atlanta University and generally brought young Lena up to believe in herself and to oppose the oppression of "Jim Crow" in every possible way.

Horne attended Booker T. Washington Junior High School in Atlanta, studied dancing, and, according to the book on the Horne family written by her daughter, Gail Lumet Buckley, "enjoyed an agreeable Atlanta life." As a teenager she went back to Brooklyn, where she attended Girls High School until her actress mother returned from a tour of Cuba, ailing and with a Cuban husband in tow, and reclaimed her. They moved in poverty to the Bronx, where Lena, at the age of sixteen, was forced by the exigencies of the Depression to drop out of school and seek employment as a dancer at New York's for-whites-only Cotton Club. She was recommended by her mother's friend, club choreographer Elida Webb, and, being young, tall, slim, and beautiful with "good, long hair," had no trouble getting the job.

At the Cotton Club she made friends with such black entertainment greats as Cab Calloway, Ethel Waters, Billie Holiday, Count Basie, and Duke Ellington. She invested a portion of her twenty-five-dollar-a-week salary in music lessons and soon was invited in 1935 to be the singer with Nobel Sissel's Society Orchestra in Philadelphia. There her father, who took her back in and became a major influence on her until his death, was managing the Belmont Hotel.

The realities of dealing with the cruelties of segregated society brought her to the decision to marry an older man whom she did not love, Louis Jones, in 1937, a union that produced two offspring, Gail and Teddy, and estranged her permanently from her mother.

She starred in the short-lived revue, *Blackbirds of 1939*, and, at twenty-three, left her husband and children to return to New York to resume her career in 1940. Later that year she became the lead singer for Charlie Barnett's band and made her first recordings for the Bluebird label: "You're My Thrill," "Haunted Town," and "Good for Nothing Joe," the latter of which became a hit. Her efforts at reconciliation with her husband failed, and she got custody of Gail while Jones kept Teddy, who subsequently died of kidney disease. She went back to New York and became the featured singer at the Cafe Society Downtown and the girlfriend of World Heavyweight Champion Joe Louis.

She met Walter White, executive director of the NAACP, in 1941, and he convinced her to accept an offer to perform at the Trocadero Club in Hollywood. It was there that she came to the attention of Robert Edens of Metro-Goldwyn-Mayer who arranged for her to audition for producer Arthur Freed. That led to her becoming the first black American woman to get a term contract with a motion picture company in Hollywood, a seven-year deal paying two hundred and fifty dollars per week to begin and clearly stipulating that she would not be asked to play stereotypical black roles.

Her first MGM movie was *Panama Hattie* in 1942, in which she appeared in a guest spot number designed to be edited out for showings in Southern theaters, the format MGM would follow in her other mixed-cast roles through her final one in *The Duchess of Idaho* in 1950.

In her only all-black film with MGM, *Cabin in the Sky*, released in 1943, Horne played the legendary temptress Georgia Brown; but the classic *Stormy Weather*, another all-black production, was done on loan to

Twentieth Century Fox and was a musical based on the thinly disguised life of Bill "Bojangles" Robinson. It was on the latter set that she met and secretly married her second husband, composer/conductor Leonard "Lennie" George Hayton, who was white and nine years her senior. She admitted after his death in 1971 that she married him for career reasons, but came to love him during their years together.

Horne was to black American soldiers what Betty Grable was to white ones during World War II. By the mid-1940s, she had become one of the nation's top black entertainers and was making one thousand dollars a week at MGM and hit a record income of $175,000 for twenty weeks at New York's Cibacabano in 1951.

Her first Broadway show, *Jamaica*, premiered in 1957, and she was a frequent guest on all the major national television shows. She was active in the civil rights movement and was present for Martin Luther King, Jr.'s, March on Washington in 1963. She performed with Tony Bennett on Broadway in 1974 and, directed by her son-in-law, Sidney Lumet, starred in *The Wiz*, the black movie version of *The Wizard of Oz*. Although she did what was billed as a farewell tour in 1980, she triumphed in *Lena Horne: The Lady and Her Music*, which at that time became the longest-running, one-woman show on Broadway.

She has received many honors in her later years, but the ones she most prizes are the Kennedy Center Award for Lifetime Contribution to the Arts and the honorary doctorate degree presented by Howard University in 1979. But in all that she has done and achieved, she still looks back upon her rearing by her Georgia grandmother as the defining experience of her full and exciting life. She was inducted into the Georgia Music Hall of Fame in 1991.

Lena Horne

INDIGO GIRLS

Amy Ray and Emily Saliers have been likened to a hand. They are a single entity in their performances as Atlanta's acclaimed acoustic, folksy duo, Indigo Girls, but they are as individually different as separate fingers on that hand in their personal likes, dislikes, and musical tastes.

Together these Grammy award winners come across as folk rockers, like Joni Mitchell or James Taylor. Individually, Ray is brash and punky, and Saliers is plaintive and soulful. Each is an established songwriter in her own right, but composing is something they do separately rather than together.

"The only way we can do a song together is if one of us goes and writes the words and then we collaborate on the music," Ray explains.

Their fifth full-length album released by Epic Records in 1994, *Swamp Ophelia*, showcased the full spectrum of their blended talents. Sailers did personal pieces like "Fare Thee Well," and Ray did some graphic meditations like "The Train," a tough take on the plights of Gypsies, homosexuals, and Jews in the Holocaust.

Since catapulting to fame from Atlanta's coffeehouse-and-bistro scene in the late 1980s, the Indigo pair have expanded from acoustic to electric tracks, stemming from Ray's interest in guitar-layered grunge and punk stylings. She says the electric instrument forces her to be much softer, finesse, and hold back in her performances because she has a tendency to "dig in [and] break strings" in the acoustic mode.

The contrast in their individual approaches to their collective music was demonstrated at the 1994 Earth Jam held in Stone Mountain Park outside Atlanta. Ray delivered a scorching, bombastic rendition of the Clash's "London Calling," while Ray joined another Atlanta folk singer, Kristen Hall, on Neil Young's plaintive "Southern Man."

Both are into message songs, particularly Ray since she visited the Holocaust Museum in Washington, D.C., and was inspired by its images to try to understand and define the pain of others through song. Another example was the cut she did with her father, "Dead Man's Hill," a song recalling her "first exposure to real evil" in witnessing two boys setting cats on fire when she was a child.

The Indigo Girls initially released their first album, *Strange Fire*, on their own label in 1987. It was reissued by Epic Records after the release of their second full-length effort, *Indigo Girls*, in 1989, and it featured a bonus track in their cover of the Youngblood's "Get Together."

Their biggest hit, "Closer to Fire," was a single spun off from their second album, and they also expanded their following with their collaborations with fellow Georgians of R.E.M. as well as with Hothouse Flowers.

Their third album, *NomadsIndiansSaints*, was released in 1990. It featured a supporting track with Mary-Chapin Carpenter and highlighted the popular titles, "Hammer and a Nail" and "1-2-3 Again."

But it was their fourth album, *Rites of Passage*, in 1992 that proved to be their best-seller, produced the hit "Joking," and spawned a massive tour.

Indigo Girls

ALAN JACKSON

At a time when Nashville seems to be dominated by packaged images turned out by the cookie cutters of commercial agents and crafty managers, Alan Jackson stands out as an impressive exception to the contemporary rule in Music City USA that stars are made, not born.

In Jackson, what one sees is what one gets—a lanky, blonde, laconic singer of songs who writes about things that ordinary people do and experience in the style of old-time country music played on fiddles and guitars and sung by the revered greats like Roy Acuff, Ernest Tubb, and George Jones.

Yes, Jackson does stand six feet, four inches tall without his hat and cowboy boots.

Yes, Jackson's hair really is blonde and long in the fashion of George Custer and Buffalo Bill Cody.

Yes, he is as modest and unassuming in person as he is reported to be by the media.

Yes, he is soft-spoken in his speech and understated in his comments and has been compared in his actual life to the western movie roles played by Gary Cooper.

He grew up in the modest circumstances of the home of a Ford Motor Company worker in Newnan, Georgia, imbued with the solid values of a household in which faith and hard work were attributes more prized than wealth and privilege. It was a life he extols movingly in his song "Home," featured on his first album.

He was a late bloomer who did not do any public singing until after he graduated from high school and did not write his first song until he was twenty-three years old. He had no idea of his potential or how to realize it until his wife, Denise, had a chance meeting with Glen Campbell when she boldly approached him in the Atlanta Airport and asked him for advice. Campbell's answer was that, if her husband really wanted to make it, they should move to Nashville.

Though Jackson had not ever been that far north before, they did just that in the mid-1980s, struggling to keep their old pickup truck running that long and arriving without a clue as to what they would do after they got there. In fact, in accepting her husband's 1993 Songwriter of the Year award from the Nashville Songwriters Association International, Denise said: "He didn't realize how bad it was really going to be."

Jackson took a low-paying job as a clerk in the Opryland mail room, and his wife followed up on her chance encounter with Campbell. He remembered her and gave Jackson a songwriting contract with his KayTeeKay Music. The monthly stipend it provided gave him the chance to quit his job, concentrate on his music, and form a honky-tonk band that performed as many as five sets a night for six nights a week.

At that time, as biographer Michael McCall put it, the odds of a tradition-minded singer like Jackson getting a record deal "were about as likely as an Appalachian yodeler opening for Kenny Rogers." In fact, George Strait, at that time was being urged to ditch the hat and rodeo belt buckle and switch to pop, and Randy Travis still was frying catfish at the Nashville Palace.

By chance, Jackson happened to meet Travis when he performed at the Palace, and the two formed a lasting friendship. When Travis hit it big, Jackson noticed that Keith Stegall had coproduced his initial hits, and he called and introduced himself. The two met and stayed in touch, and Stegall loaned Jackson his bus in the late 1980s to make a trip to open a concert for Ronnie Milsap in Mississippi.

Stegall subsequently joined with Jackson and Roger Murrah to cowrite "Blue Blooded Woman," which became Jackson's introductory single when Tim DuBois picked him to be the first performer to open under the Nashville division of Arista Records in 1989. It was a surprising choice for the man who previously had pushed the pop career of Restless Heart, but it proved DuBois's acumen in making artistic decisions that put Arista on the top of the country heap.

Jackson's uncanny capacity to come up with original and memorable lines was established with that first release. He thought up the primary lyric of the chorus, "She loves the violin. I love the fiddle," and its most distinctive line: "I live my life in Wal-Mart fashion, and I like my sushi Southern-fried."

DuBois says he chose Jackson because of "the strength of his songs." Stegall and Murrah agreed, or as Stegal said, "Alan had a way of doing things that was not really orthodox, but it worked." As Murrah put it: "It's not like we do it, but it's right. Man, that's what's going to separate him from the pack."

Jim McBride, who cowrote "Chasin' That Neon Rainbow," "Chatta-hoochee," and "Who Says You Can't Have It All" with Jackson, says

Jackson provides details for songs based upon his real experiences, especially from his travels on the Southern honky-tonk circuit. The vivid imagery of "Chattahoochee"—from stacking cans in the moonlight to fogging up backseat windows—proved he can put hot Georgia scenarios into lyrics most younger country music fans can identify with themselves. The song stayed Number One for four weeks, was performed on both the Academy of Country Music and the TNN/*Music City News* awards programs within the span of a few weeks in 1993, and was turned into an award-winning video during the same period.

Alan Jackson

It was most appropriate that his first album released in 1990 was titled *Here in the Real World* and that its title cut went to Number One because the real world produced Jackson. And it is in the real world where he is making and sustaining his success, always broadening, but never straying far from, his fundamental country roots. "Real World," the single, went to Number One and was named Song of the Year by *Music City News* in 1990. It also earned Jackson the *News'* Country Songwriter award and the Best New Male Artist award of the Academy of Country Music. The album of that title went Platinum.

He was accused of surrendering to rock influences with his "Don't Rock the Jukebox," which went Platinum and won *Billboard* magazine's Top Country Single award in 1991. But Jackson put that to rest with the comment that the only rock in it is the "solid bedrock of country's foundations," citing Hank Williams's "Move It on Over" and George Jones's "The Race Is On" as its country progenitors.

In 1992 Jackson not only was named one of *People* magazine's "Most Beautiful People" but also saw his recording of "Midnight in Montgomery," an account of his visit to Hank Williams's grave, become a classic in its own time and its video version win the Country Music Association's Video Of the Year award.

His 1993 album *A Lot about Livin'* shot up his sales from an average of nine thousand to more than forty thousand a week and stretched out his string of consecutive Number One hits to more than any other country artist in the 1990s. He consistently has won the top awards voted upon by the fans, but climaxed his recognition by winning the prestigious Entertainer of the Year award of the Country Music Association in 1995.

His album *Who I Am* was the first real insight Jackson has given into his own persona, and demonstrated that he not only is comfortable about the manner in which he has maintained allegiance to his country roots but also is steadfast in his determination to honor the past by resurrecting it.

MILLIE JACKSON

Anyone who does not understand Millie Jackson's recordings probably has led a sheltered life because the best description critics have been able to coin for them is "X-rated."

Yes, this Thomson, Georgia-born singer who specializes in telling it like it is between men and women in explicit, four-letter terms is both a rapper with a mouth and a soul singer who often is compared to Aretha Franklin, Nina Simone, and Randy Crawford. It took her a while to catch on, but she did it with a hit fourth album appropriately titled, *Caught Up*. She has been big on the adult entertainment circuit ever since.

Born in 1944 and raised by her grandfather who was a preacher, she ran away at the age of fourteen to get away from a home environment that required her to go to church six days a week and limited her television viewing to the *Tennessee Ernie Ford Show* once a week because he always ended his performances with a hymn. She finally succeeded in getting to live with her father, who had left Georgia looking for work, which he found in Newark, New Jersey. She subsequently found her own work as a model in New York City just across the Hudson River.

Her singing career started with a challenge from friends whom she had accompanied to a New York nightclub. They dared her to get up and sing with the band, which she did. And she has been singing ever since.

She was discovered by songwriter Billy Nichols and taken to MGM Records by Dioon French. Her first single, "A Little Bit of Something," was a flop, and she switched to the Spring label. Her 1973 single, "It Hurts So Good," was heard on the soundtrack of the movie, *Cleopatra Jones*.

Jackson has since sold millions of records and headlined concerts throughout the world. Her antiviolence recording, "You Knocked the Love Right Out of My Heart" received wide critical acclaim, and her soulful version of "I Can't Stop Loving You" from her *Just a Little Bit Country* album is her most requested song played on radio stations. She also has recorded duets with superstars Elton John and Isaac Hayes.

The mother of two daughters, who describes herself as "happily divorced," says she has been through most of the traumas she describes so graphically in her music.

SHOT JACKSON

When the city of Nashville and the state of Tennessee joined in proclaiming October 16, 1980 as Shot Jackson Day, a plaque was presented to the virtuoso dobro performer and acclaimed guitar designer from Blackshear, Georgia. He was declared to be "The Pickers' Pick" to the accompaniment of a standing ovation from the Country Music Disc Jockeys of America.

With characteristic modesty, the veteran picker suggested the accolade really should have gone to his long-time friend, Roy Acuff, with whose Smokey Mountain Boys he played for many years and with whom he almost was killed in an automobile crash in 1965. But for those in attendance, it was a richly deserved tribute to a man who had much to do with the development of country music through the design and manufacture of "The Sho-Bud," the world's most accepted steel guitar, and the development of "The Sho-Bro" six-string, Spanish neck guitar, as well as in custom building and repairing guitars for the biggest stars in the country music business.

Shot Jackson

"Aunt Irene" Robson was given credit by Shot for getting him started when she gave him his first guitar. Harold Bradley Jackson was fourteen, and the instrument was a $2.98 special from Sears and Roebuck. He went on to become a regular on the Grand Ole Opry, having begun there some fifty years ago, and the undisputed King of the Dobro. He performed with the Bailes Brothers, Jonny and Jack, and Kitty Wells, and joined Acuff in 1956. He and his wife Darlene sometimes performed together, and he was featured on *Hee Haw* with the Clark Family.

He and Buddy Emmons started building steel guitars as a hobby and developed a business so successful that for a while it became a part of the musical instrument division of the Baldwin Piano and Organ Company.

He was a member of the Steel Guitar Hall of Fame and a picker's picker. He died in January 1991 at the age of seventy.

STONEWALL JACKSON

Yes, his real name is Stonewall Jackson, and he really is a direct descendant of the revered Confederate general of that name. Yes, he is the only member of the Grand Ole Opry to be given a contract without first having a hit record to his credit. And yes, he writes most of his songs, including the international hit "Waterloo," and more than five hundred other titles.

Jackson is authentic country, born November 6, 1932 in North Carolina, and grew up in orphaned poverty on a piney woods, share-cropping farm near Moultrie, Georgia. He was plowing a mule at eight and pulling a crosscut saw at ten. He traded an old bicycle for a cheap used guitar and taught himself to play. After a hitch in the Navy where he gained experience and confidence entertaining his shipmates, he returned to Georgia. He worked two years on halves and cut pulpwood until he saved enough money to drive his dilapidated pickup to Nashville in 1956 to seek his fortune.

Luck smiled on him at his first stop, the studios of Acuff-Rose Publishing Company where he went to make some dubs of his songs. Wesley Rose himself heard them and set up an audition for him with George Hay, the "Solemn Old Judge" of the Grand Ole Opry who thought him "so country he's cute." After having to produce a birth certificate to prove his name was as real as his music, Jackson was sent on tour with Ernest Tubb, who subsequently called him his son. He returned to be signed to a five-year contract with the Opry without having a single credit to his name. He has been an Opry regular ever since, saying it "makes you feel that you belong somewhere."

His Opry appearance brought him a recording contract with Columbia, and his first release was "Don't Be Angry," which was one of the original dubs he did at Acuff-Rose. His first Top Ten hit was "Life to Go," which he wrote with George Jones under the agreement that the first to record it would give solo writing credit to the other. In 1959 his "Waterloo" took Jackson to the top of the pop as well as the country charts and made him an international star. He was the most played artist on radio that year and made three appearances on *American Bandstand,* which further fueled his popularity.

In 1960 he scored with "Why I'm Walking"; in 1962 had two best-sellers in "A Wound Time Can't Erase" and "Leona"; in 1963 hit with "Old Showboat"; and in 1964 went to the top with the reissue of "Angry" and the smash new "B.J. the D.J." Some of the many other hits over the years were "I Washed My Hands in Muddy Waters," "Stamp Out Lone-liness," "Give It Back to the Indians," and "Promises and Hearts." All of his numerous albums have been top sellers, and he has the reputation of never having cut a record that did not recoup its costs, a boast few of his contemporaries can make.

Now in semi-retirement, he devotes his time to his song publishing company, Turp Tunes, named for his son who is drummer in his band, the Minutemen, and to working at the Opry and playing five or six dates a month on the road. He lives the life of a "country farmer," which he remains at heart, on his "Lake Waterloo" near Brentwood, Tennessee.

Stonewall Jackson

JOHN JARRARD

In September 1995 *New Country* magazine titled its profile of Georgia songwriter John Jarrard, "Eyes That See in the Dark." No better or more accurate description of his adult life could have been stated so succinctly because Jarrard has become one of Nashville's top songwriters despite having been blinded by complications from diabetes in 1979 when he was in his mid-twenties.

But instead of feeling sorry for himself and regarding himself as handicapped, Jarrard has come to view his loss of vision as a "great blessing" because, as he puts it: "I think that just the keener sense I've developed of what life is all about as a result of not having visual distractions is worth it to me. I had to tune into myself more emotionally, mentally, and spiritually, . . . but, for that very reason, losing my eyesight has in a lot of ways been a real gift and maybe the best thing that has ever happened to me."

If, in no other way, blindness benefitted him because it closed all other career doors but songwriting to him. He had been moving up the Hall of Fame Motel's career ladder from desk clerk to assistant manager when his eyesight failed and it became obvious to him that he would have to rely upon his inner resources to make his way in the world.

Of course, if it can be said that adversity and misfortune are the two major sources of inspiration for country music writers, then Jarrard had a treasure trove of personal catastrophes to call upon for song ideas. Not only did he go blind but he also later suffered total kidney failure, which required a kidney and pancreas transplant. Then followed the breakup of his marriage of fourteen years and nearly losing his life in a serious automobile accident.

He turned out his first Number One hit, "Nobody But You," which was recorded by Don Williams and was a top hit in the country of Zimbabwe in 1983. He followed it up with a series of smashes, including: "There's No Way," "If It Ain't Dixie (It Won't Do)," "You've Got the Touch," "Katy Brought My Guitar Back Today," and "We Can't Love Like This Anymore" by Alabama; "Quittin' Time" and "Money in the Bank" by John Anderson; "Wherever She Is" and "Been There, Done That" by Ricky Van Shelton; "What's a Memory Like You (Doing in a Love Like

This)" by John Schneider; "Lonely Alone" by the Forester Sisters; "Shouldn't It Be Easier Than This" by Charley Pride; "Mirror Mirror" by Diamond Rio; "I Sure Can Smell the Rain" by Blackhawk; "My Kind of Girl" by Collin Raye; "They're Playing Our Song" by Neal McCoy; "And That Was the Easy Part" by Joe Diffie; "A Real Good Way to Wind Up Lonesome" by James House; and "Let the Joneses Win" by Pirates of the Mississippi. He also has written songs for Pam Tillis and Tracy Lawrence.

Composing was the furthest thing from Jarrard's mind when he was studying journalism and later working as a part-time disc jockey in his hometown of Gainesville. But that all changed when he fell in love with a girl who loved country music and talked him into taking her to the disc jockey convention in Nashville in 1974.

Using the station's stationery, he forged some credentials, and the two of them set out for Nashville in her beat-up Ford Capri, subsisting for three days on a bushel of apples they bought and all the free beer and hot coffee they could drink at the convention. They "sneaked into some stuff," and Jarrard got to stand next to Porter Wagoner and Dolly Parton. "I was hooked," he later concluded.

The romance did not last, but his love of country did. He started buying records and doing his homework. He discovered Kris Kristofferson, Willie Nelson, Waylon Jennings, Mickey Newberry, Billy Joe Shaver, and other great songwriters and performers. He later married, moved to Nashville, worked at the motel, and spent his off-hours pounding the pavements of Music Row trying to peddle his song ideas.

Jarrard grew up wanting an athletic career. and his ambition was to "play guard for the Knicks next to Walt Frazier." His parents gave him piano lessons as a boy, but he was allowed to quit taking them as a ninth birthday present. Until his Nashville epiphany, his sole manifestation of musical talent was blowing a harp to tunes he heard on the car radio. But when he realized that he could not sing a song and accompany himself on the harmonica at the same time, he bought himself a guitar and taught himself how to play it.

He and his friend Bruce Burch—who later made his own mark as a songwriter with such hits as "It's Your Call," "Rumor Has It," and "I Got It Honest"—used the bathrooms of empty rooms in the Gainesville Days Inn where Burch worked as a night auditor to make demos of songs they had written because they had read in some magazine that "the room in a house that most closely resembled the acoustics of a studio was the bathroom." So they huddled around the toilet and sang, played, and recorded their songs.

"A few years ago, I found one of those tapes, and it was the most awful howling that you could ever imagine," Jarrard recalls. "I determined at that point no matter how bad something was, I would never tell anyone that they couldn't make it in this business. And after hearing that tape, if I can make it, anybody can."

Most of the time Jarrard works with cowriters, such as J. D. Martin with whom he collaborated on his first hit, but when working by himself he dictates ideas, verses, and lines into a pocket tape recorder he carries all the time. He likens songwriting to farming.

"You do a lot of preparation, a lot of tilling the soil and hoeing, plowing, and fertilizing, and then you have to get away from it," he explains. "Let the seeds come up on their own, and then you can harvest it."

Although he admits to possessing a gift for constructing poetic phrases that make nifty hooks for country songs, he still regards songwriting as a "great unknown" and considers it a "risky business" for which he still is developing the "knack."

"All I know to do is just show up and write the best song I can," he elaborates. "The worst day of songwriting is better than the best day of putting in air conditioners. So I guess I've got a lot to be thankful for."

FELTON JARVIS

If any one person ever could be said to have understood and mastered all kinds of music—from country to pop, rhythm and blues to rock, and with gospel thrown in for good measure, native Georgian Felton Jarvis was that person.

Elvis Presley would have been a superstar without Jarvis's help, guidance, engineering, and production in his last years, but it was Jarvis who put the icing on the King's superstar cake. He produced his first album for Elvis in 1966, an anthology of Presley's favorite gospel songs titled *How Great Thou Art,* and it earned him a Grammy for production. The last he masterminded, *Guitar Man,* was more quintessentially Elvis than anything Presley ever did.

To turn out *Guitar Man,* Jarvis took the original unvarnished and unedited vocals done by Presley on a number of his favorite country-flavored tunes and sat down at the control board and mixed them with a set of new instrumental tracks that provided a whole new perspective to the singer's versatility. It included Presley's interpretations of such evergreen country standards as "She Thinks I Still Care," "You Asked Me To," "After Loving You," and "I'm Moving On." The title cut, "Guitar Man," featured guitarist/songwriter Jerry Reed and other notable Nashville session men.

That Presley recognized Jarvis's genius is attested by the fact that, after the success of their original album together, the singer asked the producer to leave RCA, to which he had moved in 1965, and devote his total effort to Presley's record, stage, and radio productions. Jarvis did and remained with Presley full-time until Elvis's death in 1977.

But Presley was not the only superstar Jarvis helped mold and guide. His very first studio effort was in Atlanta, where he was born and made a star out of unknown Georgia singer, Tommy Roe, with his Number One hit, "Sheila." He subsequently produced Atlantan Gladys Knight's first hit, "Every Beat of My Heart," and went on to open ABC-Paramount's ABC Records branch in Nashville in 1963. His was the expertise that helped shape the recording greatness of such other superstars as Willie Nelson, Floyd Cramer, Jimmy Dean, Jim Ed Brown, Skeeter Davis, Mickey Newberry, and Fess Parker.

Jarvis died of a stroke at the age of forty-six in 1981, and he was inducted posthumously into the Georgia Music Hall of Fame in 1987.

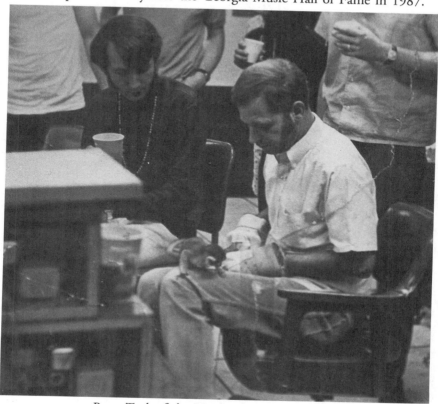

Peter Tork of the Monkees with Felton Jarvis

ANDREW JENKINS

Blind Andy Jenkins was one of the first instant celebrities created by the electronic media. A product of the broadcast pioneering by Atlanta's Voice of the South, station WSB, he had a colorful career as a writer and singer of the instant "folk songs" he composed at the drop of a headline and as a radio evangelist with a national following from Mexico to Canada. Lambdin Kay, WSB's inventive manager, gave Jenkins not only his public exposure but also his title of "Doctor."

Andrew Jenkins was born November 26, 1885, at Jenkinsburg, Georgia, and died April 25, 1956, at Thomaston, Georgia. Like his contemporary, Riley Puckett, he lost his sight as an infant because of faulty medication. A self-ordained minister, he made his living selling newspapers in Atlanta. He had a fortunate second marriage with a widowed mother of three musical children, one of whom was Irene Spain, who was to become WSB's long-time staff pianist.

With Irene and her sister, Mary Lee, and brother, T. P., he formed the Jenkins Family, one of the first folk and gospel singing groups to sing on WSB after it went on the air in 1922 with a powerful signal that carried coast-to-coast. The group attracted such national popularity that they were signed to a recording contract with Okeh Records and made their first release in 1924 of two sides titled, "Church in the Wildwood" and "If I Could Hear My Mother Pray Again."

The group subsequently recorded under the varying names of Jenkins Family, Jenkins Sacred Singers, the Irene Spain Family, Blind Andy, and Goodby Jenkins.

Blind Andy got into writing folk songs in 1925 when Okeh's Atlanta manager Polk Brockman asked him to do a song about the death of spelunker Floyd Collins in a cave in Kentucky. The result was "The Death of Floyd Collins," which he wrote in forty-five minutes. It became a minor success when done by Fiddlin' John Carson (though a copyright dispute arose between Jenkins and Carson over the song) and a major hit when recorded by Vernon Dalhart within two months of the tragic event. The Dalhart recording was backed in its second release by another Jenkins song, "The Dream of the Miner's Child," which also stirred a never fully resolved copyright dispute with the writers of the almost identical English ballad, "Don't Go Down in the Mine, Dad."

Jenkins's success with the folk song approach inspired him to go on to do similar songs like "Billy the Kid," based on the Walter Noble Burns book; "The Wreck of the Royal Palm," based on the 1926 collision of the Southern Railway fliers, Ponce de Leon and the Royal Palm, near Rockmart, Georgia; and "The Tragedy on Daytona Beach," based on the 1929 death of race driver Lee Bible. Jenkins was very careful about registering his copyrights, and, after his death, Irene was successful in pursuing royalties when Mahalia Jackson recorded his obscure "God Put a Rainbow in the Cloud," which she thought to be in the public domain.

Irene and Blind Andy also transcribed most of Fiddlin' John Carson's songs because neither he nor his daughter, Rosa Lee, could read music. One of Irene's later recollections was of her "Reverend" stepfather's requiring her to close the window before listening to some of Carson's mildly suggestive lyrics, which Jenkins referred to as "dirty words."

Jenkins's dim eyesight completely failed him in 1939, and although he knew Braille, Irene also did most of his paperwork. She recalled wistfully that had she known "Floyd Collins" was going to be such a big hit she would "have added a few grace notes to color its melodic simplicity" when she prepared the text-tune for Brockman.

Jenkins spent his final years preaching in Georgia revivals and engaging in radio evangelism on the powerful, uncontrolled radio stations across the Mexican border.

ELTON JOHN

When Elton John heard Georgia singing, he did something about it.

The flamboyant British rocker, whose fame rivals that of England's legendary Beatles who came before him, established a second home in Atlanta, buying and occupying for a substantial part of each year a luxury condominium in a posh, high-rise development overlooking Peachtree Road.

He sold the Georgia State Department of Industry, Trade, and Tourism (an agency responsible for economic development in Georgia) the rights to the words and music of his hit song, "Georgia," for a nominal fee of fifty thousand dollars.

He agreed to appear in the department's commercials for its Georgia Global Now Campaign for free and allowed himself to be filmed singing his song at the historic, restored Georgian Terrace Hotel in Atlanta.

He donated his small fee for the song rights to the Elton John AIDS Foundation, the non-profit charity that he established in Atlanta to assist the victims of AIDS and, for which, he continually engages in fund-raising activities.

DGITT commissioner Randy Cardoza said the campaign, which he described as Georgia's "most ambitious marketing effort ever," has been a "resounding success," thanks largely to John's input and participation.

Born Reginald Kenneth Dwight in Pinner, Middlesex, England, in 1947, Reg Dwight, as he was known until he changed his name at the age of twenty, was a piano prodigy as a child and won a scholarship to the prestigious Royal Academy of Music at the age of eleven. His interest in the classics waned as he was introduced to rhythm and blues and rock. While playing piano in small clubs around London, he began experimenting with his own material ranging from slow, soulful folk-blues to rapid-paced rock and rhythm and blues.

He became a charter member of the band Bluesology, writing and singing the group's first record, "Come Back Baby." In 1967 he decided to change his name—taking the John from Bluesology band member John Baldry, another young English blues-rock fan with whom he had performed since 1961, and the Elton from Bluesology saxaphone player Elton Dean—and strike out on his own.

Recognizing that he was stronger with the music than the words of songs, he advertised for a lyricist, and thus was born the team of John and Bernie Taupin (born Market Rasen), which functioned for eight years as the "perfect match" described by the critics. His first major success was the single, "Lady Samantha," in 1969. He formed a trio, later expanding it to a quartet, in 1970. He signed with the Universal Records division of MCA for American distribution, and his debut LP on MCA's Uni subsidiary, appropriately titled *Elton John,* went Gold, as did his 1971 *Tumbleweed Connection, Friends* (the soundtrack from the film of the same title), live *11-17-70,* and *Madman across the Water.*

Gold records and Number One hits followed one another in succession until the mid-1970s. The year 1973 was phenomenal, marked by the formation of his own record company, Rocket Records, with MCA handling distribution. That was the year of his Number One Gold LP, *Don't Shoot Me, I'm Only the Piano Player,* and its hit singles, "Crocodile Rock," which rose to Number One, and "Daniel," which peaked at Number Two, as well as the acclaimed and remembered Number One, the two-disc *Goodbye Yellow Brick Road. Cash Box* and *Record World* both named him Male Singer of the Year for the second straight year and joined with *Billboard* in declaring him Top Singles Artist of the Year of 1973.

In 1974 his earnings were estimated at more than eight million dollars; and, in 1975, he equalled the Beatles' feat of filling the Los Angeles Dodgers' Baseball Stadium with 110,000 fans for a concert. That was also the year that he made the cover of *Time* magazine, was honored with a star bearing his name on the Hollywood Walk of Fame, and made his film debut in the Who's rock opera, *Tommy.*

The critics began to catch up with him in 1976, some likening him and his antics with the piano to those of American rocker Jerry Lee Lewis, much to the chagrin of both performers. There were also many lampoons of his outrageous costuming, which at different times ranged from a wild-haired punk getup to a flamboyant chicken. It was the same year that his partnership with Bernie Taupin broke up on the shoals of Taupin's desire for a career in his own right. His new collaboration with lyricist Gary Osborne never worked out, mainly because of critical comparisons of his work with that of Taupin's and despite the fact that he and John registered some notable successes together.

John's vow in 1977 that he would not do any more live shows fell by the wayside in 1979 with his historic series of concerts in the Soviet Union, which turned out enthusiastic crowds in Moscow and Leningrad. The vow was completely forgotten with his reuniting of his original band for a tour in 1982 and with Taupin for a new Gold album, *Too Low for Zero*, in 1983. That was also the year he went to China, followed by an attendance-record-setting worldwide tour the next year. Despite the fact that the critics suggested his costumes made him look like "a punk Amadeus," he pulled unprecedented crowds everywhere he went and racked up two new Top Ten hits: "I Guess That's Why They Call It the Blues" and "Sad Songs."

Elton John

In 1986 he teamed up with Dionne Warwick, Stevie Wonder, and Georgia's Gladys Knight to win a Grammy for their Gold single, "That's What Friends Are For." In 1987 he went to Australia and recorded a two-disc album with the Melbourne Symphony Orchestra, *Live in Australia,* which made a surprise hit single out of "Candle in the Wind," a fan's homage to Marilyn Monroe, which was first recorded as part of *Goodbye Yellow Brick Road* fourteen years earlier.

After a brief stint with Geffen Records, he went back with MCA, and has a new look and a revitalized career as an adopted Georgian.

DOUG JOHNSON

Behind every great recording star one will find a producer with an innovative imagination and a pioneering plan for the future.

Georgia's Doug Johnson is such a person.

Johnson is a musical talent in his own right and had demonstrated a head for business that has no peer in the country music field. He moved from Atlanta to Nashville in 1987, and Music City USA has not been the same since he arrived on the scene.

The Names of the talents he has produced and developed read like a Who's Who of contry music: Patty Loveless, Joe Diffie, Collin Ray, James House, Ken Mellons, and others on the way up. Perhaps the brightest star in his crown is that of fellow Georgian Doug Stone, whom he molded into a Grammy nominee with his first recording in 1990, "I'd Be Better Off (in a Pine Box)," a tear-jerker done in the style of George Jones. With Johnson's genius calling the shots, the first three of Stone's albums—*Doug Stone, I Thought It Was You,* and *From the Heart*—all went Platinum.

Johnson was the one who produced "Kentucky Thunder" for Ricky Skaggs, "White Limozeen" for Dolly Parton, and "Extra Mile" for Shenandoah. His was the genius behind John Michael Montgomery's breakthrough "Life's a Dance" and Ty Herndon's debut, "What Mattered Most."

A native of Swainsboro and the son of Grady "Buck" and "Bunny" Johnson, Doug became vice president, A & R, of Epic Records Nashville in November 1991 and now reigns as senior vice president of that organization, where he is credited with putting Epic's roster of stars "on the cutting edge of country music for the coming century."

He has the credentials to prove that he can write as well as produce songs. He worked with the famed Lowery Group in Atlanta before heading for Tennessee and, among other credits, was the writer of "Simple Little Words" for Christy Lane.

BUCKY JONES

Perhaps there have been musical prodigies, like Mozart, who have composed more pieces in one year, but it seems hardly likely that any one composer ever has had more of his songs recorded in a twelve-month period than did Georgia's Bucky Jones in 1984—a total of sixty, most of them hits.

Jones was born at Bainbridge in the southwest corner of Georgia in 1942 and grew up in the small, county-seat town of Newton on the Flint River. He began writing songs and playing in local bands for dances, radio, and television at the age of fourteen and dates the birth of his dream of becoming a professional songwriter from his first trip to Nashville at the age of fifteen.

He humored his mother's dream for him by attending and graduating from the School of Pharmacy at the University of Georgia, but on New Year's Day of 1972, he chucked pills for composing and moved to Nashville where he quickly landed a job writing songs for the legendary Jim Reeves.

His first hit was "The Most Wanted Woman in Town" recorded by Roy Head, and his string of tune successes grew yearly until he set his high-water mark for composing in 1984.

His successes include such biggies as: "I Tell It Like It Used to Be" by T. Graham Brown; "You Don't Count the Cost" by Billy Dean; "Your Heart's Not in It" by Janie Frickie; "Only Love Can Save Me Now" by Crystal Gayle; "Touch and Go Crazy" by Lee Greenwood; "Radio Lover" by George Jones; "Standing Knee Deep in a River (Dying of Thirst)" by Kathy Mattea; "I've Got a Million of 'Em" by Ronnie McDowell; "He Broke Your Memory Last Night" by Reba McEntire; "I Could Use Another You" by Eddie Raven; "Do You Want to Go to Heaven?," "Only One You," and "War Is Hell (on the Home Front, Too)" by T. G. Sheppard; "I Meant Every Word He Said" by Ricky Van Shelton; "In a Different Light" by Doug Stone; "Blue to the Bone" by Sweethearts of the Rodeo; and "Highway Robbery" by Tanya Tucker.

Other top artists who have cut his songs include Moe Bandy, Ed Bruce, Ray Charles, John Conlee, Mickey Gilley, Tom Jones, Brenda Lee, Johnny Lee, Johnny Paycheck, Charley Pride, the Oak Ridge Boys, Joe

Stampley, Conway Twitty, and Tammy Wynette. He also wrote the theme song for the CBS Television series, *Filthy Rich*.

Jones now lives in Hanover, New Hampshire, with his wife and two children and commutes to Nashville several days each week to write by himself and with his friends and peers at PolyGram Music Publishing.

JOEL A. KATZ

As far as anyone knows, Joel Katz can't sing a lick and has never written a hit song, but his name is written big in the music industry in Georgia and around the world. An Atlanta resident, Joel Katz is the founding partner of one of the country's largest music entertainment law firms, Katz, Smith & Cohen. With offices in Atlanta and New York, their client roster includes some of the world's most well-known entertainers, music producers, record companies, concert promoters, and Fortune 500 companies.

A partial list of his clients reads like a Who's Who in the Entertainment World: John Anderson, Jimmy Buffett, Toni Braxton, James Brown, Merle Haggard, Waylon Jennings, George Jones, B. B. King, Kris Kristofferson, Kris Kross, Tracy Lawrence, L. L. Cool J., Jodeci, Lorrie Morgan, Lyle Lovett, Willie Nelson, George Strait, Marty Stuart, S. O. S., the Temptations, Tammy Wynette, and many, many others.

Katz started his law practice in 1971 after a three-year period of working as a lawyer for HUD, a law clerk for a medium-sized Atlanta law firm, and a law professor at Georgia State University. The firm's first client was James Brown, introduced to Katz by a former student. From there, Katz began representing Willie Nelson, and the roster grew to include more than fifty other artists.

In 1995, Katz was inducted into the Georgia Music Hall of Fame, the first attorney ever to receive that honor.

Throughout his career, Katz has consistently remained active in educational and industry related associations. He has been national chairman of the board of trustees for the National Recording Arts and Sciences, Inc. (NARAS), a member of the Recording Academy Television Committee, a director of the NARAS Foundation Board, chairman of the Georgia State University Music Industry advisory board, and the General Council for Farm Aid.

KRIS KROSS

Chris Kelly and Chris Smith were just two ebullient twelve-year-olds on a sneaker-buying visit to Atlanta's Greenbrier Mall five years ago when they were discovered by prodigy producer Jermaine Dupri, who was only six years their senior. Five years later they were the hip hop superstars known as Kris Kross who defied predictions that they would be a passing fad like the hula hoop and instead grew into prideful, sexy young men who are setting all kinds of records writing, performing, and recording their own hits.

They refer to themselves as the "Chrises," and their trend-setting "Krossed Out" look of wearing their stylishly-baggy clothing backwards has made them icons of first the pubescent and adolescent, and now the young adult, sets of music lovers. Between them and their mentor, Dupri, and his So So Def record label, they have made Atlanta the epicenter of hip hop and themselves into smooth role models with talent and charisma that have brought rap into mainstream and vice versa.

It was Dupri who wrote, arranged, and produced their first album, *Totally Krossed Out*, for Ruffhouse and molded them into fashion trend-setters. That album sold more than four million copies; their first single, "Jump," went double-Platinum; and two subsequent singles, "Warm It Up" and "I Missed the Bus," kept the album on the *Billboard* charts for more than fifty weeks.

So attractive and different these two young stars proved to be that they appeared twice on the *Arsenio Hall Show*; were guests on *Soul Train, In Living Color, Showtime at the Apollo, Inside Edition, Good Morning America,* the *Today Show*, and *Live with Regis and Kathie Lee*; graced the cover of virtually every teen magazine in the nation; were nominated for two Grammy and one MTV Awards and won two American Music awards; toured Europe with Michael Jackson; and headlined their own highly successful North American tour. Their second album, *Da Bomb*, was critically acclaimed and featured the single, "Alright," which went Gold, and a popular duet with Supercat, the dancehall star.

With Dupri's help, advice, and guidance, Kris Kross has become a household word and matured into a smoother, more laid-back sound with each succeeding release. The pair introduced what Dupri called "Phase

Two" of their career with a new grown-up and ready-to-rock sound with the Columbia/Ruffhouse album, *Young, Rich, and Dangerous.* Their sound has evolved as they matured into what is described as "slick and smooth" and is said to have "mellowed with age like a fine wine." In phase two the original "precocious shorties" had developed into "sexy young adults" who had wanted, and taken, more control over their music by writing and producing two of the album's eight songs: "Hey, Sexy" and "Money, Power, and Fame." They not only penned the tracks but, with Kelly on the piano and Smith on the bass, played the music themselves, and had guest appearances by their label mates Da Brat and Aaliyah.

Kris Kross

GLADYS KNIGHT AND THE PIPS

The story that Gladys Knight was born singing instead of crying is apocryphal, but it certainly is true that her first memory is of standing on a chair at the age of four in 1948 to sing gospel songs before the congregation of the Mount Moriah Baptist Church in Atlanta and that, with the encouragement of her singing parents who had been members of the famed Wings Over Jordan Choir, her life since has been one musical success after another. She, is of course, the starring personality of the black singing and dancing rhythm and blues group Gladys Knight and the Pips, which has won three Grammys from seven nominations and has recorded five Gold albums and eleven Gold and two Platinum singles, the latter two breaking all precedents by coming in the same year of 1973 on competing labels and both winning Grammys.

Gladys toured with the Morris Brown College Choir before she was five, won the National Grand Prize on Ted Mack's Original Amateur Hour when she was seven, and formed her first group at eight to sing at the birthday party for her brother Merald, who is known as Bubba. Besides herself, the group was composed of Bubba, their sister Brenda, and their cousins Eleanor and William Guest. Their performance so impressed their uncle, James Wood, that he urged them to continue professionally. Then they took his nickname "Pip" as the group's name. Since that time the original quintet became a quartet when Brenda and Eleanor opted for marriage and families and the decision was made to go with an all-male backup with the addition of another cousin, Edward Patton. Despite all the plays on the word and the jokes made about their name, the group never gave consideration to calling itself anything but "Pips"; Gladys explained that, in addition to the deserved honor it pays a kinsman who helped them so much, they also like the definition of the word as "a seed" because "we're like a seed that goes into the making of a song."

The group began touring with Supersonic Attractions and its stars Sam Cooke and B. B. King and recorded its first single, "Whistle My Love" on the Brunswick label in 1958. It had its first hit in 1961 with "Every Beat of My Heart," which not only was both an R&B and pop success but also landed them in a court battle when three different labels issued it—Huntom of Atlanta, which made it a local hit and then sold its masters to

V. J. Records, and Fury Records of New York, with which the Pips had signed a contract. Fury won the suit but not before the competing versions, one with an organ and the other with a piano background, registered Number One and Number Two on the charts at the same time and eventually sold more than one million copies collectively. The publicity helped their second Fury release, "Letter Full of Tears," become an even bigger hit and assured the success of the album of the same title and the singles "Operator" and "You Broke Your Promise." But the Pips were the ultimate losers because the company went bankrupt, and the group had several lean years while Gladys had a baby and the men had to struggle on their own in New York.

Then they went to Maxx Records and scored with "Givin' Up Is Hard to Do" in both album and single releases; and, in 1966, over Gladys's objection, they signed with Motown, which brought them not only new success but further litigation together with the anomaly of having Platinum hits for both their old and new labels after they switched to Buddah Records upon expiration of the contract with Motown in 1973.

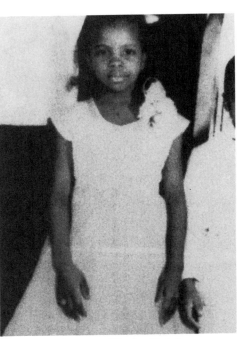

A young Gladys Knight

After minor hits with "Take Me in Your Arms and Love Me" and "Everybody Needs Love," they reached Number Two with "I Heard It on the Grapevine" in 1967. This recognition brought them appearances on the *Ed Sullivan Show*, engagements at the Copa and other nightclubs and in Las Vegas. And it was followed with Number Fifteen "The End of Our Road" in 1968, Number Nineteen "The Nitty Gritty" and Number Seventeen "Friendship Train" in 1969, best-seller "You Need Love Like I Do" in 1970, and Number Seven "If I Were Your Woman" and Record of the Year nomination for "I Don't Want to Do Wrong" in 1971. They also charted with albums titled

Nitty Gritty, Greatest Hits, If I Were Your Woman, and *Standing Ovation.* In 1972 the group had two single hits, "Help Me Make It Through the Night" and "Make Me the Woman You Come Home To," and in 1973 the single "Daddy Could Swear, I Declare" was a best-seller for several months and three albums were big successes—*Neither One of Us* making the Top Ten Pop List, *Imagination* reaching the Top Forty, and *All I Need Is Time* joining the charts.

The year 1973 was their blockbuster year. Switching to Buddah, they released their greatest hit, "Midnight Train to Georgia," which sold more than two million records and received a Grammy for Best R&B Vocal Performance. But Motown countered with a single they had done there before leaving, "Neither One of Us (Wants to Be the First to Say Goodbye)," which not only went Platinum and earned a Grammy for Best Pop Vocal Performance but also was America's Number One song of the year. (The Pips, who left Motown because they objected to the Motown practice of having other artists cover their hits and because they felt that they were not being given the same kind of attention and help given Diana Ross and the Jackson Five, subsequently sued that label for royalties they claimed they never received for that final smash single.) They had a third million seller that year in "I've Got to Use My Imagination," which made them the biggest-selling recording group of 1973.

The roll continued in 1974: "I've Got to Use My Imagination" continued a four-week run through the Top Ten; their new single "You're the Best Thing That Every Happened to Me" reached Number Three; and their recording of Curtis Mayfield's "On and On" for the soundtrack of the movie *Claudine* gave them their fourth consecutive Gold record for Buddah. In addition, the album *Imagination* brought Gladys an individual Grammy for Best Album by a Female Soul Artist. (The three Grammys Gladys and the Pips share from 1973–1974 followed previous nominations in 1967 for "I Heard It Through the Grapevine," in 1969 for "Friendship Train," in 1971 for "If I Were Your Woman," and in 1972 for "Help Me Make It Through the Night.")

In 1975 Gladys and the Pips hosted a summer variety series for the NBC Television Network, and she starred in the movie *Pipe Dreams,* for which the group also recorded the soundtrack. In 1978 they sued Buddah Records and its president, Art Kass, for $23 million because of unpaid royalties and the assignment of their contract without their consent to Arista Records. The litigation prevented them from recording for almost two years, although they continued to perform together in concerts and nightclubs. The suit was settled in 1980. Then Columbia Records bought their contract, and Gladys and the Pips entered their third decade of performing with a new album titled *About Love* on that label.

In the 1980s, the group had Platinum albums *Something Special* and *Emergency*, Top Ten hits in the United Kingdom and the U.S., and in 1987 the Gold album *Forever*. In 1989, they were inducted into the Georgia Hall of Fame.

All members of the group have, at times, made their homes in Atlanta. Gladys, who now lives in Las Vegas, has three children, two of them adults, and when asked by *Ebony* magazine to what she attributed the success of the group, she stated: "One reason we've been able to stick together is because we pray before each show—pray for strength to stay humble, courage to keep pushing, and the ability to reach people with our message."

Gladys Knight and the Pips

LEO KOTTKE

Leo Kottke, who was born in Athens, Georgia, on September 11, 1945, is one of those rare musical geniuses for whom music is an end in itself. A self-taught virtuoso on the twelve-string guitar, he is ranked among performers on that instrument as one of the foremost in the world and one of the top two or three in the United States. But he has eschewed the fortune that talent could bring him through commercial concerts and recordings to play his own music on stages of his own choosing.

He learned to play the trombone in high school in Muskogee, Oklahoma, and taught himself the flute, harmonica, violin, and guitar. He concentrated on the guitar when he came under the influence of the folk music of Burl Ives, the Kingston Trio, and Jimmie Rodgers and advanced to the music of Pete Seeger, Dan Reno, and Red Smiley.

He left college in Minnesota to work in bars and coffeehouses and in 1969 produced an album titled *12-String Blues*, which attracted some attention. Takoma Records then produced a series of fairly successful albums beginning in 1970 with *6- and 12-String Guitar* and continuing with *Mudlark* in 1971 and *Greenhouse* in 1973. Capitol Records put out his top-selling collection *Ice-Water*, which sold 200,000 copies in 1974 and followed it the next year with *Dreams and Other Stuff*. Chrysalis Records issued one titled *Leo Kottke* in 1977.

He received ovations on a concert tour of Europe, particularly in Germany in 1973, but since has chosen to live in relative obscurity in Minnesota and to perform to small audiences on his own terms.

BRENDA LEE

Brenda Lee has bridged more gaps than any other performer in modern musical history and has the records to show for it. She has sold more than one hundred million records worldwide.

Although her most ardent fans continue to think of her in terms of "Little Miss Dynamite" who rocked her way to stardom through the medium of television in the mid-1950s and 1960s, she presently has the distinction of having sold more records than any other solo female singer in the world. These include hits across the spectrum from traditional country to hard rock and back to middle-of-the-road pop.

She is credited with bringing national attention to Nashville as a pop recording center and is Music City's only true international star, having taped specifically for foreign markets in Japanese, Spanish, German, French, and Italian. She draws even larger audiences abroad than she does in the United States, particularly in Japan where she holds the attendance record.

Brenda has twelve Gold records for singles sales of one million or more and more than two dozen best-selling albums and twice that number of single chart successes.

By the time she was twenty-one, she had more than thirty-two successive chart records and, over the course of her career, has won every major music award except a Grammy, for which she has had two nominations —for "Johnny One Time" in 1969 and "Tell Me What It's Like" in 1980.

Hers is truly a "rags-to-riches" story. Although she is now rich and famous, her childhood singing often was the difference between hunger and the family's having food on the table. This was especially true after her father was fatally injured in a construction accident when she was only eight. Her mother had to go to work in a cotton mill to support her and her brother and two sisters, all of whom Brenda subsequently put through college.

Born Brenda Mae Tarpley on December 11, 1944, in Lithonia, Georgia, she grew up in nearby Conyers, where she demonstrated what her mother called "a God-given talent" as a toddler by repeating songs heard on the radio. At five she won a talent contest at the Conyers Elementary School Spring Festival by singing "Take Me Out to the Ball Game." That led to regular appearances first on "Starmakers Review," an Atlanta Saturday radio program, and, before the age of seven, appearances on *TV Ranch*, a production of Atlanta's WAGA-TV. She had to stand on a box to reach the microphone. Her first professional job was singing at a Shrine Club luncheon where she was paid twenty dollars.

A young Brenda Lee dancing with Elvis Presley

In 1955, Peanut Faircloth, a disc jockey, offered her unpaid top billing on his television program and help in getting paid bookings in the area if her family would move to Augusta. He also persuaded Red Foley and his manager, Dub Albritten, to audition her. Foley immediately signed her on his monthly *Junior Jubilee* showcase for young talent televised by ABC-TV from Springfield, Missouri, in conjunction with his regular *Ozark Jubilee*. Her popularity won her booking on the *Perry Como Show,* and she soon had appearances on the *Steve Allen* and *Ed Sullivan* shows and guest star slots with Bob Hope, Red Skelton, Danny Thomas, Dinah Shore, and others.

Albritten became her manager and, when she was eleven, arranged a recording contract with Decca Records. She then moved to Nashville, where she and producer Owen Bradley became friends and major figures in the development of the Nashville recording industry.

Her first record, Hank Williams's "Jambalaya," was cut on July 30, 1956. It was followed soon by "Dynamite," from which she got the tag that follows her today. She recorded her first Gold record, "Rockin' around the Christmas Tree," in 1958.

Albritten launched her international career by booking her in Paris at the Olympic Music Hall in 1959 and created a worldwide sensation by touting her as "a 32-year-old-midget" after the French promoter objected to signing a child. This was followed by successful engagements in Germany, Italy, and England (where she later gave a command performance for the Royal Family); a month-long tour of Brazil, where she was called

"The Explosive Girl"; and engagements in Japan and Australia, where she was mobbed by screaming fans.

Her second million seller was Ronnie Self's "I'm Sorry," which created controversy because fourteen-year-old girls at that time did not sing grownup songs about true love and heartbreak, but it bumped Chubby Checkers's "The Twist" from the top of the charts and established Brenda as a star who might be small in stature but one who had a big, bluesy voice that radiated emotion and stirred audiences.

She followed it with the hits "Eventually," "Anybody But Me," "Everybody Loves Me But You," and her third Gold record "All Alone Am I." She cut a phenomenal 256 songs by the time she was twenty-one.

Brenda Lee

In April 1963, she married Ronald Shacklett, son of a Nashville contractor, when they were both eighteen and gave birth to the first of their two daughters one year later. Brenda and Ronnie live in Nashville, and she now limits her work to six months a year, mostly in nightclubs at home and concerts abroad.

After her string of rock and pop bestsellers, she returned to her country roots in 1972 and had an immediate success with Kris Kristofferson's "Nobody Wins." Her new sound, which brought her a second Grammy nomination after eleven years, is broader and more sophisticated than her usual style, but is regarded as a progression rather than a departure from the music for which she is famed.

Standing only four feet and nine inches tall, Brenda Lee probably is the tiniest of today's music stars, but only Johnny Cash, George Jones, and Jerry Lee Lewis share her distinction of still producing country hits forty years after they first made the charts. All of them are nearly twenty years her senior.

MYLON LeFEVRE

Mylon LeFevre left his famed Georgia gospel-singing family in 1968 because he wanted "to dress differently and have longer sideburns" and to seek fame and fortune as a full-time rock 'n' roller.

Declaring he "didn't feel right about making money off God unless I was really living for Him," Mylon pulled up his family roots to record the solo album *We Believe*, (featuring "gospel words with rock 'n' roll music") with Joe South and several future members of the Atlanta Rhythm Section. He went on to form his own band, Holy Smoke, and to take Southern rock into New York long before the Allman Brothers and Lynyrd Skynyrd.

He spent four years doing 320 shows a year and trying to "get higher than anybody" with Jimi Hendrix and other musicians. In 1972 he and guitarist Alvin Lee went to England, where they recorded the album *On the Road to Freedom* with Mick Fleetwood, Ron Wood, and George Harrison as backup session players. He returned to Atlanta in 1977 to sign a contract with Warner Brothers and do a comeback concert with the Atlanta Rhythm Section at the Fox Theater on New Year's Eve.

In 1979 he sought revival of his career in an album produced by hitmaker Allen Toussaint for the Mercury label appropriately titled *Rock and Roll Resurrection.*

Presently, Mylon is an ordained minister with the Mount Paran Church of God in Atlanta.

THE LEFEVRES

There may be individuals whose impact has been greater, but of all the groups that have had major roles in the development of modern gospel music in this country, none can claim to have made greater pioneering contributions to, nor to have achieved more enduring popularity in, the evolution that has brought gospel singing out of the Pentecostal churches and into the concert halls and recording studios of the nation than the LeFevres of Atlanta. Now into their seventy-fifth year and third generation of performing, the New LeFevres, formed around the family of "Uncle Alf" (the youngest of the original LeFevres), are continuing to draw hand-clapping, foot-stomping audiences throughout the nation from the sons, daughters, and grandchildren of the fans of their inimitable forebears.

The story of the LeFevres is one of musical talent, family love, religious faith, and entrepreneurial genius in equal parts. The story began in 1921 in Smithville, Tennessee, when the children of the musical LeFevre Family—Urias (lead), Alphus (tenor) and Maude (alto)—formed a trio to sing in churches and were so popular they continued together as a performing group to sing their way through Lee College in Cleveland, Tennessee. At the time, Alphus, the member with the "built-in smile," though only twelve years old was already a champion guitarist and fiddler and well on his way to achieving his goal of being able to play any instrument made.

One of their early concerts was in the Chattanooga church whose pastor was the father of Eva Mae Whittington, an eight-year-old musical prodigy whose long black hair came closer to reaching the pedals of the church piano than her feet. There sixteen-year-old Urias was smitten with love that grew into correspondence with and culminated in marriage to Eva Mae when she became seventeen. Eva Mae, who had begun singing at her father's street-corner services in McColl, South Carolina, at the age of five, was playing the organ by ear at six when she was so small she had to sit in her father's lap to reach the keys while he pumped the pedals. She was studying classical piano at the age of eight. She succeeded the second of the LeFevre sisters, who left the trio for marriage, and served not only as pianist and singer but also mistress of ceremonies. The group traveled with her father at first, but then hired a bass singer, reformed as the LeFevres, and undertook a performing career that, with varying changes of personnel and locale and a few interruptions for reasons like illness and war, would continue with ever-increasing success and popularity throughout the twentieth century.

In 1939 they moved to Atlanta and began holding concerts for which they charged admissions of ten cents for adults and five cents for children. They quickly attracted a following, and in 1940 were signed by NuGrape and Orange Crush to do a regular radio show on WGST for fifty dollars a week, which drew more than one thousand fan letters a day and continued for ten years, with interruptions for World War II service by Urias in the Navy and Alphus in the Army. Until they returned in 1943, Eva Mae sang with the Homeland Harmony quartet; upon their return, they began traveling throughout the South for weekend concerts, while during the week Urias worked with the Georgia Power Company and Eva Mae worked in a dimestore. Although Eva Mae wanted to quit to become a full-time mother and housewife, she didn't because Urias refused to continue without her. The wisdom of this was borne out by the popularity she achieved, which culminated in her twice being named Queen of Gospel Music by the National Quartet Convention beginning in 1954 and in being elected to the Gospel Music Hall of Fame in 1978.

The first of Eva Mae and Urias's children, Pierce, was born in 1936, followed by Meurice in 1937, Andrea in 1939, Mylon in 1945, and, several years later, a retarded daughter, Monteia. In an effort to get medical help for Monteia, Eva Mae and Urias took church jobs in Philadelphia for two years and Eva Mae sold her furniture a piece at a time to pay for treatments. She ultimately had a nervous breakdown caring for and worrying about the child, but she recovered and the family moved back to Atlanta. The LeFevres went back to performing and achieved the height of their popularity in the 1950s and 1960s.

Urias proved to be an innovative manager. Under his direction, the group became the first to use more than one microphone, to use musical instruments other than the piano played by members as they sang, to wear red jackets on stage, to own and travel by custom tour bus, and to build, own, and operate their own recording studio. When the group was sidelined after a bus wreck in which Alphus suffered a broken leg, Eva Mae's children formed their own group called the LeFevreairs, which went on the road with Pierce playing the trumpet, Meurice the trombone, and all of them singing. They got good reviews, with Pierce being called "the

Pat Boone of Gospel Singing" for his smooth baritone voice. He later became a full-fledged member of the adult group.

During the 1960s the group expanded to six and at times, with the addition of various of Eva Mae and Urias's children, numbered as many as nine. Several outsiders were incorporated from time to time, and two of those alumni have gone on to achieve fame in their own right with their own groups—Hovie Lister with the Masters V and Rex Nelon with the Rex Nelon Singers.

With characteristic foresight, Urias established a television production company, Programming, Inc., in the early 1960s. This initiated the syndicated *Gospel Singing Caravan*, which was shown nationwide featuring the LeFevres, four other groups, and Eva Mae as MC. The rating of that program exceeded the combined ratings of *Red Skelton* and *Gomer Pyle*, when played in prime time. It made the LeFevres a household word throughout America and Eva Mae the foremost female gospel singer of the nation. Demands for public appearances and concerts grew. They drew record crowds at many fairs in the United States and Canada and drew overflow audiences to some of the largest auditoriums of the nation. At the height of their popularity, they were traveling more than one hundred thousand miles in more than forty states each year, had a fan club with a list of more than three thousand members, and, in addition to the *Caravan*, were appearing in three weekly television shows in Atlanta, Augusta, and Columbus, and five radio programs in Georgia.

The LeFevres also founded the LeFevre-Sing Publishing Company, the LeFevre Sound Corporation, and the SING record label. They distributed records nationally for several major groups and produced and distributed television programs for themselves, Bill Anderson, the Chuck Wagon Gang, the Rangers, and other popular groups and performers of the period.

They stayed on top until Urias retired in the mid-1970s and Eva Mae retired in 1977. Urias died of cancer in 1978, and Mylon left to pursue an individual career and enjoyed considerable rock success. But the family tradition was continued by "Uncle Alf" who, at the age of seventy-three, was heading up the New LeFevres featuring his daughter, Marla, and his son, Scott, who subsequently was named Best Bass Singer in a Midwestern talent poll. Proving that "Uncle Alf" did not lose the touch is the fact that in 1982 he received the Favorite First Tenor award in a poll taken by *Gospel Music News*. The New LeFevres complained that, although they had bridged the generation gap, they had a hard time keeping up with him.

Eva Mae continues to enjoy her status as head of the clan, and, while she no longer performs with the group, she does sing in church and gives concerts of her own. But wherever she goes, she still is hailed as the "First Lady of Gospel Music." Of her long, eventful and colorful singing career, she says:

"I sacrificed a lot to be a gospel singer. I never had a social life. I never got to spend a lot of time with my children. I feel I was anointed from my mother's womb to sing His praises and to tell of His love, but to me it was worth every minute of it. . . . If I had to do it all over again, I'd do it the same way. I am a gospel singer, and I will be a gospel singer until I die."

This gospel singer was inducted into the Georgia Music Hall of Fame in 1985.

The LeFevres

YOEL LEVI

Taking up where his renowned predecessor, Robert Shaw, left off when he retired, the dynamic Israeli conductor Yoel Levi has been credited with transforming the Atlanta Symphony Orchestra into a world-class orchestra that is consistently and universally extolled for "the clarity, virtuosity, and sonic beauty of its playing."

Since becoming its music director in 1988, Masetro Levi in 1991 led the young and dynamic Atlanta aggregation on a critically acclaimed, fifteen-city, six-country European tour and gave it the musical stature to become one of only two American orchestras to be nominated as Best Orchestra of the Year at the First Annual International Classical Music Awards in 1991–1992. Only the Chicago Symphony, among American musical organizations, can lay claim to such stellar recognition.

"Yoel Levi has built a reputation for himself and his orchestra that is increasingly the envy of his Big Five American counterparts in New York, Philadelphia, Cleveland, Boston, and Chicago," is the assessment given Levi and his baton in bringing the Atlanta Orchestra and its reputation to the forefront of world musical ranks by *Gramaphone* magazine.

Born in Romania, Levi grew up in Israel and studied at the Tel Aviv Academy of Music, where he received a Master of Arts degree with distinction, and at the Jerusalem Academy of Music under Mendi Rodan. He also studied with Franco Ferrara in Sienna and Rome, with Kiril Kondrashin in Holland, and at the Guildhall School of Music in London. He won First Prize in the 1978 Conductors' International Competition in Besancon, France, and was selected to be assistant to Lorin Maazel at the Cleveland Orchestra for six years, serving as resident conductor there from 1980 to 1984.

Before agreeing to come to the challenging post in Atlanta, he was one of the most sought-after guest conductors in the world. His appearances have included the podiums of the top orchestras in Berlin, Budapest, Copenhagen, Frankfurt, Israel, Japan, London, Munich, Paris, Prague, Rome, and Stockholm. In this country he has conducted the New York Philharmonic and the orchestras of Boston, Cleveland, Chicago, Minnesota, Philadelphia, Pittsburgh, San Francisco, and Washington. In Canada he has led both the Montreal and Toronto orchestras; and, in 1991, he was invited to conduct the Stockholm Philharmonic Orchestra in its performance highlighting the Nobel Prize ceremonies of that year.

Levi has led acclaimed performances of Mahler's Ninth Symphony with the New York Philharmonic, Orff's *Carmina Burana* and Mahler's Eighth Symphony with the Cleveland Orchestra at the Blossom Festival, Britten's *War Requiem* with the Detroit Symphony, and Mendelssohn's *Elijah* with the San Francisco Symphony. Since coming to Atlanta, he has further demonstrated his mastery of Mahler in leading his current organization's highly successful performance of Mahler's Second (*Resurrection*) Symphony in New York's Avery Fisher Hall.

Yoel Levi

He also has transformed the Atlanta Orchestra into a recording giant, leading more than twenty recordings for Telarc International devoted to the music of Barber, Brahms, Copland, Hindemith, Mendelssohn, Mussorgsky, Prokofiev, Ravel, Rossini, Saint-Saens, Schoenberg, Shostakovich, Sibelius, and Stravinsky. The reviews he and the Atlanta musicians have received for these works have been glowing:

"Barber at his best," said *DisCDigest*.

"Levi revels in the score's earthy qualities, pushing rhythms, and dynamics to their limits," the *Cleveland Plain Dealer* wrote of his exciting performance of Stravinski's "Rite of Spring."

"Yoel Levi has taken his place amongst the most eminent conductors of Sibelius," *Diapason* Magazine opined, while *Gramaphone* magazine called his interpretation of Sibelius' tone poems "raw, fiery excitement."

"Now one of America's greatest orchestras, it [the ASO] embodies virtuosity, glowing warmth, and stunningly precise ensemble," was the raving opinion of *CD Review* of London of Levi's direction of the Rossini Overtures.

Levi and the Atlanta Symphony, playing with pianist Andre Watts, subsequently have released the combined "Piano Concerto No. 1" of Tchaikovsky and "Concerto No. 2" of Saint-Saens. Their future recordings will include Beethoven's "Overtures" and Mahler's "Fifth Symphony," all expected to be best sellers.

Maestro Levi and his family have established their permanent home in Atlanta. They have become active leaders in the city's civic and cultural life, and there is every reason to believe Levi's tenure with the Atlanta Symphony will be a long and glorious one.

THE LEWIS FAMILY

For more than forty years, "The First Family of Bluegrass Gospel Music" has headlined gospel and bluegrass music festivals throughout the nation and in Canada.

The Lewis Family of Lincolnton, Georgia, averages about two hundred performances annually with about fifty of those dates being major bluegrass festivals. They add more than one hundred thousand miles annually to their bus odometer.

They do not exactly know how many albums they have recorded in their career, but they are pretty sure it is around sixty. Their fame has spread to several foreign nations where magazines write about them in languages the family members do not understand.

Typically, the family wasted no time after signing with Day Wind Records in Nashville in April of 1995. They immediately headed out for concerts in Ohio, Indiana, Colorado, Wyoming, California, Oregon, and Washington in their custom-made bus that formerly belonged to Conway Twitty.

At the heart of the group is patriarch Roy "Pop" Lewis, who marked his ninetieth birthday on September 22, 1995. He still performs with his family on the road every week.

Besides the senior Lewis, the performing members of the Lewis Family include his sons, Roy and Wallace Lewis; his daughters, Polly Copsey, Miggie Lewis, and Janis Phillips; and his grandsons, Travis Lewis and Lewis Phillips.

Staffing their records table and traveling with them for the past four decades has been Pauline "Mom" Lewis. Roy and Pauline started their musical family when they eloped and got married October 25, 1925—within days of the first Grand Ole Opry broadcast.

As major awards and honors go, the Lewis Family has had its share.

The group has sung in New York City's Lincoln Center and performed at the Grand Ole Opry, and, in 1992, was inducted into the Georgia Music Hall of Fame.

One unusual honor was being called onto Atlanta's Fox Theater stage and applauded by megastars Peabo Bryson, Elton John, and hot young rap duo Kris Kross. The occasion was their being named the Outstanding

Bluegrass Act of 1992 at the second annual Coca-Cola Atlanta Music Awards recognizing Georgia-based musicians.

"We weren't planning to go," related Polly Lewis Copsey, "but we thought, 'Shoot, it's the middle of the week, we're off, and we've got the tickets. Why not? Let's go.' We parked our bus near the stage door and watched all these limousines drive up next to us. . . . The show people were real nice to us and wanted us to go to a party afterwards at the Hard Rock Cafe, but we needed to get back to Lincolnton."

That reflects the down-home, shucks-it's-just-us philosophy of the Lewis Family. They are known to the rich and famous as well as to the poor and unknown. Their documented fans have included Elvis Presley, First Lady Mamie Eisenhower, Vince Gill, Travis Tritt, Joe Diffie, Ricky Van Shelton, and Marty Stuart.

The Lewis Family

For nearly a decade, they have hosted the Lewis Family Homecoming and Bluegrass Festival outside Lincolnton, which lures thousands of fans for a weekend of music, food, and fun.

The family turned serious about performing in the late 1940s and early 1950s as the Lewis Brothers featuring Wallace, Little Roy, Talmadge, and Esley. The latter two eventually dropped out, and the Lewis daughters eventually dropped in, along with their father.

About 1951, the family did their first recording of two '78s on the Sullivan label. They hooked up with Don Pierce, then living in California, and released some 45 rpm records on the Hollywood label. Pierce moved to Nashville and started Starday Records in 1952.

Shortly afterward, he took the Lewis family's 45 rpm recordings and put them out in a sixteen-song Starday album called *Singing Time Down South*. Future Grand Ole Opry star Bill Anderson used to play those albums as a disc jockey in Commerce, Georgia.

The group recorded many years for Canaan Records, a division of Waco, Texas-based Word Inc.

The family's weekly television show, started in 1954 on WJBF in Augusta, became one of the longest running country and gospel shows in television history, finally discontinuing in 1992. Shipping the TV show film to other nationwide stations, at one point, was young Jim Nabors, later to become Gomer Pyle on his own national show.

Whether singing on porches in Lincoln County, Georgia, or performing in major civic centers throughout the nation, the Lewis Family both live and love their music.

HOVIE LISTER

V. O. Stamps of Dallas, Texas, elevated gospel singing from churches to concert halls with his Stamps-Baxter quartets and song, "Give the World a Smile," but it was Hovie Lister, the handsome Baptist preacher from Greenville, South Carolina, an Atlantan for nearly fifty years, whose sense of style and flair for showmanship gave this music class and chic.

Believing fervently that "God didn't intend for religion to wear a long face," Lister made his Statesmen quartet, formed in 1948, one of the most popular gospel groups in America, even to the point of winning the Arthur Godfrey Talent Scouts competition of network television, without crossing that thin line between religious and secular music like contemporaries such as the Oak Ridge Boys.

Furman Bisher wrote in an article for the *Saturday Evening Post* that Lister and the Statesmen "put rhythm into religion" and were in the forefront of the groups that made all-night gospel singing a post-World War II entertainment phenomenon that could outdraw symphony, jazz and ballet concerts, circuses, basketball tournaments, and wrestling matches in most of America east of the Mississippi River and large portions of the country west of it. At the height of their popularity, they traveled one hundred thousand miles a year throughout the nation in a custom-designed sleeping bus singing to an average of twenty-five hundred, and upwards of ten thousand people per concert. They once appeared before an aggregate of sixty thousand over a five-day period during a revival in Detroit. They owned four gospel music publishing companies, operated recording and television production companies jointly with the Blackwood Brothers, and produced their own syndicated television show, *Singin' Time in Dixie*. They also recorded for RCA, including their best-selling version of "This Ole House."

Distinguished by his Clark Gable mustache, wavy hair, and toothpaste smile, Hovie, in addition to his sharp promotional instincts, is an accomplished pianist and singer, the grandson of a South Carolina music teacher who grew up playing for a family quartet, the Listers, from the age of fourteen. For a time he was featured with the famed LeFevres until he branched out on his own in the late 1940s with tenor Denver Crumpler, lead Jake Hess, bass Jim (Big Chief) Wetherington, and baritone Doy Ott as the Statesmen quartet. Jack Toney later succeeded Hess and Roland "Rozie" Rozelle, acknowledged to be one of the greatest tenor voices in gospel music, replaced Crumpler. Lister was best known for his flamboyant piano style, but he also would switch places with Ott for some emotional, crowd-pleasing solos of his own. A succession of Georgia governors designated them as Georgia's official "Ambassadors of Good Will."

Hovie Lister

Hovie founded five successful music publishing companies and had an eighteen-year recording contract with RCA and later Capitol Records. He has received eight Grammy nominations and one Grammy during his career.

He has performed in forty-eight of our fifty states and led the Statesmen to appearances on NBC, ABC, and CBS networks as a feature on the *Arthur Godfrey, Tennessee Ernie Ford,* and *Jimmy Dean* shows. He has received two honorary doctor degrees.

Lister is an ordained Baptist minister who, throughout his early years of travels, always came back to fill his country-church pulpit at the little Mount Zion Baptist Church near Marietta, Georgia, from which he refused to take any salary, insisting the pastorate helped "keep my feet on the ground." He defends the modish dress and upbeat entertaining style of his groups vigorously: "If it takes shaking my hair down, beating a piano like Liberace or Piano Red to keep these young people out of beer joints and the rear seats of automobiles, I'll do it. The devil's got his kind of entertainment. We've got ours. They criticize me, say I'm too lively for religion, but I get results. That's what counts."

Lister was the moving force in the consolidation of the Statesmen and Blackwood groups into the Masters V, which carried on in the Statesmen tradition and won a Grammy to prove it. With Lister as manager and pianist, the Masters V featured deep bassist J. D. Sumner and James Blackwood, along with former Statesmen Rozelle and Hess.

In 1984, after forty years in the gospel music field, Lister was selected to the Gospel Music Association's Hall of Fame and, in 1986, was inducted into the Georgia Music Hall of Fame. He also marketed gospel music videos as president of Reel to Reel.

BILL LOWERY

If there is any one overriding fact in the larger-than-life success story of Big Bill Lowery—the entrepreneurial genius who has made Atlanta one of the recognized recording capitals of the music world—it is that he thrives on proving that he can do what others predict cannot be done. He beat cancer when no company would insure him against it. He built radio station WQXI into the heavyweight contender that went head-to-head with the undisputed champion of the Atlanta airways, WSB. He had the last laugh on the New York publishers who predicted he would never be a successful music publisher in Atlanta. He came back from the bankruptcy of one of his early companies with a musical conglomerate bearing his name that rose in eight years to become *Broadcast Music*'s Number One publisher in 1969.

No wonder that he is known by the title of "Mr. Atlanta Music" and was the first of many Georgia greats to be selected for inclusion in the Georgia Music Hall of Fame when it was created in 1979.

Perhaps the truest measure of Bill Lowery's contributions to the world of music would be to try to imagine the voids that would exist without him. There would never have been such hits as "Young Love," "Games People Play," "(I Never Promised You A) Rose Garden," "Walk on By," "Dizzy," "Walk a Mile in My Shoes," "Don't It Make You Wanta Go Home," "Sheila," "Be Young, Be Foolish, Be Happy," "So into You," "Champagne Jam," "Down in the Boondocks," "Key Largo," "I Love the Nightlife," "Stormy," "Spooky," "Ahab the Arab," "Traces," "Be-Bop-a-Lula," "Misery Loves Company," "Reach Out of the Darkness," "Moonlight Feels Right," "Imaginary Lover," "What Kind of Fool Do You Think I Am," "Common Man," and many others among the more than six thousand titles in the catalogues of the Lowery Group of Music Publishing Companies. These titles embrace every type of music and hold twenty Gold records and have sold more than seventy-five million records since the original Lowery Music Company, Inc., received its BMI license on October 1, 1952. Neither would there have been such artists and writers as Mac Davis, Ray Stevens, Brenda Lee, Joe South, Jerry Reed, Sonny James, Billy Joe Royal, Freddy Weller, Tommy Roe, Alicia Bridges, Susan Hutcheson, Frederick Knight, Bertie Higgins, Buddy Buie, J. R. Cobb, Robert Nix,

Ray Whitley, Dennis Yost, the Classics IV, the Atlanta Rhythm Section, the Tams, Starbuck, and a host of other stars and groups.

Bill Lowery was born in the bayou country of Leesville, Louisiana. He studied radio dramatics in California at Taft California Junior College under Raleigh Borrell of the Pasadena Playhouse. After radio-announcing stints in Shreveport, Louisiana; Hot Springs, Arkansas; Oklahoma City, Oklahoma; and Wichita Falls, Texas; he became the youngest radio station manager in the nation when hired at the age of twenty-one to direct the construction and programming of radio station WBEJ in Elizabethton, Tennessee.

A trip to Atlanta to attend the Georgia Tech-Alabama Football Game in 1946 brought him to the decision to ask his employer to seek a radio station permit in Atlanta. Thus in 1946 was born out of his inventive mind the name, news direction, and programming format of station WQXI, which made "Qxie" a household word in Atlanta. With its WQX "Eye Witness News" and its pop music programming, it stole the Sunday morning listening audience and put the city's dominant station, WSB, into a ratings race from which it has never recovered.

Two years later he accepted an offer to go with station WGST as a deejay, commentator, and play-by-play broadcaster of Georgia Tech football games. He did three imaginative and popular weekday radio shows; "Mama Goes A' Shopping," "Musical Tune," and "Who's Singing," but it was his Saturday morning "Uncle Ebenezer Brown" Show, on which he played a country dialect character, that propelled him into the recording/publishing business. As "Uncle Eb" he found himself being called about local talent and referring potential recording talent to record company executives. It was thusly that he discovered the songwriting genius Joe South, who at the age of twelve walked into the studios at six A.M. one Saturday morning and talked his way onto the air.

Lowery was stricken by cancer in 1951 and, in addition to the less-than-favorable prognosis of his doctors, was unable to get insurance on himself or to buy any annuities for the protection of his family. He voted not only to beat the disease but also to make himself and his family financially secure. He followed up on the suggestion of Ken Nelson of Capitol Records that the music publishing business offered the best hope of providing his family with security.

One of the first people to contact him after he established the first of the companies now comprising the Lowery Group was songwriter Cotton Carrier, who, in 1953, brought him a gospel tune he had written, "I Have

But One Goal," which Lowery himself recorded with the Smith Brothers, Smitty and Tennessee. It became an immediate hit and gospel classic, selling more than 150,000 copies. That marked the beginning of his association with Carrier, who remained with him as general professional manager of the group until his death on July 18, 1994. It also marked the beginning of attempts of New York music publishers to lure Lowery to that city, Hal Fein of Roosevelt Music told him, "You'll never become a publisher in Atlanta or make phonograph records there."

Fein had to eat those words in less than three years when Lowery received the BMI Award in 1956 for his first million seller, "Be-Bop-a-Lula," the rock 'n' roll classic done by Gene Vincent. The next year he published the biggest seller in the history of Lowery Music Company, "Young Love," which not only was a simultaneous Number One record for both Sonny James and Tab Hunter on the country and pop charts that year, but also was revived to become an international Number One best seller by Donny Osmond in 1973. It is a song that has been recorded by literally hundreds of performers the world over and marked the beginning of a succession of Lowery hits that has continued like waves on a beach since.

Working relentlessly to realize his dream to make Atlanta "THE music capital of the world," Lowery encountered his only failure in 1961 when his National Recording Corporation (NRC) folded, not because of any failing on his part, but because of its inability to collect its money from its distributors. Starting over, he recouped and scaled new heights in the industry.

Today, the Lowery Group's many accomplishments include receiving a BMI Four-Million Performance award for "Traces"; a Three-Million Performance award for "I Never Promised You a Rose Garden"; Two-Million Performance awards for "Stormy," "Spooky," "Key Largo," "Young Love," and "Games People Play"; and One-Million Performance awards for "Down in the Boondocks," "Walk On By," "Common Man," "So into You" and "Imaginary Lover." In 1969 "Games People Play" won Grammy awards for Best Contemporary Song and Song of the Year.

The publisher takes special delight in the fact that there's a group of Lowerys running the Lowery Group. His wife Billie handles accounting, while son Butch is the CEO of Southern Tracks and daughter Terri oversees deejay mailings.

Lowery also owns and operates his own recording studio, Southern Tracks, as well as a like-named independent record label that specializes in comedy recordings including tapes by the late humorist/columnist Lewis Grizzard.

In recognition of his leadership in the industry, Bill has served twice as national president of the National Academy of Recording Arts and Sciences, is a member of the boards of directors of the National Music Publishers Association and the Country Music Association, is past president of the Country Music Hall of Fame, and serves on the NARAS Hall of Fame Elections Committee. The Bill Lowery Scholarship Fund was established in his honor at Georgia State University's School of Commercial Music in Atlanta in 1977, and in 1979 he was the first inductee upon the creation of the Georgia Music Hall of Fame. He has taken a leadership role in the yearly observance of Georgia Music Week under the sponsorship of the Music Industry Committee of the Georgia Senate and is a principal exponent of the establishment of a Georgia Recording Commission patterned after the highly successful Georgia Film Commission.

A rotund man of physical proportions equal to his reputation and achievements, Lowery, with his flowing mane of silver hair, takes delight in being described as "Santa Claus without a beard," and sets great store by his reputation for being "the type individual that knows no defeat and is always certain that anything can be accomplished."

Mitch Miller and Bill Lowery

CURTIS MAYFIELD

Curtis Mayfield, a native of Chicago and a long-time resident of Atlanta, is a multifaceted talent whose induction into the Georgia Music Hall of Fame in 1993 could be credited to his achievements in any one of the several musical fields in which he has excelled: singer, recording star, composer of movie sound tracks, producer of hit records for others, and thoughtful lyricist on the problems of race in particular and the nation in general.

He is perhaps proudest of his reputation among African-American citizens for "singing what all the brothers feel," including his big hit of 1970 expressing anger about racial injustice, "If There's a Hell Down Below, We're All Gonna Go." Generally, his soft, high-pitched voice has been one of moderation in society and faith in religion, the latter a reflection of the deep religious faith of his grandmother.

Among music lovers, Mayfield is best known as the lead singer and driving force behind the Inspirations, one of the seminal groups in the field of soul. He and his Chicago neighbor, Jerry Butler, started the ensemble as the Roosters; they subsequently became the Impressions and recorded the classic R&B hit, "For Your Precious Love." Their record company changed the group's name to Jerry Butler and the Impressions, and the group temporarily dissolved in internal dissension until Mayfield made enough money to bring it, without Butler, to New York to record his Top Twenty pop hit for ABC-Paramount, "Gypsy Woman," in 1961.

Finding favor and popularity with R&B audiences, he went solo in 1969 and was ranked eighth among male vocalists by *Billboard* magazine. In 1970 he issued two LP albums, *Curtis* and *Curtis Mayfield Live*, for his own custom record label, Curtom. The latter featured the hits "Hell Down Below," "Mighty, Mighty," "We're a Winner," "Stare and Stare," "Stone Junkie," and "I Plan to Stay a Believer." He started off 1972 with the hit single, "Get Down," and moved from there to composing movie scores, an endeavor in which he had some of his most spectacular musical successes.

Among the movies he scored were *Superfly, Claudine, Let's Do It Again, Sparkle, Short Eyes*, and the Sidney Poitier-Bill Cosby film, *A Piece of the Action*. The *Superfly* soundtrack album went Gold, as did the singles of "Freddie's Dead" and the movie theme. Georgia's Gladys Knight and the

Pips recorded his *Claudine* material, and that work earned him nominations for an Oscar and a Golden Globe award. The Staple Singers hit Number One on *Billboard*'s pop singles list with its rendition of the *Let's Do It Again* title song. Mayfield not only scored *Short Eyes* but also had a featured acting role in it.

Mayfield had a succession of hit albums during the latter part of the 1970s and the early years of the 1980s, and in 1978 produced Aretha Franklin's hit album, *Almighty Fire*. He made a succession of concert tours in the 1980s and in 1983 reunited the Impressions, including both Jerry Butler and Fred Cash from the group's two previous incarnations.

During his comeback tour, Mayfield was injured when stage lighting fell and struck him. The accident was nearly fatal and left him paralyzed from the neck down. Nonetheless, he made significant progress in trying to resume his recording career.

Curtis Mayfield was inducted into the Georgia Music Hall of Fame in 1993.

ROBERT McDUFFIE

When the world-renowned violin virtuoso Yehuti Menuhen needs a chair partner for a sextet, he passes over his illustrious contemporaries for a brilliant younger Georgian, Robert McDuffie of Macon, who at age twenty-five was being heralded by the critics as the most promising of the rising new school of young American violinists. But if Bobby McDuffie had his druthers, he would rather be playing "The Star Spangled Banner" at the beginning of one of the games of the Atlanta Braves, of which he is a self-pronounced "fanatic."

Although a late bloomer by the standards of Menuhen who made his debut at the age of seven, McDuffie's performance at the Metropolitan Museum in New York in December 1983 was reported by *The New York Times* as "so polished and poised" that there was almost a sense of nonchalance. *The Washington Post* called him a player "with power and abandonment." Whatever the adjectives, it has been unanimously conceded that he is one of the foremost musicians in the new musical shift of the strongest and most talented violinists from Europe and Russia to the United States.

Since leaving Macon at the age of sixteen to study under the acclaimed Dorothy DeLay at the Julliard School of Music in New York City, McDuffie has amassed a record of credits that would be impressive for a performer twice his age.

At nineteen he was guest soloist with the New York Pro Arte Chamber Orchestra on a tour of the Soviet Union and was invited back three years later as an individual to solo with major Russian orchestras.

He was guest soloist with the American Symphony Orchestra on its tour of Greece, toured the United States with the Danish Symphony and Czech Philharmonic Orchestras, and has performed with the Chicago, St. Louis, and Baltimore Symphonies and at the Ravinia Music Festival.

He played with Menuhen, president of the Royal Philharmonic Orchestra, at Carnegie Hall and was invited by him to England to be a sextet chair partner in March 1983 and back again for a similar performance with him in the Great Performers Series in February 1984.

Contemporary American composer David Diamond wrote a violin sonata for and dedicated it to him and arranged for him to perform Samuel

Barbre's Violin Concerto in a private presentation for that terminally ill composer.

Renowned violin teacher Jens Ellerman of the Cincinnati Conservatory of Music gave him a two-hundred-and-twenty-five-year-old Gagliano violin.

Leonard Bernstein adopted him as a protege and often consulted with and advised him about his work and career before his death.

Former U.S. Supreme Court Justice Harry Blackmun invited him to perform at a party for the justices of the Supreme Court and their guests and became one of his foremost patrons and friends.

He was named Summer Artist-in-Residence at the Apsen Music Festival in Colorado where he scheduled rehearsals around watching Braves games on cable TV.

Since in classical music the road to success is the exact opposite to that in country music where the would-be star first strives to make a hit record and then tour, McDuffie is touring to develop the stature and demand that will result in lucrative recording contracts. He spends only about twelve weeks a year in his small, austere one-bedroom apartment on Broadway in New York City; once, to pay rent on the apartment, he musically accompanied a belly dancer at a party in New Jersey. But most of the time he plays with symphony orchestras and in concerts at factories and airports as part of the Affiliate Artists Program. He competed in the Naumburg International Violin Competition in 1981, which he lost because of a "memory slip," but his performance brought him a coveted invitation to play with the Chicago Symphony, considered to be America's best orchestra at the Ravina Music Festival.

The son and brother of gifted keyboard artists in Macon, McDuffie flunked piano and started playing the violin at the age of six, becoming a local celebrity performing for civic clubs and churches in the Macon area. However, in his early teen years he was much more interested in playing baseball and once was caught using a tape recording of himself to try to fool his mother into thinking he was practicing while he actually was on the ballfield. Believing that he had exceptional talent if only given the proper instruction and opportunity, Mrs. McDuffie took him out of school and placed him in the hands of Mrs. Lay in whose home he lived until his graduation from Julliard. It was there, McDuffie relates, that he developed the discipline to practice four hours a day and, as he put it, "where I got 'the fingers.' "

Described by music critic Larry Fennelly, "as regular a guy as you could meet this side of the Athens KA House" and as one who "has the quiet confidence of those who are good at what they do but haven't let it disturb their composure or swell their head," McDuffie is modest and self-effacing in discussing his success, talent, and technique. His style has been described as "intense and dramatic," but he emphatically denies that he is "hot-dogging" when he holds out his right foot and shakes his head while playing emotional passages. He prefers twentieth century music to Tchaikovsky and Mendelssohn and tries to give even the old masters what he calls "a fresh approach."

McDuffie performs more than one hundred concerts worldwide each season and has appeared as a soloist with many of the world's finest symphony orchestras. In 1991 he performed at La Scala in celebration of Gian Carlo Menotti's eightieth birthday, an engagement specifically requested by the great composer.

He has been profiled for *CBS Sunday Morning*, NBC's *Today Show*, *PBS Charlie Rose*, and *The Wall Street Journal*, and was nominated for a Grammy in 1990.

He and his wife, Camille Taylor McDuffie, and their children, Eliza and Will, reside in New York City.

Robert McDuffie

CLAYTON "PAPPY" McMICHEN

Clayton "Pappy" McMichen was a great fiddler with an ego to match, and his success in infusing jazz, Dixieland, and other progressive techniques into traditional rural music made him a pioneer crossover artist who was a major figure in the development of country and western music in its popular present-day forms.

While he was clearly a leader in the establishment of musical trend, won numerous championships with his fiddling virtuosity, and could claim considerable credit in the development of the careers of such stars as Jimmie Rodgers, Merle Travis, and Gene Autry, his own somewhat erratic course and sometimes abrasive personality cost him true stardom of his own.

Born into the third generation of a musical Scotch-Irish family, on January 26, 1900 in Allatoona, Georgia, McMichen learned to play the fiddle at the age of eleven from his uncles and father, who played Viennese waltzes for formal balls as well as reels for square dances. He moved to Atlanta to work as an automobile mechanic and to form bands. They were known as the Hometown Boys' String Band and the Lick the Skillet Band. He followed within days the appearance of Fiddlin' John Carson on radio station WSB in 1922, but later claimed that he predated Carson's performance by broadcasting earlier over Georgia Railroad's station, which programmed privately for the entertainment of the passengers of its trains. That same year he dethroned Carson as Georgia's Fiddlin' Champion.

In 1926, at the request of Columbia Record's Frank Walker, McMichen was chosen by Gid Tanner to be lead fiddler for the Skillet Lickers band, which he formed to record on Columbia Records and which quickly became the most popular string band in America. Throughout that relationship McMichen was to prove himself as difficult to get along with as his music was beautiful. He was constantly in friction with his fellow performers about personal credit and musical style. He was always wanting to experiment with new forms of what he called "modern music," particularly jazz, and to incorporate progressive treatments into their arrangements. From time to time he would form bands of his own to try his new approaches, one of which was known as McMichen's Mellow Men.

He considered Tanner's musical talents meager and insisted that he record off mike; consequently, Tanner was often inaudible. Although he conceded that it was the sweet tenor voice of "Blind" Riley Puckett, a member of his first band, that sold the Skillet Lickers' records, he demanded the addition of his name to that of Puckett's on the labels of the band's recordings on the contention that the band's name was taken from that of his original group. He promoted Jimmie Rodgers to Okeh Records when Columbia Records, to which he and the Skillet Lickers were under contract, declined to sign him in competition with Puckett.

Clayton "Pappy" McMichen

He got into a number of disputes over songs he claimed to have written and was denied a copyright on "Bile Them Cabbage Down," which was declared to be in the public domain after he claimed to be its author.

He was a musical pioneer. Perhaps his greatest musical innovation was the development of the multiple-fiddling technique, which was employed by the Skillet Lickers and which was the forerunner of western swing, an idea he said came from the symphonic orchestra he admired. He wanted to play popular songs on country strings rather than city horns and was the first to employ a clarinet in a country band; he composed and arranged music that he called "hot" country or "country" jazz.

When the Depression caused the Skillet Lickers to break up, he formed his Georgia Wildcats, which from their base in Covington, Kentucky, played McMichen's brand of country jazz with a Dixieland beat to record houses and on major radio stations around the country.

He played fiddle for Jimmie Rodgers on his first and many other records, and Rodgers made a hit of Pappy's "When It's Peach Picking Time in Georgia." Pappy discovered Merle Travis, a seventeen-year-old in the coal-mining town of Drakesboro, Kentucky, and let him make his first recording with the Wildcats. He helped Red Foley get his first job and got Gene Autry and his band signed at radio station WHAS in Louisville, Kentucky, from which Gene left to make his first movie. Pappy worked as a disc jockey before retiring in 1954 and came out of retirement briefly to appear as the star of the Newport Folk Festival in 1964.

Pappy was for many years recognized as the Fiddling Champion of the United States, having won his first title in 1926 and his last in 1952. He died at the age of sixty-nine in Battlesboro, Kentucky, on January 3, 1970.

JAMES MELTON

The range of Georgia's handsome, personable tenor James Melton of Moultrie embraced the total musical spectrum. He was equally adept at singing folk songs such as "Shortenin' Bread" in dialect and performing demanding operatic roles such as those of Tamino in *The Magic Flute* or Ottavio in *Don Giovanni*. At the time of his death at the age of fifty-seven in 1961, United Press International reported him to be "one of the most popular music personalities ever produced by the United States."

He not only was one of the most highly acclaimed singers of the Metropolitan Opera for a decade but also was perhaps even better known to the American public as a multimedia star of movies, radio, and television whose career spanned more than thirty years.

A graduate of the University of Georgia, where he was a classmate of the colorful Bill Tate, and a performer in the summer operas produced by Hugh Hodgson, Melton went to New York in 1927 armed only with talent and charm and brass to match and obtained an interview with showman S. Z. (Roxy) Rothafel by singing outside Roxy's office door until he admitted him. Roxy put him under contract as one of "Roxy's Gang at the Roxy Theater." Soon thereafter he began radio appearances in which he was an immediate success, with his repertoire ranging from black spirituals and folk songs to show tunes and operatic arias.

He began nationwide concert tours in 1930, made his Town Hall debut in 1932, and did twenty-eight concerts with the great George Gershwin in 1934 in which he specialized in songs from *Porgy and Bess*, which he later always included as highlights of his concert programs.

Standing six-foot-two with blue eyes, black, wavy hair and a baby face, Melton was a natural for the movies and starred in a number of musicals for Warner Brothers beginning in 1935. But because his all-consuming ambition was to sing in grand opera, he left Hollywood to join the Cincinnati Summer Opera in 1938 and became a member of the Chicago City Opera later that same year; he remained with that organization until he obtained an audition with the Metropolitan in 1942. The Met's Bruno Walter was impressed and asked him to study the piquant role of Tamino, which Melton committed to memory in five days and in which he made his debut to critical acclaim three weeks later.

He performed fifteen times a year for the Metropolitan for the next ten years, and his success was credited with ending the prejudice of that company against the admission of singers from the popular field.

Throughout his ten seasons with the Met he also gave up to fifty concerts yearly throughout the nation and starred in such popular radio shows as the Texaco Star Theater, the Telephone Hour, and the Harvest of Stars. After he left the Metropolitan, he established a touring nightclub act that enjoyed great success in major cities, and he made an easy transition to television to star on the Ford Festival on the NBC network in 1951 and 1952.

James Melton

He devoted his spare time to the collection of antique automobiles, fire engines, and stagecoaches, and when that collection of more than a hundred vehicles outgrew the confines of his home in Norwich, Connecticut, he established the Melton Museum at Hypoluxo near Palm Beach in 1953. The Museum became one of Florida's major tourist attractions.

Whenever Melton traveled, he extolled the virtues of Southern cooking and had a standing order with the Biltmore Hotel for a meal of country ham, blackeyed peas, turnip greens and potlikker, cornbread, and sorghum syrup whenever he visited Atlanta, and he always delighted in hosting his high-toned New York musical colleagues to such gustatory experiences. His pet peeves were improperly cooked collards and cornbread prepared with sugar.

Melton delighted in being compared with both Caruso and Barnum at the same time, and he never hesitated to tell reporters how much he enjoyed singing and the life that went with it.

"Singing is the first thing and the most important thing," he told *Atlanta Journal Magazine* book editor Frank Daniel in 1948. "I like to please the people who listen to me sing. I'm having a good time and I don't know why I shouldn't admit it."

He died in New York City of lobar pneumonia and was buried in Ocala, Florida.

JOHNNY MERCER

Any list of American's ten greatest songwriters would include the name of Johnny Mercer of Savannah, Georgia. Most authorities rank him as the greatest lyricist the nation has produced. A recitation of the titles of his hits beginning with "Lazybones" with Hoagy Carmichael in 1933 and running through "Good Companions" with Andre Previn in 1974 constitutes by itself a graphic history spanning the four momentous decades from the Great Depression to the Space Age.

With 701 published songs, ninety film credits, six Broadway musicals, four Academy awards from fifteen nominations, and thirty-seven Hit Parade songs of which thirteen were Number One, he is Georgia's undisputed premier musician of all times. His life appropriately has been honored by his posthumous induction into the Georgia Music Hall of Fame and the enshrining of his works and memorabilia in the Johnny Mercer Room established in the Georgia State University library in Atlanta.

Mercer won his first Oscar in 1946 for "On the Atchison, Topeka, and the Sante Fe," written with Harry Warren for MGM's *The Harvey Girls*, and repeated in 1951 for "In the Cool, Cool, Cool of the Evening," done with Carmichael for Paramount's *Here Comes the Groom*. Then he received two in a row with Henry Mancini for "Moon River," from Paramount's *Breakfast at Tiffany's*, in 1961 and "Days of Wine and Roses" from the Warner Brothers film of the same title, in 1962.

Others of his Academy award nominations include "Jeepers Creepers" in 1939, "Love of My Life" in 1941, "Blues in the Night" in 1942, "That Old Black Magic" in 1943, "My Shining Hour" in 1944, "Ac-Cent-Tchu-Ate the Positive" in 1945, "Something's Gotta Give" in 1956, "The Facts of Life" in 1960, "Charade" in 1964, "The Sweetheart Tree" in 1966, and "Life Is What You Make It" in 1971.

He had six straight Oscar nominations from 1941 to 1946, four of them consecutive hits written with Harold Arlen, who, with Mancini, was one of his two most successful collaborators. Critics noted that Mercer's Southern background was the perfect complement for Arlen's cantorial one. These two produced some of the enduring classics of American music, particularly "Blues in the Night," for which Arlen persuaded Mercer to move the line "My Momma done told me" up to the opening.

It is impossible to single out any one Mercer song as most popular, but two of his most memorable ones for which he did both the words and music were "I'm an Old Cowhand," from the 1935 movie *Old Man Rhythm*, one of the two films in which Mercer appeared, and "G.I. Jive" from World War II.

A reading of the list of his Hit Parade songs between the years of 1935 and 1955 is a nostalgia trip for anyone over fifty; in addition to the above-named and the Oscar-winning tunes, the list includes "Eeny Meenie Miney Mo" in 1935; "I'm Building Up to an Awful Letdown," "Goody Goody," "Lost," and "Dream Awhile" in 1936; "Too Marvelous for Words" and "Have You Got Any Castles, Baby?" in 1937; "Bob White, Whatcha Gonna Swing Tonight," "Daydreaming," and "You Must Have Been a Beautiful Baby" in 1938; "Could Be," "Gotta Get Some Shuteye," "And the Angels Sing" (Bing Crosby's favorite), and "Day In–Day Out" in 1939; "Fools Rush in Where Angels Fear to Tread" in 1940; "Tangerine," "I Remember You," "Skylark," and "Dearly Beloved" in 1942; "Laura," "Dream," and "Out of This World" in 1945; "Wait and See" and "Come Rain or Come Shine" in 1946; "Glow Worm" in 1952; "P.S. I Love You" in 1953; and "Autumn Leaves" in 1955.

Among others of his works that have become standards are "Hooray for Hollywood," "Mister Meadowlark," "You Were Never Lovelier," "I'm Old Fashioned," "Hit the Road to Dreamland," "One for My Baby and One More for the Road," "How Little We Know," "I Wonder What Became of Me," "Any Place I Hang My Hat Is Home," "Early Autumn," "When the World Was Young," "Song of India," "Spring, Spring, Spring," "Midnight Sun," "Love in the Afternoon," "If I Had My Druthers," "Satin Doll," "The Bilboa Song," "Emily," "Summer Wind" and "Happy Ever After."

Born to wealth on November 18, 1909, John Herndon Mercer attended a fashionable Virginia prep school and was forced to drop out of college by the bankruptcy of his father's real estate business precipitated by the economic crash of the late 1920s. He vowed to himself at the time that he one day would pay off his father's debts, a promise on which he was able to make good in the early 1950s when he sold his interest in Capitol Records, which he founded in the early 1940s, and sent a Savannah bank his personal check for $300,000 to reimburse all the creditors or their heirs with interest.

His action was a headline story of its day and further reinforced the reputation Johnny had made for himself as an honorable and affable man liked by everyone, a man who could work successfully with the most temperamental composers and artists and whose trademarks were his cherubic face, broad, gap-toothed grin, and the Greek fisherman's cap he loved to wear.

He was a devotee of jazz and blues from the days when he, along with his cousin Walter Rivers and their boyhood black friends, would sneak into the black neighborhood of Savannah to listen to "race" recordings on an old Victrola at Mamie's Record Store. Johnny was cited for his "love of music" in the yearbook of Woodbury Forest Preparatory School, and at the time he left to seek his fortune in New York City at the age of nineteen, he was an admirer of the music of Louis Armstrong and Paul Whiteman and the plays of Noel Coward. He listed as his heroes Victor Herbert, Irving Berlin, George Gershwin, Walter Donaldson, Gus Kahn, Isham Jones, and W. S. Gilbert, whom he called his "idol."

His outgoing personality got him a job as a runner delivering papers and securities on Wall Street, but he hung out on Broadway and around Tin Pan Alley and showed up at every audition he could. He attended the one for *The Garrick Gaieties*, where they tried to discourage him by saying they needed songs instead of singers. There he met songwriter Everett Miller, with whom he teamed up to write "Out of Breath and Scared to Death of You," which was incorporated into the show. It became his first published song and led to his first professional job as a contract composer with Miller Music.

He also met and fell in love with one of the dancers in that show, Elizabeth "Ginger" Meechan, whom he married in 1931. During their lifelong union they adopted two children, Jeff and Mandy. Ginger and Bob Bach joined in doing his biography *Our Huckleberry Friend*, after his death on June 25, 1976.

The biggest disappointment of his career was his failure to do a smash stage musical or to scale the heights of Broadway in the six attempts he made between 1946 and 1963. In 1932 he worked with E. Y. "Yip" Harburg, to whom he later would refer as "my guru," in collaboration with Arlen on the revue *Americana*, and Jerome Robbins sent him to London to do one of Lew Leslie's *Blackbirds*. He and Arlen wrote *St. Louis Woman* in 1946, but it failed when Lena Horne dropped out after NAACP objections, although it did make a star of Pearl Bailey. He and Robert Emmet Dolan had a flop *Texas, Li'l Darlin'* in 1949, and in 1951 he did both words and music for *Top Banana*, a Phil Silvers takeoff that ran for 350 performances and was released as a film, but which did not achieve major hit status.

His biggest stage success was with *Li'l Abner* in 1956, which he did with Gene de Paul following their triumph with the classic screen musical *Seven Brides for Seven Brothers*; it lasted for 693 performances and was made into a movie. He and Arlen tried again in 1959 with *Saratoga*, based on the Edna Ferber book, but it sank under the weight of bad reviews. A second attempt with Dolan in 1963 with *Foxy*, written for Bert Lahr, closed shortly after it moved to New York's Ziegfeld Theater from Alaska. His last effort was his collaboration in England with London Symphony Orchestra conductor Andre Previn on *The Good Companions* in 1973; it produced some memorable music but was lambasted by London critics for lyrics that were "not British enough."

Mercer's major triumphs were scored in the fields of movies, radio, and recording. He got his first big break in 1932 when he won the Pontiac

Johnny Mercer

Youth of America Contest to appear on Paul Whiteman's Kraft Radio Program. Whiteman liked him so much that he kept him on for a year to write, emcee, and sing with his orchestra. His success in jointly writing both words and music to "Lazybones" with Carmichael in 1933 and single-handedly producing the hit "I'm an Old Cowhand" for the movie in which he starred with Buddy Rogers in 1935 led to a contract with Warner Brothers and a stint in Hollywood with such greats as Richard Whiting, Harry Warren, Ziggy Elman, Jerome Kern, and Gordon Jenkins. With Arlen and Carmichael he produced an unequalled succession of Oscar-winning songs and other hits.

He also was in great demand on radio and, in addition to Whiteman's show, worked on the Benny Goodman Camel Caravan, Bob Crosby's Show, Your Hit Parade, the Pepsodent Show as Bob Hope's replacement (on which he enhanced his identity singing the commercial, "Poor Miriam . . . forgot to use her irium"), his own Johnny Mercer's Music Shop, and numerous morale-building broadcasts to the Armed Forces during World War II.

He joined with songwriter-producer Buddy DeSylva and Hollywood record store owner Glen Wallichs in founding Capitol Records in 1942; he became its first president and built it into the nation's largest recording company by the time he sold out his interest in the early 1950s. He not only was one of the most important stars using his own label but also helped make recording greats of such artists as Peggy Lee, Nat "King" Cole, Paul Weston, Paul Whiteman, Stan Kenton, Margaret Whiting, Les Paul and Mary Ford, Ella Mae Morse, Freddy Slack, Bobby Sherwood, and the Woody Herman Band. His wife wrote in her book that he quit the business because "the receptionist wouldn't know who he was" when he walked into the office. His profits made him independent for the remainder of his life and allowed him to pay off his late father's debts.

After musical trends passed him by, he devoted his last years to founding and being first president of the Songwriters' Hall of Fame in New York. He also served as president of the National Academy of Television Arts and Sciences and was a director of ASCAP. He received the Ed Wynn Humanitarian award, was commissioned an Admiral in the Georgia Navy, served on the White House Record Library Commission, and was proudest of the honor bestowed upon him by the board of commissioners of Chatham County in changing the name of the Black River in his home county to that of Moon River. His hobby was riding trains, which he did as frequently as possible, both coast-to-coast and to and from his beloved Savannah, to which he went often to refresh himself.

There have been many attempts to analyze the secret of his success in writing memorable and enduring lyrics. Fred Astaire attributed it to the fact that Mercer had "the common touch expressed in uncommon lyrics." Mel Torme said it was that he wrote in "the idiom of his decades." President Gerald Ford said it was that "his phrases were full of affection for people everywhere." Irving Berlin, who would have to be his closest rival for the title of "Greatest American Songwriter," attributed it to his high literacy in knowing when and when not to use "all those six and seven-syllable words" and the fact that "he's very sentimental and knows how to use tender corn." Or, as was stated at the ASCAP Mercer tribute in 1978: "Song was his life, and his life was a song—'free and easy' was his style, but hard-working professionalism was his excellence. He approached romance and farce with a wry, fresh viewpoint. He always held something back, too. His lyrics will never dull from outmoded mawkishness. He was the greatest of American lyricists."

Whatever the reason, he managed to capture the soul of America with words and music and, had none of his illustrious predecessors and successors ever existed, he singlehandedly would have put the state of Georgia into the pages of the musical history of the world.

RONNIE MILSAP

The talents of blind troubadour Ronnie Milsap fortunately are sufficiently colossal to be spread over the three states of North Carolina, Georgia, and Tennessee, which all claim him, with enough left over for the remaining forty-seven to join them in applauding one of the most admired and respected entertainers of the second half of the twentieth century.

Born blind by congenital glaucoma in Robbinsville, North Carolina, on January 16, 1944, and abandoned by his mother as an infant, Ronnie was reared by his grandfather, Homer Frisby, in Hayesville, North Carolina, just across the state line from Young Harris, Georgia, where he later graduated from Young Harris College.

His musical genius was discovered and developed with classical training at the Morehead School for the Blind in Raleigh, North Carolina, where he was a violin virtuoso at the age of seven, a master of the piano at eight, an accomplished guitarist at twelve, and a performer on all instruments except brass (which he found "boring") by the time of his graduation.

But it was in Georgia where he decided to pursue his personal choice of a musical career rather than the legal one picked for him by North Carolina authorities who awarded him a full scholarship to attend law school at Emory University. It was in Georgia where he met and married Joyce Reeves, who has been his adoring wife for more then thirty years and who became his "eyes." Ronnie and Joyce, the daughter of a Douglas, Georgia, poultry businessman, lived on the edge of poverty out of a motel in Gainesville, and he "paid his dues" by playing whatever kind of music was needed in whatever kind of club or dive in the Atlanta area that would hire him. It was in Georgia, too, where he developed into the anomaly of a white man who could sing rhythm and blues songs like a black man and who played with such great black artists as Jerry Butler, Jackie Wilson, Ben E. King, and B. B. King at the Royal Peacock on Atlanta's Auburn Avenue. His talent won him a contract with Scepter Records for which he recorded the Ashford and Simpson single "Never Had It So Good," which reached Number Five on the R&B Charts in 1966 and brought him engagements on the black circuit, including playing at the Old Howard Theater in Washington, D.C., with stars like Smokey Robinson and the Miracles and Little Anthony and the Imperials.

Fellow Georgian Chips Moman, composer of "Luckenbach, Texas," which later was to become the anthem of Willie, Waylon, and the other outlaws, lured Ronnie to Memphis, Tennessee, in 1969 to work as a recording session keyboardist by day for big names like Elvis Presley, Petula Clark, B. J. Thomas, and Dionne Warwick, and to perform by night at T.J.'s, the famous Memphis hangout. Ronnie did the background piano work for Elvis's recordings of "In the Ghetto," "Suspicious Minds," and "Kentucky Rain," and he so impressed Presley that he soon became the King's favorite pianist for his private parties at Graceland.

However, he was dissatisfied with his inability not only to get anyone to record his music but also to establish his own identity, and he was seeking ways to get back into his first love of country music when he came to the attention of Jack Johnson, Charley Pride's manager, who told Pride about him. Pride caught his act when Ronnie was playing in Los Angeles in 1970 and called him to tell him, "Come to Nashville. I'll help you if I can." Thus came about the supreme irony in Ronnie's odyssey to superstardom—he, a white man whose major credential was being able to sing like a black man, was being given his big boost up the ladder to success by a black man who already had achieved his stardom by singing like a white man.

It was not a pleasant or easy transition, however, because Milsap had signed a long-term contract with T.J.'s and was unable to obtain his release from it. When he decided to leave anyway, he was sued, and he and Joyce lost everything, including the home they had bought in Memphis. They arrived in Nashville in 1972 as broke as the day they first hit the road in Georgia.

Fortunately, Roger Miller signed him as resident singer for the rooftop lounge of his King of the Road Motor Inn; the compensation included a room for them and their infant son Todd, and Pride and Johnson made good on their promise to arrange a contract with RCA, the company for which Pride recorded.

His first single, "I Hate You," made the charts in 1973, and the same year his second, "The Girl That Waits on Tables," rose to the Top Ten. In 1974 he scored the first of the twenty Number One hits he was to do over the next eight years with "Pure Love," the composition of a struggling young songwriter named Eddie Rabbit. He had two other Number One hits that year, "I'd Be a Legend in My Time" and "Please Don't Tell Me How the Story Ends." The latter won for him the first of his four Grammys for Best Male Country Vocal Performance, the Country Music

Association's Male Vocalist of the Year award, and *Billboard* magazine's Best New Male Artist award. Coming within two years of his entry into the country and western music field, the awards brought comments of "overnight success" and criticism of "failure to pay his dues" from the unknowing, which prompted Joyce to observe: "If he's an overnight success, it was a long night."

He went on the road with Pride and remained with him for more than a year before striking out on the concert circuit on his own. He was invited to join the Grand Ole Opry in 1976 and proceeded to turn out an unending string of Top Ten hits over the next several years: "Too Late to Worry, Too Blue to Cry," "Daydreams about Night Things," "She Even Woke Me Up to Say Goodbye," "What Goes On When the Sun Goes Down," and "Stand by My Woman Man" in 1976; "It Was Almost Like a Song" and "What a Difference You've Made in My Life" in 1977; "Let's Take the Long Way around the World" and "Back on My Mind Again" in 1978; "Nobody Likes Sad Songs" and "In No Time at All" in 1979; "Why Don't You Spend the Night," "My Heart," and "Smokey Mountain Rain" in 1980; "Am I Losing You," "There's No Gettin' Over Me," and "I Wouldn't Have Missed It for the World" in 1981; and "Any Day Now," "I Love New Orleans Music," and "Inside" in 1982. He also did the movie soundtrack for *Bronco Billy,* which included the hit "Cowboys and Clowns," and has been in great demand as a guest on all major television shows.

A six-time Grammy winner, he has had more than forty Number One singles. He holds more awards from the Country Music Association than any other single male artist and is the first three-time winner of both the CMA Vocalist and Album of the Year awards, having received the former in 1974, 1976, and 1977 and the latter in 1975, 1977, and 1978. He is the only four-time winner of Album of the Year for a Male Performer. In 1977 he swept the Country Music Association awards when he received the awards for Entertainer, Male Vocalist, and Album of the Year, and he holds virtually every other country music award for which he is eligible, including *Billboard* magazine's Bill Williams Memorial award as Artist of the Year in 1976, Special "Break-through" award for Outstanding Artist Achievement in 1981, Male Singles Artist awards for 1976 and 1980, and Overall Singles Artist award for 1976. In 1990, he was inducted into the Georgia Music Hall of Fame.

He received the *Record World* Top Male Vocalist award in 1976, Male Country Single Artist award in 1980, the *Cash Box* magazine Most Artistic

Achievement and Male Country Singles Artists awards in 1979, Male Singles Artist award in 1980, Male Vocalist of the Year for Country Single award in 1981, and Top Male Vocalist in 1982. He has been accredited on RCA with six Gold albums and one Platinum album and the only Gold braille album ever to be awarded to any artist.

Although he is sightless and has known poverty both as a child and adult, Milsap refuses to write or sing sad songs. His outlook is positive; his personality, outgoing; and his only peeves are those with people who want to discuss his feelings about his blindness and fans who invade the privacy of his home in the fashionable Nashville suburb near the governor's mansion and the homes of the late Minnie Pearl and Tammy Wynette. Having never been sighted, he does not miss what he cannot comprehend and has trained himself to be so self-sufficient that, having paced it off in advance, he can work at ease all over a stage without stumbling or faltering. One of his favorite "stunts" is to astound his audiences by walking to the edge of the stage and teetering on the brink while cracking jokes about the time he fell into the orchestra pit and "saw stars."

At the beginning of his career he was addicted to rhinestone-studded costumes in flashy colors, but in recent years has replaced the glitz with open-necked shirts, embroidered jeans, and monogrammed glasses. His musical styles have become softer and more subdued also; and, while his albums and programs still have a mix of country, rock, gospel, and rhythm and blues, he is tending more and more to do mainstream pop songs with broad appeal and is considering assembling a large orchestra to back his Las Vegas style reviews. Versatile is the word most often used to describe his music, and he says his one criterion for selecting any song he performs is "Is it people music?"

Critics generally concede that had he stayed with the Mozart and Bach on which he was trained he could have been another Van Cliburn. However, he doubts such ever would have happened, noting that he was suspended several times at blind school for playing Jerry Lee Lewis's "Whole Lot of Shakin'" instead of the "Minuet in G" and that his teachers finally relented and let him and three other blind students form a rock group known as the Apparitions. He says he regards music "as my identity in this world"; he calls himself a "modern day Huck Finn" and explains, "He envisioned everything in his head. So do I." Most who know of him and his fabulous talent and success over great odds would say the best description of him is the title of his smash hit—a legend in his own time.

Milsap was inducted into the Georgia Music Hall of fame in 1990.

Zell Miller and Ronnie Milsap

MOREHOUSE COLLEGE GLEE CLUB

The members do not get paid or receive academic credit, but the men who make up the Morehouse College Glee Club of Atlanta would fight, if necessary, to get and keep their places in it.

It is a plum assignment that takes them to the far corners of the world and gains them audiences with the mightiest of leaders everywhere. They have sung to presidents and bishops, toured Africa, and helped part the Iron Curtain with concerts on Radio Free Europe. They are the official ambassadors of their school, the alma mater of such great leaders as the late Dr. Martin Luther King, Jr., and have been a major factor in the spread of its fame as one of the foremost institutions of higher learning for black men.

The Club has a long and distinguished history that dates back to the early years of the twentieth century when Morehouse was the Atlanta Baptist College. If its lineage is traced back to the establishment of the progenitor of the Morehouse College Quartet, which is one of its component parts, it can map its roots back to the Reconstruction days of 1870. In its present incarnation it had its beginning in the spring of 1911 with a concert given by the school glee club and orchestra under the direction of Miss Georgia Starr, the school's music teacher at that time. The glee club had ten or twelve members, and there were five or six men in the orchestra led by a student, Edmund Jenkins from South Carolina, who reportedly could play all of its instruments.

The survivors of those groups were those who came together under the leadership of Kemper Harrelds, who came to the campus as Miss Starr's successor in the fall of 1911. He directed its programs until he retired in 1951 and turned over his baton to his outstanding pupil, Wendell Phillips Whalum. Except for the years 1961–1963 when he completed work on his doctorate, Dr. Whalum was the Fuller E. Callaway Professor of Music at Morehouse until his death in 1987. He was succeeded by Morehouse alumnus, Dr. David Morrow, who has held its podium since that time.

During its illustrious history under its three acclaimed directors, the Morehouse College Glee Club performed for the late President Franklin D. Roosevelt at Warm Springs, Georgia, in 1932; won international acclaim as one of only three groups in the world to participate in the Second

International Choral Festival at New York City's Lincoln Center in 1969; was selected by the Department of State in 1972 to tour the African countries of Senegal, Ghana, Uganda, Nigeria, and Ethiopia; videotaped the Polish Solidarity Anthem, which was aired by the United States Information Agency over Radio Free Europe on the "Let Poland Be Poland" program broadcast December 13, 1982, to mark the first anniversary of the communist imposition of martial law on Poland; performed at convocations honoring Bishop Desmond Tutu, Leah Tutu, and Robert Mugabe; and sang with the combined choruses of the Atlanta University Center to pay tribute to human rights activist, and now South African president, Nelson Mandella when his United States tour came to Atlanta.

The Club is the official singing organization of Morehouse College and is at the call of the college's president to perform for special occasions and ceremonies throughout the year. Along with local concerts, it makes an annual spring tour of two to three weeks, encompassing ten to twelve cities throughout the United States.

The Club has ninety-seven student and four honorary members, the latter being Dr. Robert Shaw, Dr. Leonard de Pour, Dr. Hugh M. Gloster, and the late Dr. Benjamin E. Mays.

CHIPS MOMAN

The man who made Luckenbach, Texas, famous is from LaGrange, Georgia. Chips Moman is his name, and he wrote that hit song for Willie Nelson and Waylon Jennings.

Throughout his childhood Chips was surrounded by music. Every member of his family sang or played an instrument. When he was fourteen years old, Chips moved to Memphis, Tennessee, where he began a career as a major figure in the early development of rock 'n' roll, the popular return of soul music, and the expansion of country music.

In 1972 he moved back to Georgia and built a studio in Atlanta. Almost immediately he began making hit

Chips Moman

records. The next step in his musical odyssey was Nashville. There he distinguished himself in every facet of the music business: songwriter, producer, publisher, and record company executive.

As a record producer, Chips turned out hits for such superstars as Elvis Presley, Willie Nelson, Waylon Jennings, B. J. Thomas, Johnny Cash, and Kris Kristofferson.

He wrote his first song "This Time" at fourteen for Troy Shondell while sitting on his front porch in LaGrange. It was the first of many Top Ten hits he has written. Others include "Dark End of the Street," "Do Right Woman," "Hey Won't You Play Another Someone Done Somebody Wrong Song," and "Luckenbach."

His music productions include such well known songs as "Suspicious Minds," "Always on My Mind," "Hooked on a Feeling," "Hello Love," and "In the Ghetto."

Many honors of musical achievement have been bestowed upon Chips, including Producer of the Year in 1982 and membership in the Georgia Music Hall of Fame in 1992.

REX NELON

For twenty years Rex Nelon's was the booming bass that stirred audiences for the LeFevres. Since forming his own Rex Nelon Singers twenty years ago, he and his group based in Smyrna, Georgia, have been winning awards right and left, including a Dove award, Gospel Music's equivalent of the Grammy, for *One Step Closer*, the Best Traditional Gospel Album of the Year in 1981. They have had a total of ten Dove nominations since 1977, as well as being the Grammy nominee for Gospel Album and Best Gospel Performance Traditional for their *Feelings* in 1980.

Rex Nelon (top center) and the Nelon Singers

The Southern Gospel Music Association voted the Nelon Singers the Best Mixed Gospel Group of the Year in 1982, and its members hold the following *Singing News* Fan awards: Rex, Favorite Gospel Bass Singer, 1980; Kelly Nelon-Thompson, Queen of Gospel Music, 1980 and 1981; and tenor Jerry Thompson, featured on Song of the Year, 1981. The group holds Fan awards for Song of the Year, "Come Morning," for 1980, and Favorite Group of the year, Number One Vote Getter, and Favorite Song of the Year, "Sweet Beulah Land," for 1981. All individual singers as well as the band were nominees for best in their categories in 1982.

JESSYE NORMAN

With a silvery voice covering a fantastic three-octave range from E-flat below Middle C to E-flat above High C, Jessye Norman of Augusta, Georgia, was acclaimed throughout Europe as the greatest operatic soprano since Kirsten Flagstad and Brigit Nilsson for thirteen years before her American debut. In 1983 she made up for lost time at home by receiving two nominations for Grammy awards and joining the New York Metropolitan Opera for its centenary season.

The daughter of the late Silas Norman, an Augusta insurance executive and one of the early black candidates for public office in that city, Jessye began singing in the Mt. Calvary Baptist Church at the age of seven. Her father was Sunday School superintendent there for twenty-eight years. She won a number of talent contests and participated in sit-ins in Augusta while attending Lucy Laney High School. She pursued her college studies in music first at Howard University and then at the University of Michigan under the tutelage of French baritone Pierre Bernac. In 1968 she won a singing competition in Munich, Germany, and received a three-year contract with the Deutsche Opera in Berlin, where she made her operatic debut in the role of Elisabeth in *Tannhauser*. However, after a recital in London, she decided her voice was not suited for Wagner and asked for her release. She settled in England, where she wrote for *The London Times* and developed a performing and recording repertoire of parts ranging from contralto and mezzo to lyric or dramatic soprano. Her death scene as Dido in the BBC Promenade Festival performance of *The Trojans* by Berlioz, which packed Royal Albert Hall, was acclaimed by British critics as "ravishing, grandoise, luminous, and voluptuous." She also won highest praise for her lieder recitals at the Edinburgh Festival and her Haydn and early Verdi.

In 1982 she was named Musical America's Musician of the Year and appeared on the cover of *International Directory of the Performing Arts*. She was also nominated for Grammy awards in two categories.

Three years later in 1985 she sang at the inauguration of President Ronald Reagan. And, in 1989, when the French celebrated the two hundredth anniversary of Bastille Day, Miss Norman concluded the event by singing "Le Marseillaise" at the base of L'Arc de Triumphe to millions of television viewers.

Although she has homes in New York and England and has traveled around the world, she maintains strong ties to Augusta where she still has relatives.

GRAM PARSONS

Gram Parsons did not live to see fruition of the objective that was the obsession of his short, tragic life—the unification of all segments of the pop music audience into the country rock movement of which he is regarded a principal pioneer. But the memory of this haunted young musical genius, who grew up in Waycross, Georgia, and whose body was stolen and cremated by friends after his untimely death in California at the age of twenty-six, is being perpetuated by his protege Emmylou Harris, who has championed his cause, popularized his music, and achieved in her career the fame that was denied him in his.

He was born Cecil Conner on November 5, 1946 in Winterhaven, Florida, the son of country singer and songwriter "Coon Dog" Conner, who committed suicide after moving his family to Waycross where he operated a packing plant. His mother married wealthy New Orleans businessman Robert Parsons who changed young Conner's name to Gram Parsons and lavished on him the trust fund that financed the dissolute lifestyle that killed him.

After mastering the piano and guitar at early ages, he ran away from home at fourteen; was playing in a folk band with Jim Stafford in Greenwich Village at sixteen; passed the entrance examination to Harvard at seventeen, only to drop out after five months because of his preoccupation with LSD trips; and formed his own band, the International Submarine Band, which distinguished itself with one purist country album on Lee Hazlewood's label that flopped and now is a rare collector's item.

Gram migrated to California where he joined the acclaimed rock group, the Byrds. With Chris Hillman, he convinced the band to experiment with country music and to record *Sweetheart of the Rodeo*, the first real country rock album. This brought the Byrds an invitation to appear on the Grand Ole Opry where they sang Gram's own composition "Hickory Wind," which later was to be featured with great impact by Emmylou on her 1979 album *Blue Kentucky Girl*.

The Byrds left him stranded in England after he objected to accepting an invitation to tour South Africa, and he formed friendships with Keith Richards and Mick Jagger of the Rolling Stones that continued until his death. Jagger wrote the song "Wild Horses" about and for him, as later did Emmylou with her composition "Boulder to Birmingham."

In 1969 he and Hillman formed the landmark country-rock group, the Flying Burrito Brothers, whose first LP, *The Guilded Palace of Sin*, which featured their joint composition "Sin City," won critical acclaim, including the praise of Bob Dylan, but was too far ahead of its time for acceptance by the majority of either country or rock fans. Gram did three albums, including some of his best songs on *Guilded Palace*, before leaving the Burritos to concentrate on solo work after being severely injured in a motorcycle accident in 1970.

Although getting more into drugs and drink, he was given a contract by Warner Reprise on the strength of a possible album with Merle Haggard, but Haggard backed out. Parsons assembled a new band featuring Harris, the Alabama girl he had met while she was singing folk songs in and around Baltimore and Washington, D.C. and whose high soaring voice was just what Parsons needed for perfect harmony for his country singing. They did two albums of mostly Parsons songs, *GP* and *Grievous Angel*, neither of which was successful, but which gave Emmylou a treasure of future songs for her own career.

After his wife left him, he died presumably of a heart attack at Joshua Tree Inn in California's Yucca Valley while on a weekend of drinking and drugs with a group of friends. Before an autopsy could be held, his body was stolen from the Los Angeles International Airport by his manager and friends and, in accordance with a previous understanding, was cremated at the base of Cap Rock in Joshua Tree National Park before it could be sent home.

Parsons in death has become a cult figure, and Emmylou has included at least one of his songs in each of her albums and never fails to tell her audiences that they should "look behind me to all that was going on with Gram and the Burritos." As for Parsons, he said while working with the Burritos that all he wanted to do was "take the sweetness and down-home feeling of country music and create goose bumps."

HANK PENNY

Although he objected to the term and was critical of those to whom it applies, Herbert Clayton "Hank" Penny was a musical "outlaw" before being an outlaw was cool. And because he was a rebel with a streak of puritanism, his musical ideas were before their time early in his career and out of date later in his career. Consequently, all but the most avid country music buffs revere Bob Wills and love Roy Clark but are unaware that it was Penny who perfected the western swing techniques of Wills and taught Clark much of what he knows about guitar picking and country comedy.

But one place where he still is remembered and beloved is in Atlanta and the area covered by the Voice of the South, radio station WSB, over which Penny and his Radio Cowboys were stars of the daily noontime Crossroads Follies from 1938 to 1943.

A young, mostly self-taught, ambitious Birmingham miner's son, Penny was fresh from a stint with Lew Childre of station WWL in New Orleans, where he became an ardent fan of Wills' music, when he put together a new sound in Atlanta, Georgia. It was built around Noel Boggs, a jazz-minded steel guitarist whom he lured away from New Orleans, and Georgian Boudleaux Bryant, a classical violinist with the Atlanta Civic Symphony whom he converted to a lover of country music. And it was punctuated by the percussion of his own distinctive rhythm guitar tuned an octave higher than normal.

Also at this time Penny began alternating his new swing-style music with his own brand of country comedy for which he would later bill himself as "That Plain Ol' Country Boy from Rimlap, Alabama."

Penny's dream of going to the Grand Ole Opry was shattered by the Opry's refusal to accept Boggs's electric steel guitar because it was not in keeping with traditional country music, an irony underscored by the fact that Penny subsequently criticized the Opry for being "too hokey" and endangering the more traditional forms through the "overproduction" of the Nashville Sound.

He and his band did record a number of the songs they made popular at WSB for ARC, Okeh, and Columbia Records, including "Won't You Ride in My Little Red Wagon," "Hawaiian Honeymoon," and "Lonesome Trail Blues" before disbanding because of the draft.

Declared 4-F, Hank left Atlanta and went to Cincinnati in 1943 and became the top performer on the WLW Boone Country Jamboree and Midwestern Hayride. There he formed a close friendship with the great Merle Travis, who later persuaded him to move to the West Coast. He also began a stormy relationship with Syd Nathan, who signed him as a charter artist for his King Records where he cut his greatest hits and with whom Hank broke in 1947 because of a demand that he record songs that he felt were "too risque."

Hank Penny

While on the West Coast, he made four musical western movies with Charles Starrett and returned to radio with his Penny Serenade Show and as a comedian on ABC Radio's weekly Roundup Time. He got into television as a stand-up western comic, first with Spade Cooley, whose music he also admired and emulated, and then with Dude Martin, as well as with his own Hank Penny Show in Culver City. His new band, the Penny Serenaders, and then the California Cowhands, gained a reputation as one of the finest western swing bands in America. It featured a female singer, Jaye P. Morgan, who later became famous as a pop singer.

He recorded the classic "Steel Guitar Stomp" and "Remington Ride" and had his biggest hits with "Get Yourself a Redhead" in 1946 and

"Bloodshot Eyes" in 1949. He also was a partner in the Palomino night-club in North Hollywood, which he gave away before it became the fore-most country music club it is today.

He moved to Las Vegas in 1954 where he played both jazz and coun-try music at the Golden Nugget for seven years. It was a magnet for young country talent, the most famous of whom was Roy Clark.

In 1961 Hank Penny came back to Atlanta, where he had first become so popular, to record an instrumental jazz LP for NRC.

From 1963 to 1970 he lived in Carson City and worked mostly at Harrah's. Then he tried to crash Nashville for the second time, and the producers of *Hee Haw* turned him down because they said they already had a guitar-playing comedian in Hank's protege, Roy Clark.

A broken man, he spent the next three years in Wichita, Kansas, as a disc jockey at station WFRM owned by a former western band leader who was an old friend.

In 1975 he and his fifth wife, Shari, returned to the San Fernando Valley where he now lives in semi-retirement, working in an occasional movie and dreaming of forming another band to resurrect the greatness that would have been his but for the fate of timing and his uncompro-mising stubbornness.

"PIANO RED"
WILLIAM (WILLIE LEE) PERRYMAN

Ask any person on the street who recorded the first rock 'n' roll record and odds are you will get one of three responses—Bill Haley and the Comets, Elvis, or the Beatles—all wrong. The correct answer is William (Willie Lee) Perryman of Hampton, Georgia, a black rhythm and blues and barrelhouse pianist who, as Piano Red, helped make old Underground Atlanta famous with his performances at Mulenbrink's Saloon and, as Dr. Feelgood, is one of the best-known and most-sought-after acts on the college fraternity circuit.

"Red," as he preferred to be called, cut that pioneer disc for RCA Victor and producer Steve Sholes (who later made a rock recording star of Elvis) in 1950. It was a 78 rpm titled *Rockin' with Red (Rock, Rock, Rock)* that earned Red a Gold record in 1951. Because it was regarded as a "race" record and such songs were not played on white radio stations of the period, it was listed on the rhythm and blues charts and overlooked by rock historians. In fact, it was so much a progenitor of rock that it was a hit before disc jockey Allen Freed took the term "rock 'n' roll" from the idiom of the black streets and introduced it into the national vocabulary on a white-oriented station.

But history is being corrected thanks to the efforts of the Lowery Group and producer Sonny Limbo, who issued an album of Red's best-known songs in 1978 titled *First Piece of the Rock*, including a new performance of the 1950 original, and thanks to the Georgia Music Hall of Fame, which inducted him into membership in 1983, thus immortalizing him in the company of such other black Georgia musical greats as Ray Charles and Dr. Thomas A. Dorsey. His work and style also has attracted the attention and admiration of Mick Jagger and the Rolling Stones who often visited and consulted with him. And one of his minor hits of the early 1960s, "Mr. Moonlight," was covered and made even more popular by the Beatles.

Following up on the success of his original rock disc, Red had a string of R&B hits, including "Right String Baby But the Wrong Yo-Yo," "Red's Boogie," and "Laying the Boogie." His recording successes led to his popular live radio shows on station WAOK in Atlanta and his album, *Dr.*

Feelgood. His subsequent nightclub act, Dr. Feelgood and the Interns, has put him and his band in great demand on college campuses, a popularity that continues to the present. All of his recordings have been even more successful in Europe than the United States, and he is a popular concert performer in England, France, Germany, Holland, and Switzerland. His crossover popularity soared as his Underground Atlanta performances won him widespread acclaim and following among white adult audiences in Georgia's capital city.

"Piano Red" Perryman

Red was born the son of a sharecropper on a farm near Hampton in Henry County and developed his innovative style of blues and rock piano playing and songwriting and singing in the honky tonks of Decatur Street in segregated Atlanta. He died April 25, 1985.

RILEY PUCKETT

Though they may not remember his name, there are few Americans over the age of sixty who cannot recall being enthralled at one time or another in their youth by the lyric tenor recordings of Georgia's Riley Puckett or being hummed to sleep to the tune of his "Rock-a-Bye-Baby."

The "granddaddy" of the crooners, the first of the recorded yodelers, and the originator of the wild bass run guitar style that was the forerunner of the bluegrass and rock techniques, Puckett was one of the first superstars of the infantile recording industry in the 1920s. Probably the most versatile artist of his time, he established himself as a virtuoso instrumentalist, composer, folk-singer, balladeer, and minstrel.

Born May 7, 1894, in Alpharetta, Georgia, and blinded at the age of three months by the wrong medication used for a minor eye ailment, George Riley Puckett graduated from the Georgia Academy for the Blind and learned to play the five-string banjo at the age of twelve and then the guitar in order to have a means of livelihood.

As a performer he attracted a following with contemporaries like Fiddlin' John Carson, Gid Tanner, and Clayton McMichen. He appeared on Atlanta's radio station WSB in its infancy in 1922 and played with Carson on "Little Old Log Cabin in the Lane" before any recordings were made. Tanner invited him to go with him to New York to make the first recordings of Southern artists for Columbia Records to offset those made a year earlier by Carson for Okeh Records and then to join him as one of the Skillet Lickers, the wild Georgia string band that dominated the recording industry through the 1930s.

Puckett billed himself as "King of the Hill Billies", toured the United States, performed on the Grand Ole Opry, and, in addition to WSB, appeared on such pioneer radio stations as WCKY in Covington, Kentucky, WLS in Chicago, WSM in Nashville, and WMAZ in Macon, Georgia. Columbia Records so valued his services that the firm gave him and his wife, Blanche, a honeymoon trip to New York in June 1925 and presented him with a big phonograph and a thousand records as a wedding gift.

All the band members agreed that it was Puckett's singing more than anything else that made the records sell, and it was his incomparable backup style with the guitar that gave the band its unique sound. He was one of the original five-finger pickers, a style used by the finest guitarists of today, and he set the trend for heavy contrapuntal bass runs that later developed into bluegrass.

He made frequent use of double or quadruple-time runs with the thumb pick held with thumb and forefinger and used the flat pick in the way now emulated by Doc Watson; he shunned chromatic notes in favor of clear, easily heard single-note work. He developed the devices of hesitating so that one of the four basic beats came half a beat late and of strumming the strings upward. His simple solo style is characterized as "pre-Carter Family" to distinguish it from Maybelle Carter's bass melody notes and up-and-down brushing technique.

His singing style was heavily influenced by blues and pop singers and, at times, showed considerable black influence. And, while he was most noted for his sweet spellbinding tenor, he had a tremendous range and could sing any four parts of a quartet. Like Jimmie Rodgers, whom he predated as a recording yodeler by three years, he could sing a blues or pop song without sounding as out of place as did many of his "hillbilly" contemporaries. After the final disbandment of the Skillet Lickers in 1934, he shifted his recording repertoire from essentially traditional to mostly popular hit tunes. He had moved close to the mainstream of Northern urban popular music by the time of his untimely death from blood poisoning in East Point, Georgia, in 1946.

His classic, "Sleep Baby Sleep," which also is known as "Rock All Our Babies to Sleep" and "Rock-a-Bye-Baby," was recorded September 10, 1924, and featured the first recorded yodeling. He did a bottleneck style recording of "John Henry" and had an extensive repertoire of familiar lyrical songs and fiddle tunes like "Little Brown Jug" and "Ida Red"; he made ballads out of original folksongs like "Frankie and Johnny," "Bully of the Town," and "Casey Jones."

He recorded new ballads like Bob Miller's "Twenty-One Years" and Carson Robinson's "Altoona Freight Wreck." He did the traditional "Prisoner's Song" as "All Bound Down in Prison" and wrote "Put My Little Shoes Away," "Ada from Decatur," and many more. He made a whole nation, particularly the women, grow sentimental with such perennial favorites as "Silver Threads among the Gold," "Down by the Old Mill Stream," "Wait Till the Sun Shines, Nellie," "Old Spinning Wheel in the Parlor" and scores of others that today trigger nostalgia in the over-sixty age group.

Probably no artist of his era has had as many of his songs played throughout the United States by country musicians nor has had more hits that always will be country and western standards than this blind genius.

George Riley "Blind" Puckett was inducted into the Georgia Music Hall of Fame in 1986.

Riley Puckett

GERTRUDE "MA" RAINEY

Gertrude Malissa Nix Pridgett of Columbus, Georgia—known in musical annals by her married, professional name of Gertrude "Ma" Rainey, is the unchallenged "Mother of the Blues."

She may have been outshone and outrecorded by her younger protege, Mamie "Bessie" Smith, but it was her colorful singing and spectacular stage shows during the 1920s and 1930s that launched the development of the classic "Chicago" blues. She left a legacy of more than ninety records to prove it. In his unpublished autobiography her fellow Georgian, Dr. Thomas A. "Georgia Tom" Dorsey (who was her accompanist and arranger and director of her Georgia Wild Cats Jazz Band before he went on to make history in his own right as the "Father of Gospel Music"), documented her role in founding "city" blues.

Gertrude "Ma" Rainey

Rainey made her debut at the age of twelve and six years later became the "Ma" to William Rainey's "Pa" when she married the older showman. They put together a flamboyant stage show in which she made awesome entrances wearing gowns weighing as much as twenty pounds, touched off by her trademark necklace of five, ten, and twenty dollar gold pieces. Dorsey wrote in his memoirs of her performances:

"When she started singing, the gold in her teeth would sparkle. She was in the spotlight. She possessed her listeners; they swayed, they rocked, they moaned and groaned, as they felt the blues with her."

She almost missed out on the immortality she earned because she started performing before recorded music became the rage; and Smith, whose style was profoundly influenced by the example and tutelage of Rainey, was on the scene when the opportunity presented itself. However, when the Chicago-based Paramount label looked around for its own blues artist to offset Smith, they found Rainey, who already had been touring with her blues show for twenty-one years and was thirty-seven when she first entered a recording studio in December 1923.

A favorite entrance of hers was to begin singing from inside a box-like prop built like an old-fashioned Victrola (as early phonographs were called) and then to make an electrifying entrance singing the "Moonshine Blues." In other sets she would burst onto the stage, as the bass drum rolled like thunder and the stage lights flickered like lightning, and belt out:

I see the lightning flashing,
I see the waves a dashing . . .
I got to spread the news;
My man has gone and left me.
Now I've got the stormy sea blues.

She continued to tour until 1933 and managed two theaters in Rome, Georgia, after her retirement from the stage. She died December 22, 1939, and is buried in the family plot in Columbus's Porterdale cemetery.

"Ma" Rainey finally got her just due when she was inducted into the Rock and Roll Hall of Fame in 1990 and the Georgia Music Hall of Fame in 1992.

EDDY RAVEN

It was in the school auditorium of Cobbtown, in the middle of the Georgia Tobacco Belt halfway between Metter and Reidsville, that young Edward Garvin Futch made his first stage appearance in the winter of 1961. He decided then and there that he would rather write and sing songs than work for his Uncle Troy making flues for tobacco-curing barns in Metter.

That was when he decided to call himself Eddie Raven and set out on the checkered course of life that first saw him writing hit songs for others and finally become a performer of hits for himself. He now is recognized everywhere as a featured star on the weekly series of the Nashville Network, *Yesteryear*.

Raven's music has followed varied influences over four decades, from teen-pop in the 1950s, rock in the 1960s, country in the 1970s, and his own melding of country, rhythm and blues, calypso, and Cajun since. Basically, he always has come back to his Cajun roots, which date from his birth in Lafayette, Louisiana, and to which he returned to finish high school after following his truck-driving, guitar-playing father to homes in Savannah, Metter, and Baxley, Georgia, and Orlando, Florida, during his developing years.

His father encouraged his musical inclinations and ambitions, and he made his first recordings while in Georgia in teen-rock style for the small and obscure Cosmo label. Upon returning to Louisiana, local record producer/performer Bobby Charles, known for his hit "See You Later, Alligator," scored a local hit with Raven's "Big Boys Cry." He also performed with brothers Johnnie and Edgar Winter of Texas for a time, but his career was going nowhere until his old friend and fellow Cajun, Jimmie C. Newman, introduced him to his contacts at Acuff-Rose Publishers in Nashville.

That was the beginning of Raven's string of country hits written for others, beginning with "Country Green" and "Touch the Morning" for Don Gibson, "Good Morning, Country Rain" for Jeannie C. Riley, and the late-career smash, "Back in the Country," for Roy Acuff. He also scored with "I Don't Want to Talk It Over Anymore" and "The Latest Shade of Blue" for Connie Smith.

ABC gave him a recording contract after catching his showcase performances at Nashville's King of the Road Motor Inn in 1974, and he had a minor hit of his own in "The Last of the Sunshine Cowboys" that same year. The year before, he and Don Gant had written the song, "Thank God for Kids," which no one but Raven believed was destined to be a hit. He recorded it himself with little success but persisted in pitching it until, nine years later, the Oak Ridge Boys registered their superhit with it.

That led to a deal with RCA in 1984 after brief stints and some minor successes with Monument, and then Electra, Records. His first RCA single, "I Got Mexico," which he co-wrote with Paul Worley, went to Number One and led off a string of seventeen consecutive Top Ten singles for him. They included Number Ones "Shine, Shine, Shine," a R&B-style cut introduced on the syndicated *Dance Fever* television program in 1987; the Cajun-inspired "I'm Gonna Get You" in

Eddy Raven

1988; calypso-beat "Joe Knows How to Live" from the latter part of that same year; and the autobiographical "Bayou Boys" and "In a Letter to You" in 1989. He did the latter two top-rated recordings for Universal Records and had later hits on the Capitol label. He recently recorded for Liberty and in 1994 went with the Intersound Entertainment label for which he turned out an album titled *Wild Eyed and Crazy*.

They still remember him in Metter as Eddie Futch for his play as an offensive end on the Metter Bulldogs football team.

OTIS REDDING

Otis Redding of Macon, Georgia, who perished at the age of twenty-six in a tragic airplane crash in 1967, probably did more in his brief but brilliant career as the writer and singer of sentimental soul ballads to build a bridge between black and white music in America than any other performer. As Jerry Wexler of Atlantic Records put it in 1968: "Otis is tremendously responsible for the fact that . . . the young white audience now digs soul the way the black does."

Redding, who was born in Dawson, Georgia, on September 9, 1941, decided after his family moved to Macon that becoming an entertainer was the one way he could escape the dead-end, lower-class existence into which he had been born, and he set out to develop himself along the lines of his idols, Sam Cooke and fellow Maconite Little Richard.

He cut a Little Richard-styled number, "Shout Bamalama," for Bethlehem Records in 1960 that went nowhere, but he began paying his dues as a "gofer" and sometime performer for Macon's Johnny Jenkins and the Pinetoppers. He got his big break at a recording session for Stax Records in Memphis, Tennessee.

When the Pinetoppers wound up with forty minutes of recording time remaining, someone suggested that Otis sing, and Stax President Jim Stewart agreed. He started out with a Little Richard-type number, but Stewart stopped him and said the last thing the world needed was another Little Richard and suggested instead that he sing something slow. Redding responded with a rendition of his own "These Arms of Mine" about which Stewart was mildly enthusiastic and agreed to record and release it. After a slow start, it eventually rose to Number Twenty on the rhythm and blues charts and sold seven hundred and fifty thousand copies, and it put the shy, but ambitious twenty-one-year-old Redding on the road to stardom.

Stewart signed Redding to a long-term contract and created a new label, Volt Records, for his release, which found increasing favor with black record buyers and concertgoers. When his "Mr. Pitiful" reached Number Ten in 1965, it gave him the name by which he was thereafter known. His soul ballads had a pleading urgency and were characterized by sentimental lyrics, which usually implored a girlfriend to forgive or come back to him.

Two other singles that year—the slow and aching "I've Been Loving You Too Long" and the classic soul shaker "Respect"—established him as a star. His version of "Respect" went to Number Four R&B and Number Thirty-Five Pop, but the general public really learned who Otis Redding was when Aretha Franklin covered it and carried it to a smash Number One two years later.

The advent of the Rolling Stones gave him and modern soul a further boost when that group covered his slow and sad "Pain in My Heart," and he reciprocated by covering their "Satisfaction." That latter experience gave rise to the rumor that Redding was the original author of "Satisfaction" and had sold it to the Stones for $50. The truth of the matter, however, was that neither Redding nor any of the people at Stax/Volt Records could decipher Mick Jagger's lyrics from the 45 RPM recording of it they had bought; so Otis wrote his own version. Whatever the case, the Redding cut soared to Number Four and propelled him in another big leap into the white market.

Otis Redding

He became in great demand on the black concert circuit and was said to have Harlem and Watts "locked up," but he refused to follow the more commercial style of superstars like James Brown. Redding insisted that the stomp beat and communication had to be the predominant features of modern soul and that his songs were going to be simple, direct, honest, and concise. The critics said his style reached "artistic fruition" in late 1966 with his album *The Otis Redding Dictionary of Soul*, which was pronounced the "best example of modern soul ever recorded" and proved that assessment by making it with the pop audience.

He stuck with his determination not to change his music and proved the wisdom of his judgment with his success with soul ballads like "Try a Little Tenderness," blues like "Hawg for You," and the revival of the Beatles' "Day Tripper." The only concession he made to the more traditional format was with his Number Sixteen "Shake" in 1967. That same year he formed his own record company, Jotis, and his own music publishing firm, Redwal, and produced his protege, Arthur Conley, in a Gold record and Number Two hit, "Sweet Soul Music," which they cowrote with Sam Cooke.

His overseas record sales topped even those in the United States, and France rated him one of the world's top singers in its polls for both 1966 and 1967. England's *Melody Maker* magazine's naming him Top Male Singer of 1967 in that country dethroned Elvis Presley's eight-year reign with that title. He made several appearances on Dick Clark's *Where the Action Is* and on a number of other major TV shows, went on a month-long R&B tour that grossed more than two hundred and fifty thousand dollars, and was the star of the Monterey Pop Festival of 1967. The demands upon his schedule became so great that he purchased a twin-engine Beechcraft to facilitate meeting them, and that plane carried him to his death in the icy waters of Lake Monona while en route to a concert in Madison, Wisconsin, on December 10, 1967. The crash claimed the lives of all but one member of his musical group, Ben Cauley of Memphis, who heard two cries for help but was unable to save anyone else except himself.

Three days before the tragedy, Otis recorded the song he had written with Steve Crooper, "(Sittin' On) The Dock of the Bay," in Memphis. Released a month after his death, it went to Number One on both the R&B and Pop Charts and sold more than four million records; it won Redding two posthumous Grammy awards in 1968 for Best Male Rhythm and Blues Vocal Performance and Best Rhythm and Blues Song. An album of the same title went to Number Four, and seven other songs issued posthumously all made the charts, including Number Six "I've Got Dreams to Remember," Number Ten "The Happy Song," and the cover of James Brown's "Papa's Got a Brand New Bag."

Through the work of Aretha Franklin and contemporaries, the crossover trends started by Redding became the new wave that has erased many of the boundaries separating pop and soul music and accelerated the merger of black and white music into a truly integrated American art form.

In 1981, Redding was inducted into the Rock and Roll Hall of Fame.

JERRY REED

"Hearing Things" would get most people a trip to the funny farm. But when Jerry Reed "kept hearing things in my head," he translated them into the hot licks that earned him a one-way ticket out of the poverty of the Atlanta Exposition Cotton Mill Village to worldwide acclaim as the "Guitar Man" who has written more than four hundred songs and as Burt Reynolds's sidekick in the movies.

Born Jerry Reid Hubbard on March 20, 1937, he developed his unique "Finger-picking" style of playing on a beat-up guitar that his mother bought for him for seven dollars when he was five years old. She taught him his first chords while he was sitting on the stovewood box in the family kitchen. He dropped out of school to supplement the family income by tending looms in the cotton mill by day and to perfect his picking technique, usually for free, in the gin mills of the area by night.

He might still be a "lint head" but for a policeman friend who introduced him at the age of sixteen to Bill Lowery. The Atlanta music mogul was impressed by both his enthusiasm and his resemblance to the late James Dean and took him to Hollywood in 1955 where Lowery persuaded Capitol Records executive Ken Nelson to put him under contract.

In California Jerry cut some "rockabilly" tracks and wrote "Crazy Legs," which Gene Vincent recorded in 1956. But mostly he was frustrated and discouraged until his two-year stint in the service when the Army put him in its Circle A Wranglers, a country group it used for recruiting promotion.

During this time he wrote an instrumental number that was recorded by Chet Atkins, who invited him to come to Nashville to work as a session man after his discharge. When he had trouble limiting himself to the discipline of Army life, Atkins urged him to write the things he heard in his head.

In 1961, he established himself as a coming songwriter when another native Georgian, Brenda Lee, chose his "That's All You Gotta Do" to be her hit record of "I'm Sorry." He followed that with the two minor hits of "Goodnight Irene" and "Hully Gully Guitars."

He was signed as a solo act by RCA in 1965 and produced a first album called *The Unbelievable Guitar and Voice of Jerry Reed.* Jerry has said that he found the album embarrassing, but it contained the rocking "Guitar Man." Elvis Presley recorded the song and made a big hit in 1967 with Reed playing the guitar, an accomplishment that gave him the "Guitar Man" handle by which he continues to be known.

Presley scored another success with Jerry's "U.S. Male," and further Reed hits written for others included "A Thing Called Love" recorded by Johnny Cash, "I Promise" by Tom Jones, and "If It Comes to That" by Englebert Humperdinck.

Jerry's own recordings then became hot sellers: "Tupelo Mississippi" in 1967, "Remembering" in 1968, "Are You from Dixie" in 1969, and "Talk about the Good Times" and "Georgia Sunshine" in 1970. In the latter part of 1970 he came out with the hit "Amos Moses," which made the Top Ten and brought him a nomination for Instrumentalist of the Year by the Country Music Association. His recording of "When You're Hot, You're Hot" was a Number One Country song in 1971 and won him a Grammy as Top Country Vocalist in 1972, and his "Lord, Mr. Ford" reached the top in 1973.

He had won the first of his two Grammys in 1970 for the instrumental album he did with Chet Atkins when Atkins subsequently introduced him to Glen Campbell. Glen invited him first as a guest and then as a regular for three years on his popular television show, *The Goodtime Hour*. That exposure in turn attracted the attention of Burt Reynolds, who auditioned and signed Jerry for the role of Wayne in the film *W. W. and the Dixie Dancekings* in 1973, and the "good ole boy" chemistry between the two led to further parts for Jerry in *Gator* and both *Smokey and the Bandit* movies. In the first Jerry wrote the hit soundtrack song, "East Bound and Down." He later did the movie *High Ballin'* with Peter Fonda for which he also penned the hit title song. So far he has seven movie credits, including *Hot Stuff* with Dom DeLuise and Suzanne Pleshette. He also has done a television film *Concrete Cowboys* and a television mini-series with Claude Akins, *Nashville 99*.

In addition to his two Grammys, Jerry has two Country Music Association Instrumentalist of the Year awards and twenty-one BMI awards for both country and pop performances.

He tried five times to complete his high school education, but finally gave up because he kept "just sitting there running guitar licks in my head." After deciding, however, that his "life's work was going to totally revolve around my music," he has undertaken the serious study of music theory.

Jerry Reed

He met his wife, Priscilla "Prissy" Mitchell, who now is a talented backup singer, at the age of seventeen when he was doing a one-night stand at Lithia Springs, and they were married by the time he was eighteen. They and their two daughters live in a Georgian mansion in Nashville. The older daughter, Seidina, has a promising career as a singer in her own right, prompting Jerry to say, "Seidina scares me to death. She's got so much talent—just like her mama."

A laid-back, good-natured wisecracker, Reed takes little other than his music seriously and keeps his professional and private lives strictly separated. His only love besides family and music is fishing, but he makes it emphatically clear that "the only thing I'll not quit doing is playing a guitar."

He was inducted into the Georgia Music Hall of Fame in 1987.

ANTONIO "L. A." REID

They all laughed when Antonio "L. A." Reid said he and his partner, Kenny "Babyface" Edmonds, were going to Atlanta in 1989 to establish a major recording label.

But they are not laughing now that LaFace Records, which the two of them founded, is the only custom label to be listed for two consecutive years by *Business Week* magazine among its list of the nation's top five labels in new music releases. In fact, they concede that it is no misnomer that LaFace now is being referred to in the trade as the "Motown of the South."

Reid and Edmonds have succeeded not only because they work hard at, and have a broad vision of, their business, but also because they understand from personal experience the performing, as well as the producing, side of the business.

Originally from Cincinnati, they formed the R&B funk band, the Deele, and began writing and producing songs together in the early 1980s in Los Angeles. They released their debut album, *Street Beat,* for Solar Records of Los Angeles in 1983, turning out hit singles with "Body Talk" and "Just My Luck." Two albums later, they scored R&B hits with "Two Occasions" and "Shoot 'Em Up Movies," which inspired inquiries from across the recording spectrum and gave birth to what became known as the "L. A./Face Sound." It was the sound that gave the music world the classic hit "End of the Road," which stayed on the *Billboard* charts for a record-breaking fourteen weeks, as well as the acclaimed cuts "Superwoman," "Roses Are Red," "My, My, My," "Roni," and "Miracle," which brought a total of three Grammys and a long list of other industry awards to Reid.

Asked why the two chose Atlanta for their upstart label, Reid responded that he found the Southern city appealing because it has "a great deal of political power rooted in the black community." Perri "Pebbles" Reid, his multiPlatinum-recording-artist wife, cited the same attributes when she established her own Savvy Records there in 1993.

While the recording industry stood around scratching its collective head, LaFace was building a roster of not only hit artists but also hit producers. They included superstar Toni Braxton, who brought the firm sales of more than four million records and herself two Grammy, two American Music, and one Soul Train awards. Others numbered among LaFace's big talents are multiPlatinum-selling, Grammy-winning TLC, the Gold-selling rap group OutKast, and hot, young producers Jermaine Dupri and Dallas Austin.

Reid beams when he is compared to his icons Berry Gordy and Clive Davis. He said he is inspired by their proven ability to discover and develop timeless stars not tied to a single demographic or creative medium.

"LaFace is not locked into one look, one sound, or one creative approach," he says. "There are many aspects to being black and we are the rhythm of black culture in its every form."

He notes that "landmark music" historically has been generated in cities outside New York and Los Angeles and that Atlanta has given LaFace "the opportunity to develop both our company and artists away from the prying eyes of the industry."

"Motown has Detroit, Philadelphia International has Philly, Prince has Minneapolis, and LaFace has Atlanta," Reid declares, pointing out that he has produced the records that prove it.

Antonio "L. A." Reid

R.E.M.

Not even the members of R.E.M., the alternative band that sprang from the campus of the University of Georgia in Athens to become a worldwide musical phenomenon, can define with precision what it is they do that is so different and attracts such a large and enthusiastic following. So its fans can be forgiven if they, too, cannot articulate what the group has that turns them on and out.

Their music is variously described as artful and challenging, with emotive, elliptical lyrics, or bold and brawny, played loudly on the electric guitar. Sometimes it is likened to punk rock. It is said to have set the standard for alternative bands of the 1990s such as Pearl Jam and Offspring. As Denise Sullivan, author of the book, *R.E.M.—Talk about the Passion*, put it: "They've done everything their own way, on their own terms, and that's really rare."

The band was formed in Athens in 1980 by a quartet of the most disparate individuals anyone might assemble anywhere—lead singer Michael Stipe, bassist Mike Mills, drummer Bill Berry, and guitarist Peter Buck. Mills was the brainy preppie who hung out with other straight-A students. Berry was the cool dude who ran with the seedy element. Buck was the guitar virtuoso who still takes his mother and wife to awards shows. And Stipe was, and remains, the far-out loner with the shaved head, goatee, and Dr. Seuss-type hat whose goal is to have his production company, Single Cell, make movies in the mode of Oliver Stone.

Stipe, who is the band's dominant personality, disappeared for two years of introspection in 1991 after making R.E.M. close to a household name with his rendition of "Losing My Religion."

R.E.M. could be said to be an amalgam of sound and statement—set aside by the subject matter, as much as the music, of its songs. It has dealt with such provocative topics as Bible-thumping televangelists, American "imperialism," domestic violence, and the transformation of artistry into commerce by pop culture. Nowhere is this characteristic of its songs more apparent than in its 1994 CD, *Monster*, which features the haunting track, "Let Me In," done in the style of Kurt Cobain, the late lead singer of the grunge trio Nirvana, and dedicated to actor River Phoenix who died of a drug overdose. Both were Stipe's personal friends. Their deaths, he admits, caused him to "kind of lose my mind for awhile."

The first single of *Monster* is "What's the Frequency, Kenneth?" using the phrase uttered by the men who beat up newscaster Dan Rather in New York in 1986. *Time* magazine's Christopher John Farley wrote that that album "demonstrates that R.E.M. still knows the frequency."

R.E.M. almost came to its demise on its much-heralded European tour in 1995 when drummer Berry collapsed with a brain aneurysm in Switzerland and had to undergo life-threatening surgery. The tour abroad had to be cut short with the band's future in doubt, but Berry had a strong recovery. The band bounced back with a highly successful, nineteen-city American tour that grossed more than fifty million dollars.

The sales of their albums have skyrocketed since 1983 when R.E.M.'s debut issue sold more than five hundred thousand copies. Its 1992 offering, *Automatic for the People*, sold more than three million copies, and one of its tracks, "Everybody Hurt" earned the band four MTV video music awards. *Monster's* sales have hit six million and are still climbing. This popularity has earned R.E.M. as many as six and seven Grammy nominations in a single year.

R.E.M.'s Bill Berry, Michael Stipe, Peter Buck, Mike Mills

LITTLE RICHARD
(RICHARD PENNIMAN)

The life of Little Richard, the "King of Rock and Roll" from Macon, Georgia, is a story stranger than fiction. Who could dream up a biography that has a black boy from the Deep South who started his career in seedy nightclubs, developed into a musical prodigy, sped up the R&B of blacks and turned it into the rock 'n' roll of whites, taught Paul McCartney to "sing," wrote songs for Elvis Presley, and then walked away from the limelight of the recording industry to become an ordained minister in the Seventh Day Adventist Church—all by the age of twenty-five?

Born December 5, 1932, Richard was one of twelve children born to Leva Mae and Charles (Bud) Penniman of Macon, Georgia. After the death of his father, Richard became the breadwinner in the family by washing dishes in the Macon bus station and working other jobs. A devotee of rhythm and blues and the new postwar swing form, boogie-woogie, Richard was determined to have a musical career and performed in clubs in Atlanta, New Orleans, and other Southern cities. In 1951, the eighteen-year-old Richard came to the attention of Zenas "Daddy" Sears at an Atlanta audition, which Sears had organized. Richard impressed the legendary industry insider and, by winning the talent contest, received a contract from RCA under the Camden label.

He made four recordings in October 1951, including a boogie-woogie number and a "moaning" urban song of his own, and added four more in January 1952. Reissues of these reveal him to have had a strong, clear voice and to be the writer of lyrics that tell a definite story. He spent the next two years playing small black nightclubs in the South, experimenting with what was to become his version of rock, and noting as he did that it was whites rather than blacks who responded to his material.

While he was cutting some traditional blues songs for Specialty Records in New Orleans in 1954, the producers heard him play his "Tutti Frutti" during a break and asked him to record it. It sold two hundred thousand copies in the first week and a half and went to the top of the charts at the end of 1955; it stayed there through the spring of 1956 and earned him a Gold record.

That success thrust him into the national spotlight where his multi-colored outfits and pomaded pompadour stunned staid music critics. He kept up a steady string of hits including "Long Tall Sally," "Slippin' and Slidin'," "Rip It Up," "Ready Teddy," "The Girl Can't Help it," "Lucille," "Send Me Some Lovin'," "Jenny, Jenny," "Miss Ann," "Keep A-Knockin'," "Good Golly, Miss Molly," "Lawdy, Miss Clawdy," "Oooh! My Soul," "True, Fine Mama," "Baby Face," and "Kansas City."

Eighteen of his singles had sales in the neighborhood of one million each during the fifties, and his lifetime total had exceeded thirty-two million by the end of the seventies. His songs were recorded by Elvis Presley, Buddy Holly, Tom Jones, Pat Boone, and Paul McCartney, each of whom had at least one hit with a Little Richard composition. He also did soundtracks for three movies. His group gave starts to stardom to such greats as Jimi Hendrix, Otis Redding, Joe Tex, and Billy Preston.

The course of his life was changed, however, while he was en route to Australia, where his music had a major impact. An engine in his plane caught on fire over the ocean, and he promised God to enter the ministry if the plane landed safely. It did, and he removed all his rings, threw them into the sea, and returned to Alabama to earn a divinity degree and be ordained in the Seventh Day Adventist Church.

But he was lured back into performing in 1963 by invitations from the then relatively unknown Beatles and the Rolling Stones to tour with them and play his music in Europe, where it had remained highly popular. He arranged the Beatles' first recording contract with VJ Records and "taught Paul McCartney that little 'oooouu' that he throws in songs like 'I Saw Her Standing There.' "

He returned to the United States to appear before throngs of young rock fans in places like the Whiskey-A-Go-Go on Sunset Strip and at the famed Coconut Grove. He resumed recording with Okeh Records in 1969 and made the charts with "Poor Dog," "I Need Love," and "Hurry Sundown" as he did with his LP *The Explosive Little Richard.* In 1972 his Reprise album *King of Rock 'n' Roll* was on the charts for a number of months.

But his later records never sold as well as his early ones, and his popularity during this comeback portion of his career was centered largely in rock-revival concerts that attracted standing-room-only crowds of teen-aged rockers who wanted to see and hear the man they had heard about from the Beatles, Stones, and Tom Jones.

In the eighties, Little Richard, who now lives in Riverside, California, returned to his religious fervor and the revival circuit. The one thing that riles him is the claim of others to be the originators of rock 'n' roll. As he stated to the magazine *Rolling Stone* on that subject: "Like Ford was the founder of the Ford . . . I'm the founder of rock and roll. You understand me? Which was first named Rhythm and Blues. I speeded it up and they called it Rock and Roll."

A serious automobile accident in 1986 did not keep him from coming out with the religious—"not gospel," he said—song "Lifetime Friend." He also appeared in a film that year, *Down and Out in Beverly Hills,* and continues to make many guest appearances on television and stage.

He was inducted into the Georgia Music Hall of Fame in 1984.

Little Richard

TOMMY ROE

The phrases "typical American boy" and "bubble gum music" were the ones most often used to describe Tommy Roe of Atlanta, Georgia, and the songs he wrote and recorded in the 1960s and 1970s. The pop rock tunes turned out by that clean-cut graduate of Brown High School, however, turned into some of the biggest hits of the 1962–1972 decade and earned for him the royalties that bought the thirty-acre farm near Cumming, Georgia, to which he returned in the early 1980s as home base for his hoped-for second career in making movies.

Born May 9, 1943, Thomas David Roe was a contemporary of Atlanta rock stars Billy Joe Royal and Joe South. Roe, ironically, was a bigger hit in England than in America and found it necessary to move there to establish his stardom back home.

He developed a fine singing voice, formed his own dance group called the Satins, and began writing original compositions for them while he was still in high school. One of those songs done while he was in the tenth grade was "Sheila," which went nowhere on its first recording for Judd Records in 1960, but became a Number One hit when picked up and promoted by ABC-Paramount Records two years later.

Because his follow-up records did much better in England than in the United States, he left his Georgia job as a General Electric technician and moved to England to become one of Europe's top in-person performers. He continued recording for ABC, which issued his *Tommy Roe* and *Something for Everybody* albums in 1963; these also sold far better overseas than in America. His single "Sweet Pea" was one of the top sellers in England in 1966, as were his albums of the same title that year and *Phantasy* in 1967. He also appeared in concert with the Beatles, who admired and played his music.

An invitation to appear on Dick Clark's new ABC-TV rock show, *Where the Action Is*, brought him back to America and stimulated his popularity with young rock fans in this country to the point where he accomplished the sensational feat in 1969 of placing four consecutive recordings in the Number One spot on the national best-seller lists—reissues of "Sheila" and "Sweet Pea," "Hooray for Hazel," and "Dizzy," which he wrote and recorded with fellow Atlantan Freddy Weller, whom he met while Freddy was playing lead guitar with Paul Revere and the Raiders. All four sold more than one million copies each and earned him Gold records.

He and Weller scored again in late 1969 with "Jam Up, Jelly Tight," which took its title from an expression his father always used to describe things that were OK. This recording made the Top Ten and Gold record status in January 1970. His album *Twelve in a Roe* was a best-seller for the first six months of that year, as was his single "Pearl" during the summer. His single and album, *We Can Make Music*, were hits in the late 1970s, and his single "Stagger Lee" made Number Twenty-four nationally in late 1971. ABC also issued retrospective albums of his songs: *Beginnings*, *Sixteen Greatest Hits*, and *Greatest Hits*, and he added another single "Mean Little Woman" to the charts when he switched to MGM Records in 1972.

During the late 1960s Roe had one of the country's most successful nightclub and concert acts. He appeared at Disneyland, the Hollywood Bowl, and the Sahara Hotel in Las Vegas, and made extensive annual tours of England and Europe. He also was featured in a number of joint concerts with Joe South and Billy Joe Royal, including their SRO performance at the Greek Theater in Los Angeles in the summer of 1970. He was a popular guest star on television and headlined such shows as those of Ed Sullivan, Mike Douglas, and Virginia Graham.

Although continuing to write songs and running his total number of tunes to more than two hundred, he took a break from show business in the late 1970s and moved to Malibu, California, to contemplate his future. It was during that time that he was divorced from the woman he married while living in Great Britain. In California he began to think seriously about reviving his original boyhood ambition of making and acting in movies. He tried his hand at acting in little theater in Los Angeles, appeared in a production of *Star Spangled Girl* in Lubbock, Texas, and guest starred in some television sitcoms.

He married French actress Josette Banzet and returned to Georgia in 1982 to live on the farm he had bought in Forsyth County with his earnings from his first hit with "Sheila." He also joined producer-director Bill Warren in making the movie *Hopefully Yours* in Cartersville and Athens, in which he starred and introduced four of his songs. He also resumed concert engagements and appeared with such other veteran rock stars as Rick Nelson, Chuck Berry, and Bo Diddley. He also made plans for further movies.

The wave of nostalgic about 1960s rock in the 1980s gave a boost to his performing career, and in 1986 he was inducted into the Georgia Music Hall of Fame.

Roe characterizes his music as country rock and attributes the wholesome image of it and of himself to following the advice of his parents when he first began traveling for concerts as a teenager: "Do the right things, and stay away from the bad things."

Tommy Roe

DAVID ROGERS

Atlanta's David Rogers fell into the "almost-but-not-quite" category of country music stardom and is a good example of a fine talent having difficulty breaking out the herd of aspirants who compete for fame and fortune in the country music industry. His recordings consistently made the charts, from "Forbidden Fruit," his first in 1967 to "Hold Me" in 1983. Some critics called him country music's "finest ballad singer," but the really big break always eluded him.

Born March 27, 1936, he resisted his father's ambition for him to be a doctor, traded his camera for a guitar, and secretly taught himself to pick while in grade school. He began playing for local clubs in Atlanta when only sixteen. He supported himself selling pots and pans door to door and as a draftsman while developing his style working in Kathleen Jackson's Longhorn and later Egyptian Ballroom nightclubs.

Jackson financed a demo tape that fellow Atlantan Pete Drake sold to Columbia, which signed him to a five-year contract. Some of his chart records were "I'd Be Your Fool Again," "I'm in Love with My Wife," "A World Called You," "I Wake Up in Heaven," "She Don't Make Me Cry," "Ruby, You're Warm," "Need You," "Whispers and Grins." In 1973 "Just Thank Me" made the Top Twenty, and in 1974 "Loving You Has Changed My Life" made the Top Ten. His album *Farewell to the Ryman* was well received as was his *Best of David Rogers* by Music Masters.

Pete Drake was a big influence on this talented stylist, who, according to Drake, "really believed in country music." He died in 1993.

KENNY ROGERS

Of all the women Kenny Rogers has loved and left or sung with, about, or to, the two who have had the most profound impact upon his incredible life and career are Georgians in their roots or origin—one a real-life Georgia peach from Athens and the other the bigger-than-life creation of the late songwriter Roger Bowling of Dillard, Georgia.

The former is Marianne Gordon, the "*Hee Haw* Honey" who became the mother of his idolized, Georgia-born second son, Christopher Cody, and for whom he built the showplace farm near Athens where they raised and showed prized Arabian horses until the breakup of their marriage. The latter is "Lucille," the depressed and discouraged Ohio farm wife with no last name, who, in Bowling's blockbuster ballad that became a megahit for Rogers, deserted her husband, children, and crops in the field to seek the good life in the bright lights and bars of the big city.

Before he met Marianne in an appearance in the mid-1970s with the folk-tinged pop vocal group he had formed, The First Edition, on the syndicated *Hee Haw* television program in Nashville, Rogers, by his own admission, had measured success solely in terms of money. He was flat broke, living on an insurance settlement from the theft of his wardrobe, and struggling to survive. He and Marianne, a *Hee Haw* regular and successful star of commercials for Clairol, Ford, Max Factor, Pillsbury, Coca-Cola, Muriel Cigars, and other then-popular products, hit it off from the start, and she set about inspiring him to concentrate on establishing himself as a country singer. They were married in 1977.

Rogers wanted a vehicle similar in vein to the Mell Tillis's song, "Ruby, Don't Take Your Love to Town," with which he had had a Top Ten pop hit in 1965. He sought out Marianne's fellow Georgian, Roger Bowling, who had put him on the country charts for twelve weeks in 1976 with "While the Feeling's Good," and Bowling gave him "Lucille," a classic country story ballad that he had cowritten with Hal Bynum. It turned out to be what Rogers himself called "the catalyst for a whole new career." It took off like a skyrocket, giving him his first Number One country hit as well as a Top Five pop hit and earning him a 1977 Grammy for Best Male Country Vocal Performance.

It spawned a string of successes beyond his wildest expectations; but, perhaps more importantly, it—and the love of Marianne—brought about a reversal of Rogers's outlook on life, an ironic realization that happiness, not success or making big bucks, was the "most important thing in the world to me."

But the dollars and the honors came rolling in, along with a continuous string of Grammys and chart-topping recordings. The very next year, he and a young songwriter named Don Schlitz hit it just as big with "The Gambler," which won a Grammy for Schlitz for Best Country Song of 1978 and spawned a phenomenally popular series of television movies for Rogers in the title role. He repeated the process with Roger Bowling and his song, "Coward of the County," in 1980. He was not able to carry his Midas touch over to the big screen with *Six Pack*, although that big-screen vehicle did give him a Number One country record, "Love Will Turn You Around," and won him the 1982 American Music Best Country Single award.

Kenny Rogers

He followed "Lucille" with a seemingly unending string of hits, and because he crossed and recrossed so many musical lines, the word "countrypolitan" was coined by the critics to describe his easy-going, good-natured, throaty, self-deprecating delivery of musical material of all genre.

If any one of his musical directions could be said to top the others, it would have to be his series of love-song duets with some of the top women singers in the business, most particularly the late Dottie West. Beginning with the smash "Every Time Two Fools Collide," they had a Number Two hit with "Anyone Who Isn't Me Tonight," a Number One single and Grammy nomination with "All I Ever Need Is You," a Number Three hit with " 'Til I Can Make It on My Own," and "You Needed Me," for which West already had won a Grammy for her earlier single of that title. The two of them became so popular that their joint concert in Michigan's Pontiac Silverdome drew more than sixty thousand fans, most of them cheering women.

He also had big successes with the Number Ten cut "We've Got Tonight" with Scottish singer Sheena Easton, "Islands in the Stream" with Dolly Parton, and the Top Five "Don't Fall in Love with a Dreamer" with former fellow New Christy Minstrel Kim Carnes of "Bette Davis Eyes" fame. He and Marianne also cowrote "We Don't Make Love Anymore."

Although he now has it made as a mainstream artist who is equally at home in Vegas or before a country audience, Rogers grew up in Depression-era poverty in Houston, Texas, learning to sing in a church choir and teaching himself to play the guitar to the accompaniment of another neighborhood kid, Mickey Gilley. Beginning with the Scholars, a rockabilly outfit he formed while in high school, he dropped out of college to perform in succession with a light-jazz trio and the New Christy Minstrels, with which he made some recordings for Mercury. He and fellow minstrel Mike Settle formed the First Edition and scored a major pop hit with "Just Dropped In (To See What Condition My Condition Was In)," which was revived after he became a star in his own right. The group became Kenny Rogers and the First Edition in 1968, and its management was taken over by supermanager Ken Kragen when they landed a spot on the *Smothers Brothers Comedy Hour,* one of the most popular television shows of that time. The rest is musical history.

BILLY JOE ROYAL

Georgia's Billy Joe Royal left the boondocks of Valdosta, where he was born, for the suburbs of Atlanta in 1951 when he was six years old, but the music of his early years stayed with him, and his recording of "Down in the Boondocks" fourteen years later sold more than two million copies. It made him a concert superstar whose performances of music alternatively described as "country-soul" and "country rock" have brought him ovations from stages as diverse as those of the London Palladium, the Greek Theater of Los Angeles, and the Flamingo Hotel of Las Vegas.

One of the foremost of the young performers who developed around the songwriting and producing talents of Atlanta's great Joe South, Royal got his start singing "Zippy-dee-doo-dah" for a school PTA meeting shortly after his family moved to Marietta.

After learning to play the guitar and piano first under the influence of traditional country performers and then of major rock artists, he formed his own band to play for dances and parties while attending Marietta High School. Billy Joe and the Corvettes were playing small clubs by the time he graduated and shortly thereafter landed a two-year booking in Savannah.

Out of his friendship with South developed the recording sessions that produced the smash "Down in the Boondocks" in June 1965 and resulted in a recording contract with Columbia Records, which issued an album of the same name that made the charts, as did a second LP, *Billy Joe Royal*, released in November 1965. Guitarist Freddy Weller, who played for Royal's rock version of "Boondocks," also made a hit of it under his own name on the country charts.

His recording successes brought Royal many bookings in major cities throughout the United States and abroad. While in London to do the Palladium, he was invited to a Royal Garden Party, where he was presented to the British monarch, and his appearances at the Flamingo caused *The Hollywood Reporter* to describe him as potentially rivaling Elvis Presley and Tom Jones as a Las Vegas attraction.

In November 1967, the third and last of his albums produced by South was released. It was called *Hush* and took its name from the title of the wailing hit of the *Billy Joe Royal* album. For his next LP in 1969 he switched to Buddy Buie at Studio One; Buie produced *Cherry Hill* and followed up with another in 1971.

Most of Billy Joe's other singles made the charts, including "I Knew You When" and "I've Got to Be Somebody" in 1965, "Heart's Desire" and "Campfire Girls" in 1966, "Every Night" in 1970, and "Tulsa" in 1971. His relatively low output of recordings in the late 1960s and early 1970s was due to his heavy schedule of concerts and television appearances, the latter of which included appearances on such shows as those of Barbara McNair, Tom Kennedy, and David Frost.

In 1987 his album *The Royal Treatment* was certified Gold.

Royal makes his home in Atlanta where he works on his music and pursues his favorite pastime, breeding horses.

Billy Joe Royal

ART SATHERLEY

Imagine a world without "San Antonio Rose," "Back in the Saddle Again," and "You Are My Sunshine." That is what things would be like in country music if Thomas A. Edison had not hired an urbane Brit named Arthur E. Satherley and turned him loose with his Paramount Records to seek out and record black blues and white hillbilly talents—music that was anathema to the sophisticates and speakeasy habitues of the Roaring Twenties and the Depressed Thirties.

As a roving talent scout for the Edison organization and later for Plaza Music's American Recording Corporation (ARC), he scoured the boondocks of Georgia, the Southeast, and Southwest for unknown talents, whose songs he recorded, and persuaded Sears, Roebuck to sell their records. It was in that role that he became, if not the father, at least the midwife of what we know today as "western swing." It was he who found Bob Wills and the Texas Playboys in Tulsa, first recorded them in Dallas in 1935, and gave their signature instrumental the title, "San Antonio Rose."

It also was Satherley who came to Savannah and then spent time in Atlanta in the late 1930s seeking out Hank Penny and the Radio Cowboys who were playing their perfected version of "western swing" on radio station WSB's Crossroads Follies. It was his idea to use Penny and his musicians as a hedge against the temperamental Wills who was always threatening to pack up his band and head back to Oklahoma. Wills did not leave but was left alone to do his own thing his own way by Satherley, whom Wills subsequently affectionately dubbed "Uncle Art." Penny, under Satherley's guidance, went on to become a star on ABC Radio and a big hit on the Las Vegas scene.

During his talent hunts, which might be likened to a prehistoric Ed McMahon Star Search, Satherley, who wound up as vice president of the Columbia Broadcasting System, which purchased ARC in 1939, is credited with discovering and bringing to New York the Carter Family in the mid-1930s and, a decade later, producing such all-time country classics as: Gene Autrey's "Back in the Saddle Again" and "You Are My Sunshine," Roy Acuff's "Great Speckled Bird," Bill Monroe's "Blue Moon of Kentucky," Patsy Montana's "I Want to be a Cowboy's Sweetheart," Little Jimmy

Dickens's "A'Sleepin' at the Foot of the Bed," Al Dexter's "Pistol Packin' Mama," Ted Daffan's "Born to Lose," and Tex Ritter's "Rye Whiskey."

Counted among Satherley discoveries also are Adolph Hofner, the Prairie Ramblers, the Hoosier Hot Shots, Bob Atcher and Bonnie Blue Eyes, Earl Flatt and Lester Scruggs, Roy Rogers, Johnny Bond, George Morgan, Lefty Frizzell, Marty Robbins, Johnny Cash, Carl Smith, Ray Price, and the Statler Brothers. He also discovered and recorded a number of great blues musicians, including Brownie McGhee and Big Bill Broonzy. He retired in the early 1950s, but the assistant he trained, Don Law, took over where he left off in Nashville and, along with Chet Atkins, is credited with developing the Nashville Sound of today.

Satherley, who left his native Bristol, England, for what he regarded the "American frontier" in 1913 at the age of twenty-two, never looked back. He had the good luck to get a job with the Wisconsin Chair Company, which was absorbed by the Edison Companies, and it was but a short jump from there to the music business when Edison made him assistant secretary and put him in charge of Wisconsin Chair's recording subsidiary, Paramount.

He spent his quiet retirement years preparing a taped anthology of his musical achievements with commentaries on each that he specified not be released until after his death, which came at the age of ninety-six in 1986. He was inducted into the Country Music Hall of Fame in 1971.

ROBERT SHAW

The only thing that can be said with certainty about Robert Shaw, the colorful and tempestuous retired music director and conductor of the Atlanta Symphony Orchestra, is that he provokes strong feelings from admirers and detractors alike, and virtually no one is neutral about him, his credentials, or his work. On the one hand, he is widely regarded as the world's greatest living conductor of choral music, and media critics generally write about him in lavish terms, sometimes acclaiming him a genius; on the other hand, singers and musicians complain about his ferocious temper tantrums, and his audiences sometimes were turned off by his experimentation with a contemporary repertoire.

But whatever the assessment, none deny that in his twenty years at its helm, Shaw transformed the Atlanta Symphony from a parochial ensemble, which was the outgrowth of a youth orchestra sponsored by the Atlanta Music Club with an annual budget of only three hundred thousand dollars, into a nationally recognized, full-time, professional musical organization. The symphony under his direction consisted of eighty-eight members backed by a chorus of two hundred and fifty, had an RCA recording contract, was funded in excess of six million dollars a year, and drew SRO audiences from the Kennedy Center to Carnegie Hall and won rave reviews from the toughest critics in New York, Chicago, Boston, and Washington, D.C.

Shaw was born in Red Bluff, California, in 1916, the second of five children in the singing family of a minister in the Christian (Disciples of Christ) Church. He went to Pomona College with the intention of either entering the ministry himself or becoming a teacher of comparative religion. That plan changed, however, during his junior year in 1937 when he met Fred Waring, who came to the campus to make a film with Dick Powell, was impressed by Shaw's direction of the College Glee Club as a substitute for an ill professor, and invited him to come to New York to organize a similar group. Shaw agreed and began the next year. He worked as Waring's righthand man until 1945 and also formed his own collegiate chorale in 1941. This group brought him to the attention of Arturo Toscanini, who asked him to prepare choruses for all of his major concerts and, despite Shaw's total lack of orchestral experience, invited him to be a guest conductor of the NBC Symphony Orchestra in 1945. That experience prompted Shaw to hire Julius Herford of Indiana University to tutor him in musical analysis and conducting technique in a personal cram course of forty to sixty hours a week over the next several years. About the same time, composer William Schuman, then president of the Julliard School of Music, named him to be director of choral music of that institution despite the fact, as he later told him, that "You were terribly, terribly ignorant." Shaw's fame spread to the point that he soon was leading workshops on choral conducting and guest conducting throughout the nation; and, in 1948, he founded the Robert Shaw Chorale, which basically was a pickup organization built around a nucleus of experienced choral singers with whom he was to achieve fame through concerts, recordings, and guest appearances on radio programs and later on television.

His first post as a conductor was with the San Diego Symphony Orchestra from 1953 to 1957, a summer appointment that he combined with six weeks of annual choral workshops at San Diego State College. In 1956 he became associate conductor of the Cleveland Symphony Orchestra under the legendary George Szell, whose conducting techniques he adopted and adapted and whom he strongly defended against Leonard Bernstein's charge of being the "last of the great tyrants of the podium." His last year there, 1967, overlapped his first as music director in Atlanta, where he succeeded the founding conductor, Henry Sopkin, and diagnosed its problem as "not so much promoting the orchestra as educating the audience."

His leadership in Atlanta—where, contrary to the prevailing trend of jet-setting (or, as Shaw calls them, "suitcase") conductors, he insisted upon being a highly visible resident involved in what he termed the "social matrix"—brought a steady upgrading in orchestra personnel, salaries, and programming and the recruiting of the best voices from the churches and colleges of the Atlanta area for his Atlanta Chorus. His educational efforts, which he described as "marching not just over the next hill but over the next mountain range," centered on his attempt to develop a modern repertoire mixing Bartok, Hindemith, and Stravinsky, and Beethoven and Berloiz. This proved to be too much for many conservative tastes and brought him criticism for performances that were said to be too extroverted and tedious. Critics likened them to "two tomcats fighting on a fence at midnight." The resulting decline in season ticket sales culminated in an effort by the board of directors to fire him in 1972, but editorial criticism by the Atlanta newspapers and the formation of a citizens committee to spur ticket sales by checks made personally to Shaw brought a reversal of that decision and an overhaul of the symphony's administrative and business procedures after Shaw accused the front office personnel of being "musically and aesthetically unknowledgeable and uncommitted."

Having won that battle and subduing his critics to the degree that he experienced no further serious problems with his tenure or programming, Shaw concentrated on building the orchestra's national image with wide-ranging concert tours and the development of choral spectaculars he called "emotional omni-umgatherum" such as his reading of the requiem masses and the thundering Beethoven Ninth. The most respected critics applauded the precision, rhythm, and vitality of the Orchestra's performances under his direction. Paul Hume of *The Washington Post* called his ability for "sustaining the basic rhythmic foundation" in all of his works "a rare gift" in which other musicians stand in awe, a capacity sustained by recording studios that found it necessary to time his takes by a stopwatch to assure exact and consistent tempo in all parts of each selection. John von Rhein of *The Chicago Tribune* and Robert C. Marsh of *The Chicago Sun-Time* agreed that the Atlanta Orchestra under Shaw was better than either the Boston or Chicago orchestras, and Irving Lowens of *The Washington Star* said Shaw's musicians "simply outplayed . . . [and] outclassed" their Washington counterparts.

Stories of the Shaw temper are legion—from throwing his glasses across the stage to berating the quality of individual performances to stalking off the podium when doors were left open. Some of his most talented singers and musicians quit because of his tantrums, one being quoted as saying Shaw gots so angry he sometimes became "totally irrational." He wrote open letters of comment and encouragement to his performers, a collection of which comprises a major portion of the biography done by Joseph A. Mussulman.

Shaw deplored the cynicism he saw creeping into American orchestras and expressed concern about the discouragement talented musicians experienced because of the scarcity of employment opportunities, the uncertainty of regular work, and woefully inadequate compensation. He saw the answer to the problem in the creation of what he called a "Society of Musical Arts" of upwards of two hundred musicians and singers in each major metropolitan area who would be involved not only in the city's symphony orchestra but also in opera, chamber music, oratorio, cantata, and musical education.

In 1988, after twenty-one years as music director and conductor of the Orchestra and seeing his dream fulfilled of building the Atlanta Orchestra into a major American orchestra, the maestro stepped down and became music director and conductor laureate.

Throughout his career, Shaw has received abundant recognition for his work. His honors include thirteen Grammy awards, England's *Gramophone* magazine award, a Gold record for the first RCA classical recording to sell more than a million copies, honorary degrees and citations from forty U.S. colleges and universities, four ASCAP awards for service to contemporary music, the first Guggenheim Fellowship ever awarded to a conductor, the George Peabody Medal for

Robert Shaw

outstanding contributions to music in America, and the Gold Baton award of the American Symphony Orchestra League for "distinguished service to music and the arts."

He was a 1991 recipient of the Kennedy Center Honors, the nation's highest honor for those "who, through a lifetime of accomplishment, have enriched American life by their achievement in the performing arts." He was named Musician of the Year in the 1992 edition of *Musical America*, the international directory of the performing arts, and during the same year was awarded the National Medal of Arts at a White House ceremony. He was the 1993 recipient of the Conductors' Guild Theodore Thomas award and was inducted into the Georgia Music Hall of Fame in 1988.

HAROLD SHEDD

If Harold Shedd gambled with money the way he does with talent, he already would have broken the banks in both Atlantic City and Las Vegas. His unerring ability as a producer to turn unknowns who are talented and different into Gold, and often Platinum, recording artists is legendary on Nashville's Music Row.

One has to look no further than the successes of supergroups like Alabama and the Kentucky Headhunters, both Shedd discoveries. He heard about the former when they were playing in Myrtle Beach, South Carolina, went to see and hear them, and took them under his wing. In ten years he turned that band into one of the most honored and profitable in the business. The latter he signed on after hearing them sing the Waylon Jennings's song, "Only Daddy That'll Walk the Line," which was written by South Georgian Jimmy Bryant. Shedd produced the song just as he heard them sing it, with the results that it sold two million records, won a Grammy, and made the Headhunters Vocal Group of the Year.

Born in Bremen, Georgia, near the Alabama stateline, Shedd had a fourteen-year stint in radio, starting out as a disc jockey and working his way up to engineer, sales manager, and owner of the station. He relocated to Nashville and moved into jingle and commercial production, becoming co-owner of a recording studio by 1979. His successes with Alabama, Reba McEntire, Glen Campbell, Roger Miller, Mel Tillis, K. T. Oslin, Louise Mandrell, Dobie Gray, and others brought him a call from PolyGram, which turned him into a record executive, first at Mercury Nashville and now as president of Polydor Nashville.

Shedd, who also is a musician and performer in his own right, is said to have developed his own strain of country music described as "the country sound with a touch of gospel." He swims upstream against the "herd instinct," which prompts his contemporaries to try to cover or better the successful sounds of new performers who click with the fans. He looks for something that is "a little on the offbeat side" and regards it as a "challenge" to "break into new things" and succeed with new, young acts.

An excellent example of the type talent he seeks is Toby Keith, the Platinum singer-songwriter he brought with him when he moved from Mercury to Polydor. He knew that Keith would have a long and successful career when his first release, "Should've Been a Cowboy," was an instant success and marked him in the company of "people who will be like Alabama and George Strait."

His goal is to make Polydor "not the biggest, but the best" record label in Nashville. He has proved his point by filling his company's roster of performers "with unique artists that offer something new to the country audience."

Shedd was inducted into the Georgia Music Hall of Fame in 1989.

LYNYRD SKYNYRD

One can get up an argument either way as to whether the Southern hard rock booze band Lynyrd Skynyrd was for real or the product of a put-on hype of its charismatic founding leader, singer, and songwriter Ronnie Van Zant. But the color and controversy of its performance, from its discovery in an Atlanta bar to its demise in a tragic plane crash in Mississippi, had a major impact upon both the music and social outlook of disaffected youth of the seventies, particularly in the South.

The outgrowth of the My Backyard Band started by Van Zant and guitarists Gary Rossington and Allen Collins in Jacksonville, Florida, in 1965, Lynyrd Skynyrd dates from the group's expansion to include bassist Leon Wilkenson, keyboardist Billy Powell, lead guitarist Ed King, and drummer Robert Burns (later replaced by Artimus Pyle).

The group's unusual name was the respelled version of a high school gym teacher, Leonard Skinerd, who made them get haircuts. Described by critics as looking like "The Furry Freak Brothers doing a guest shot on Star Trek" and notorious for their hard drinking, they gravitated from Florida clubs to Atlanta. There their lightning quick three-guitar riffs and their joyously unreconstructed Southern style—complete with unfurled Confederate flag—attracted a loyal and rowdy following at Funocchio's. The producer Al Kooper signed them to record for his Sounds of the South Records.

Their records, some of which were done in Buddy Buie's Studio One in Atlanta, became best-sellers, such as "Second Helping," which earned a Gold record; "Sweet Home Alabama," their classic response to the Southern slanders of Neil Young; and "Free Bird," a tribute to their idol, Georgia's Duane Allman.

Van Zant's powerful lyrics of social commentary articulated the rage of working-class Southern youth about the good life it was impossible for them to achieve, but proved to touch responsive chords in disaffected young people throughout the nation.

The band was at the peak of its popularity and in the midst of a nationwide tour that would take it to Honolulu and culminate in a concert at New York's Madison Square Garden when the plane in which it was traveling to Baton Rouge, Louisiana, crashed near McComb, Mississippi, on October 20, 1977 killing Van Zant, guitarist Steve Gaines, singer Cassie

Gaines, and an assistant manager. Seriously injured were Rossington, Collins, Wilkenson, and Hawkins. Ironically, the group hated to fly and usually traveled in a custom bus, but had to take a charter flight to meet its Louisiana schedule.

The survivors retired the name Lynyrd Skynyrd in tribute to the victims and reconstructed themselves two years later as the Collins-Rossington Band.

Then in 1987, a decade after the fatal plane crash, a reorganized Lynyrd Skynyrd group did a memorial concert in Nashville. Original band alumni Collins, Rossiter, and Wilkenson appeared along with Ronnie Van Zant's brother, Johnny. They also released an MCA album called *Legends*.

CARL SMITH

Carl Smith was a string bass player with a robust, energetic voice who perfected the talents that made him the Number Twenty all-time country record seller during a career that stretched from the late 1940s into the early 1980s. He went from twice-daily radio broadcasts over station WGAC in Augusta, Georgia, and in two-to-three dollar-a-night concerts in every schoolhouse within nightly driving range of that East Georgia city to the stage of the world-famous Grand Ole Opry.

He and his band, the Smokey Mountaineers, lived and performed in and around Augusta in the late 1940s, after he was discharged from the U.S. Navy. He still comes back every year to Augusta to show off the champion cutting horses he raises, trains, and shows from his farm in Tennessee in the annual Augusta Futurity, which attracts horse fanciers from all over the world.

Smith was born in 1927 in Maynardsville, Tennessee, the hometown of the late Roy Acuff, who was his boyhood idol, along with Ernest Tubb and Bill Monroe. He learned to play the string bass at the age of seventeen and in 1944 spent his summer vacation on a musical internship with radio station WROL in Knoxville. After high school he went into the Navy; he then spent a year learning the ropes of broadcasting and country music in Georgia.

Then it was back to WROL where he played bass with Skeets Williamson and honed his musical skills to the point that his colleagues sent one of the acetate demo recordings he did to station WSM, the fountainhead of country music, in Nashville. He was invited to do a guest shot on the Hank Williams show, which resulted in his being signed to do a WSM morning show and to work on the Grand Ole Opry. According to his biography, he was one of the final stars created by the Opry's now long-gone star-making system.

Producer Don Law at Columbia Records also received one of Smith's demos and signed him to a recording contract in 1950 that resulted in his first hit, "Let's Live a Little," which reached Number Two in the summer of 1951. This was followed by the two-sided Top Ten record "Mr. Moon" and "If Teardrops Were Pennies," and his first Number One recording,

"Let Old Mother Nature Have Her Way," which stayed on top for eight weeks.

In March of 1952 he recorded a song given him by Ernest Tubb, "(When You Feel Like You're in Love) Just Don't Stand There," which also held the Number One spot on the charts for eight weeks. He had another Number One in "Are You Teasing Me?" later that spring.

From then on, it was one Top Ten after another until, by the time of his retirement in 1984, he had seen ninety-three of his singles on the charts, forty-two of which were Top Ten releases and six went to Number One. During his career he sold more than fifteen million records. His last performance that made the charts was in 1978, and in 1984 he decided that he was "burnt out" and "didn't enjoy performing any more," and chose to retire with honor in his prime rather than "drop dead not able to carry a tune in a bucket" like some of the elder statesmen of country who refused to quit.

He still is remembered for such titles as "It's a Lovely, Lovely World," "Our Honeymoon," "That's Just the Kind of Love I'm Looking For," "Just Wait 'Til I Get You Alone," "This Orchid Means Goodbye," "Do I Like It," and his cover of Porter Wagoner's "Trademark." His "Hey Joe," a Number One cut in 1953, was resurrected nearly three decades later in a popular parody by Moe Bandy and Joe Stampley.

Perhaps the best known of his many hits are "Let's Live a Little," "Foggy River," "Deep Water," and "Mr. Moon."

Smith's first wife was June Carter, now Mrs. Johnny Cash, and they produced a namesake daughter, Carlene, who now performs as Carlene Carter, having taken her mother's maiden name. His band, the Tunesmiths, established itself as one of the best in country music with such top musicians as guitarist Sam Pruett (formerly with Hank Williams's Drifting Cowboys), steel guitar virtuoso Johnny Sibert, and drummer Buddy Harmon.

His interest in horses, which became his second career after retiring from country music, began with the purchase of his first horse in 1952 and got underway in earnest when he acquired his first cutting horse in 1964.

He and his wife, Goldie—a former country star in her own right who, as Goldie Hill, had a number of hit singles in the 1950s, including "I Let the Stars Get in My Eyes" and "Say, Big Boy"—live on a forty-acre spread near Nashville where they produce championship cutting horses that they show in competitions all over the country, highlighted by the Augusta Futurity.

THE S.O.S. BAND

The S.O.S. Band is the direct opposite of the signal of distress with which the uninitiated often associate its name.

To the contrary, the initials of the eight-member Atlanta-based music group that specializes in a fresh, space-age mixture of live pop ballads, hard-driving funk, and jazz-flavored dance tunes stands for Sounds of Success. These sounds were designed by Los Angeles music producer Sigidi, and they achieved success through the discovery and management of Atlanta promoter Bunnie Jackson Ransom.

S.O.S. had its beginning with Santamonica, the house band of the mid and late seventies at Atlanta's Regal Room, which developed the reputation of having one of the hottest live shows with the performances of singer Mary Davis of Savannah, keyboardist Jason Bryant of Atlanta, drummer James Earl Jones III of Philadelphia, and saxophonist Billy R. Ellis of Cleveland.

They invited Mrs. Ransom to catch their act, and she was so impressed with the band's penchant for originality that she called their work to the attention of Clarence Avant, president of Tabu Records, who put them under contract and signed Sigidi to shape their sound. He added bassist John Alexander Simpson III, lead guitarist Bruno W. Speight, saxophonist Willie "Sonny" Killebrew, and trumpeter Abdul Raoof and later replaced James as drummer with Jerome Thomas.

The group's first single "Take Your Time (Do It Right)" was a fabulous across-the-board-hit. It sold two million records to earn a Platinum record and achieved simultaneous Number One rankings on the pop, soul, and disco charts, the later for fourteen consecutive weeks in 1980. The S.O.S. album of the same title sold more than eight hundred thousand copies to earn Gold status, and, on the strength of those successes, the group went on national tour with the Isley Brothers and the Commodores.

As with the first, Tabu joined with CBS Records to issue second and third albums in 1981 and 1982—the former being titled *S.O.S. Band Too* and the latter *S.O.S. Band III*. *Too* produced a hit single in "Do It Now" and received considerable publicity for its inclusion of the band's own tribute to Atlanta's murdered and missing children, "Do You Know Where Your Children Are?" *III* was recorded at Master Sound and Axis Studios in Atlanta and was produced by Gene Dozier and Ricky Sylvers with Leon Sylvers serving as executive producer. It featured songs written by the group's members and Dozier, who is noted for his horn arrangements on albums by Shalamar and Dynasty. It headlined the single "High Hopes" penned by Jimmy Harris and Terry Lewis of the Time. The two Sylvers joined the venture from production of albums for Shalamar, the Whispers, and Dynasty.

The S.O.S. Band

In its later recordings, S.O.S. has expanded from its typecasting as a dance band and has gotten into message songs like the one about Atlanta's children and energetic expressions of the love theme with such Mary Davis tunes as "There Is No Limit." Under the direction of Sigidi, it has put together a fresh mid tempo sound balancing a heavy bottom with a sophisticated string ensemble and strong horn charts on the top, all overlined with vibrant vocals delivered in a gospel-tinged style.

The Los Angeles Times called them "one of the most promising R&B groups around." The judgment of *Black Music* is that S.O.S. has a "very polished soul sound . . . a mix of disco and soul that's a sure fire formula." Mexico's *Sonida* calls their style "the sound of today."

In 1980 *Cash Box* magazine awarded the group five of its top end-of-the-year awards: Most Promising Group in Black Singles, Top New Group on Black Singles, Most Promising Group on Black Albums, Top New Group on Black Albums, and Most Promising Group on Pop Singles.

JOE SOUTH

The one thing on which both the despairing admirers and the admiring detractors of Joe South, Atlanta songwriter and guitarist, agree is that his capacity for putting meaningful words to memorable music was sheer genius.

South started picking out notes on his father's guitar at the age of eight, talked Atlanta music producer Bill Lowery into putting him on radio station WGST to sing some of his own songs at the age of twelve, was playing in Pete Drake's band with Jerry Reed and Ray Stevens and performing on the Georgia Jubilee at the age of fifteen, and was picking backup for stars like Bob Dylan, Aretha Franklin, Fats Domino, Eddy Arnold, Simon and Garfunkle, Solomon Burke, Conway Twitty, Marty Robbins, and Wilson Pickett at the age of seventeen.

Joe South

He could have made a career and a fortune as a virtuoso studio guitarist, but he found working under the direction and discipline of others "too frustrating." He signed on as the first artist under contract to Lowery when Bill left his deejay job to set up his own music publishing and recording firm, NRC, in Atlanta. South said he had things he "was really aching to say," and Lowery encouraged him to put them into words and music.

His first song to be recorded was "Let Me Tell You about Love" by Ric Cartey, which was released with less than success in 1956 by RCA. The second was a hit he prefers to forget—"The Purple People Eater Meets the Witch Doctor." It was put out by Lowery in 1958, made the Top Thirty, and got South an invitation to appear on Dick Clark's television show. He made it with the first of his message songs with "Concrete Jungle" in the early 1960s and moved to Nashville, where, although he was in great demand as a session musician, he became discouraged with his inability to sell his own songs and returned to Atlanta and the Lowery fold in 1966.

In two years he wrote and produced a series of hits including "Down in the Boondocks," "I Knew You When," "I Gotta Be Somebody," and "Hush" for Billy Joe Royal, and "These Are Not My People" for Johnny Rivers.

In 1968 he decided he could do better recording his own materials and signed with Capitol Records, which produced a regional hit with "Birds of a Feather" and a chart album in *Introspect,* which contained Joe's classic: "Games People Play," the prospects of which were not realized until other performers began to record it. Capitol reissued the album under the title *Games People Play* in 1969, and both it and the single became Gold records for South, earning him Grammys for Song of the Year and Best Contemporary Song, as well as bringing a third Grammy to saxophonist King Curtis for the Best Rhythm and Blues Instrumental Performance. "Games" was recorded by more than one hundred and twenty-five other major artists.

South's biggest year was 1971 when his "(I Never Promised You A) Rose Garden" became a Number One hit recorded by Lynn Anderson and won a Grammy as the Most Performed Song of that year. It is the best-selling country song in the history of Columbia Records. By 1982 it had been played on the air more than two million times and was declared the "biggest country song of the decade" by *Billboard* magazine.

He had further successes with his own singles of "Mirror of Your Mind" and "Walk a Mile in My Shoes." The latter was recorded by Ray

Stevens and featured by many major artists, including Harry Belafonte and Lena Horne in their 1970 television special. His album, *Don't It Make You Wanta Go Home*, and its title song, which was written during a recording session, caught the surge of environmental concern in 1970, and his "So the Seeds Are Growing" moved onto the charts in 1971.

The suicide of his brother, Tommy, started Joe on a downhill slide. He stopped working and went to Hawaii for two years, where, in his words, "Polynesian paralysis set in." When he returned to Atlanta he found musical trends had changed, and an album released in 1975 did not do well.

But he has continued to write and perform. In the 1980s his "I Knew You When" was revived by Linda Ronstadt and went high in the pop charts. Wherever Joe goes he is received well by those who have stood in awe of his genius for years and have pulled for his success.

He was inducted into the Georgia Music Hall of Fame in 1981.

Joe South and Governor Zell Miller

RAY STEVENS

If there were a decathlon in the music industry, Ray Stevens would have to be a leading contender, because his versatility embraces every aspect of the business.

He not only is a singer, a multi-instrumentalist, a composer, a lyric writer, an arranger, and a producer but also is equally at home in the fields of pop, country, blues, rock, ballads, comedy, and social commentary as well as having a background in classical piano and music theory.

His roots as a total artist are in the cotton mill town of Clarkdale, Georgia, near Atlanta, where his mother started him at the age of five on the piano with Bach and Chopin. He spent all his spare summer hours around the jukebox at the mill swimming pool and listened to Kitty Wells, Lefty Frizzell, Ernest Tubb, and Eddy Arnold, and on Sunday nights he listened to the great radio comedians like Jack Benny and Red Skelton.

When the family moved to Albany when he was ten, his background was broadened by the rhythm and blues of Ray Charles, Fats Domino, the Clovers, and the Drifters. As a teenager in Albany, he formed his own dance combo and worked as a disc jockey.

While pursuing a music degree at Georgia State University in Atlanta, he played in a combo with Jerry Reed and Joe South and was introduced by his Sunday School teacher to music publisher Bill Lowery, who recorded his first song, "Silver Bracelet," which became a minor hit on Prep Records. He also changed his name from Harold R. Ragsdale (which Lowery said sounded "like a dog's name") to Ray Stevens by using his middle name and his mother's maiden name.

He developed his flair for comedy by doing bits of his own material during intermissions at the dances played by his combo.

While a junior in college, he recorded for Mercury Records and scored almost immediately with hits like "Jeremiah Peabody's Polyunsaturated, Quick Dissolving, Fast Acting, Pleasant Tasting, Green and Purple Pills," "Ahab the Arab," and "Harry the Hairy Ape." His first "Sergeant Preston of the Yukon" had to be withdrawn because of the objections of the company holding the rights to the television show of that name.

Ray Stevens

After working at Monument Records as an A&R man, he overcame the early stereotype of being only a novelty composer with his sardonic and controversial "Mr. Businessman" and followed it with a string of hits: "Along Came Jones," "Gitarzan," and the enduring classic, "Everything Is Beautiful." It was recorded with the backings of his daughters' school chorus and earned him the first of his two Grammys and honors from BMI for more than one million performances.

Then came the rollicking antics of Ethel in "The Streak," which sold more than five million records, and his second Grammy for his rendition of "Misty," which was an unplanned, spur-of-the-moment improvisation picked up by an engineer when Ray and his band "were just fooling around in the studio."

Shriners' Convention, his sensational first record with RCA, sold more than two hundred thousand copies the first week and made the Top Ten in the second. It is a showcase of Stevens's versatility: he wrote the entire script, did all the background vocals, played most of the instruments, sang all the voices in different octaves and supervised the overdubbing and multi-tracking; thus he not only proved his own genius but also permanently "enshrined" Coy and Bubba into American folklore.

All of his more than twenty albums demonstrate the breadth of his talent and evidence his astounding success in running the gamut between the absurdly humorous and the deadly serious without damaging his credibility as an artist.

His recordings have made him in great demand as a guest performer on television, and he has appeared on the *Merv Griffin, Glen Campbell, Dean Martin,* and *Andy Williams* shows and had his own program when Andy signed him as his summer replacement.

He also has experienced tremendous success in television commercials and never misses an opportunity to express his positive feelings about life and his strong belief in America. He attributes most of his success to the perspective he gained in being born and recorded in Georgia and the South and the exposure that the blues and folk music that is integral in the culture of the region gave him. He was inducted into the Georgia Music Hall of Fame in 1981.

DOUG STONE

Doug Stone has been performing since the age of seven when an ambitious mother pushed him out onto the stage during a concert to sing a duet with Loretta Lynn.

He had to change his name from Brooks to Stone to avoid confusion with the rising star of Garth Brooks, but he has established himself as a mellow country crooner who is known as "Mr. Sensitive" among the followers of neo-honky-tonk balladry. In fact, he often is referred to as the "Dean Martin of Country Music" because of his unique flair for communicating the fragility of a broken heart with his delicate baritone voice and laid-back style.

Stone grew up playing five instruments and, by the age of fifteen, was writing his own songs and performing at skating rinks and any other venues to which he could wrangle invitations in and around his hometown of Newnan, Georgia. Upon graduation from high school, he took a day job as a diesel mechanic while performing in local clubs and establishing a recording studio in his home at night.

He was ready to seize opportunity when it presented itself in the form of a visit from a Nashville manager who, after being alerted to Stone's promising talent by a local friend, came to Newnan to catch his performance at the local VFW Hall. The manager liked what he heard and introduced Stone to his fellow Georgian, Atlanta producer Doug Johnson who originally hailed from Swainsboro. The two entered into a production relationship that continues to the present.

They dazzled everybody by hitting the Top Five and earning Stone a Grammy nomination with his first record, a George Jones-style tearjerker titled, "I'd Be Better Off (In a Pine Box)" in 1990. They followed up with a string of Number One hits—"I See You in a Different Light" and "A Jukebox with a Country Song" in 1991, "Too Busy Being in Love" in 1992, and "Why Didn't I Think of That?" in 1993.

But Stone's career almost ended in his own pine box in 1992 when he was forced at the age of thirty-five to undergo quadruple bypass surgery to correct a life-threatening heart condition. But he did survive, regained his strength, and bounced back with the hit album appropriately titled *From the Heart*. It was followed by the equally popular albums *More Love* in 1993 and *Faith in Me, Faith in You* in 1994.

The reviewers found interesting analogies between the *Faith* album and Stone's experience in undergoing heart surgery at an unusually young age. They were particularly intrigued by its opening number, "You Won't Outlive Me," which *Country Music* magazine's Michael McCall opined "might well have been chosen because he identified with it rather than because it furthered his well-marketed image as a balladeer."

Whatever the motivation, the album was received as the "most varied . . . and strongest" of Stone's career and was interpreted by McCall as "making his tenderness appear to be backed by a heart that pumps as well as bleeds."

With a trademark voice best described as a "tender sob," Stone may be regarded by some as "mushy," but he has succeeded in communicating the fragility of a broken heart like no country artist since Conway Twitty. It is true that, unlike Twitty, he has not tried to achieve a balance of vulnerability with virility, but he has proved himself to be the most vulnerable soul in country music, one who identifies with the faith and values of the fans who applaud his style and lyrics.

He also gives the lie to those who say he lacks spunk and spirit with his animated performance style that features odd dance moves that have been described by one reviewer as "a cross between Michael Jackson, a hillbilly Fred Astaire, and John Travolta of the famous 'Staying Alive' era."

Doug Stone, Zell Miller, and Bill Anderson

SWANEE RIVER BOYS

The Swanee River Boys broke out of the pack of six gospel quartets operating out of Chattanooga, Tennessee, by adding the "something extra" of diversification of repertoire to include a winning mix of gospel, folk, western, Negro spiritual, and popular songs.

With the broadcasting help of the fifty thousand watts of radio station WSB of Atlanta, Georgia, they became immediately before, during, and after World War II one of the most popular precursors of today's male singing groups like the Statler Brothers and the Oak Ridge Boys.

Though they never had a hit recording and they disbanded more than thirty years ago, their group continues to be remembered fondly by everyone old enough to recall its days as a headline act on the prewar and postwar radio network programs Checkerboard Time, sponsored by the Purina Feed Company, and the Circle Arrow Show, sponsored by the Western Auto Company. Many will remember the Thanksgiving of 1947 when they and Atlanta opera singer Beverley Wolfe created a national sensation by finishing second and first in that order on the popular NBC radio network talent show, The Big Break.

Although they prided themselves in sharing equally in both responsibilities and credit, the Swanee River Boys credited Bill Carrier who was born July 16, 1913, near Arthur, Kentucky, and since 1965 has lived in Smyrna, Georgia, with being the moving force in their formation. It was he who teamed with a fellow graduate of the Vaughan School of Music, Stacy Abner of Wedowee, Alabama, to form the quartet known as the Vaughan Four to sing over radio station WNOX in Knoxville, Tennessee, and to star with Archie Campbell (later of *Hee Haw* fame) on that station's Mid-Day Merry-Go-Around in 1938. Over the next two years the group evolved into its permanent composition of Carrier as baritone and guitarist, Merle and Buford Abner as bass and lead singers respectively, and George Hughes of Texarkana, Arkansas, formerly of the Rangers Quartet and the teacher of Singing Cowboy Jimmy Wakely, as high tenor.

After changing their name at Merle's suggestion to Swanee River Boys, they moved to Chattanooga to broadcast over radio station WDOD's Noon Day Frolic and their own fifteen-minute show sponsored by the patent laxative, Black Draught, and broadcast remote by Nashville's station

WLAC. They incorporated humor with Buford as their comedian. Testimony to their popularity was the overwhelming response of 3,298 requests to an offering of a free photograph of the group. It was there that Carrier met his wife, Willene Daniel, daughter of gospel songwriter Roland J. Daniel, who had come from Crossville, Alabama, for an audition.

Swanee River Boys

It became clear, however, that if they were to make it as full-time professional musicians, they would have to break out of the plethora of gospel groups operating out of Chattanooga. They accepted Carrier's suggestion that they broaden their repertoire to include songs of the type made popular by the Sons of the Pioneers, spirituals done in black dialect, traditional folk songs, popular ballads, and patriotic and seasonal songs. The approximately three hundred songs they committed to memory were almost evenly divided between gospel and secular titles, but the requests they received on tour ran almost two-to-one in favor of the secular material. The meticulous logs kept by Carrier showed they had performed 508 times when they were signed in the spring of 1941 to an exclusive, five-year contract by J. Leonard Reinsch to appear on WSB after the Cox organization brought him from WLS in Chicago to reorganize the country music programming of the Voice of the South.

At WSB they starred with Hank Penny, Pete Cassell, James and Martha Carson, and Billy's younger brother, Fiddler Cotton Carrier, on the Saturday Night Barn Dance, and every afternoon on the Little Country Church House. Their most requested song was, "I've Found a Hiding Place" followed closely by "Dese Bones Gwinna Rise Again" and "Carry Me Back to Ol' Virginny," the latter done so convincingly in Negro dialect by Buford that many listeners thought they were black. In late 1941 they were invited to join the transcribed Checkerboard Time and made regular trips to St. Louis, Missouri, to make those recordings. Their popularity as concert artists skyrocketed, and they made more than fifteen hundred appearances during their time with WSB, which continued until Merle and Buford entered military service in late 1943.

Billy and George tried non-music-related jobs in Louisville, Kentucky, but returned to Atlanta in 1944 to reform the Swanee River Boys with Leroy Abernathy of Canton, Georgia, who later would go on to become a member of the Gospel Music Hall of Fame, and Bill Lyles who later would become a member of the famed Blackwood Brothers Quartet until his tragic death in an airplane crash. Then in 1946, the original group got back together and, after a brief stay with WSB, went to WBT in Charlotte, North Carolina, and then to WLW in Cincinnati. There they worked in both radio and television and starred on the Circle Arrow Show until Billy left the group in January 1952 and the remainder disbanded later that year. They made their only recordings during that last year, four sides for MGM while Billy was with the group and ten sides for King after his departure.

Billy and Willene Carrier had their own Sunday program on radio station WPFB in Middletown, Ohio, for ten years while Billy worked at non-musical jobs; and, after they moved to Smyrna, for three years they performed with their son Larry on Atlanta station WYZE every Sunday.

THE TAMS

Five young black men with the single ambition to rise out of the Atlanta ghetto into which poverty had them trapped pooled their vocal talents to develop a unique a cappella singing style and their meager financial resources to buy matching multi-colored tam-o'-shanters to top their street attire of T-shirts and jeans. In the fifties, they became the acclaimed singing and dancing group called the Tams.

They made musical history in rhythm and blues in the sixties and in beach music in the seventies and eighties. Four of the original members were still going strong when they received the Beach Music of the Decade award at the first Annual Beach Musical awards ceremonies held in Myrtle Beach, South Carolina, in 1982.

Lead singer Joseph Lee Pope, baritone Charles Walter Pope, and tenor Horace (Sonny) Key started singing together in high school. They persuaded bass singer Robert Lee Smith, who collected rents in the boarding-house where they practiced, and lead singer Floyd Ashton to join them when they decided to form a vocal group to sing for tips and whatever else they could get in small clubs and at private parties around Atlanta.

Because they were averaging only about $1.25 a night when they worked, they decided their act needed some distinction; so they pooled their earnings until they could afford to buy the set of bright, matching tam-o'-shanters that gave them their name.

Two songwriting students at Georgia Tech, Cliff and Ed Thomas, caught one of their acts and persuaded the group to make a demo tape in their dormitory room at Tech. They, in turn, took the tape to Atlanta music producer Bill Lowery. The tape featured three of their original compositions, and Lowery liked the latter two—"It's Alright (You're Just in Love)," and "Disillusioned"—so much that he and Joe South produced the group's first single of them on the Arlen label. The songs became a local hit, and the Tams followed with four more singles. Because of the difficulty Ashton had in recording lyrics at the initial session, he was dropped from the group, and Joe Pope became the group's permanent and only lead vocalist until Joseph Jones joined them later.

The Tams

Believing the group had more than local potential, Lowery called them to the attention of ABC/Paramount Records, which signed them to a long-term contract and made their first single "What Kind of Fool (Do You Think I Am)," which on its release in October 1963 became an instant Number One hit.

It was followed by such favorites as "You Lied to Your Daddy," "Silly Little Girl," "I've Been Hurt," "It's Better to Have Loved a Little," "Shelter," "A Little More Soul," "Love, Love, Love" and "Hey Girl, Don't Bother Me." This last song, when later released in England, became a Gold record on the Probe label and made the Tams even bigger stars there than in the United States—an amazing result considering the tune was written on the spur of a moment to fill an album. Their biggest hit of all came in 1968 with "Be Young, Be Foolish, Be Happy," an original composition by Ray Whitley and J. R. Cobb.

With their new wealth, they bought themselves flamboyant outfits, featuring violet and orange vests, flowered shirts, and rainbow bell-bottom pants to complement their trademark. They also hired Albert Cottle, Jr., of the Queen City Gospel Singers to join them as choreographer and additional vocalist. With fancy new steps to match their colorful new costumes, they not only became one of the most popular acts on the R&B circuit, where they won favor with the soul audiences, but also became favorites on college campuses. *Billboard* magazine in 1966–1967 listed the group as one of the Top Ten Favorites among college music fans.

Their LPs also did well: *Presenting the Tams* made the Top Ten on the R&B hit lists, and *Hey Girls, Don't Bother Me* and *Time for the Tams* showed on the charts in the sixties. In all, ABC released nineteen singles and five albums, and Lowery did *Best of the Tams* on his 1-2-3 label released by Capitol, which also released a "Tams Medley" single. In 1971 the group's switching to Dunhill Records resulted in the sensational English release of "Hey Girl, Don't Bother Me."

In 1970 the Tams signed a management contract with Carolina Attractions and, under the guidance of Harold Thomas, developed into one of the hottest beach music acts in that medium. As a result they received the top beach music award at the first of the annual presentations in that category in 1982. They were recognized in 1992 with the Mary Tallent Pioneer award at the Georgia Music Hall of Fame banquet at the World Congress Center. Joe Pope died in March of 1996; the surviving members live in Atlanta and, before Pope's death, were still performing.

GID TANNER
AND THE SKILLET LICKERS

When music historians sit down to sort out the what and why of twentieth-century American Music, they will have to accord high ranking to the influence of Gid Tanner on all of its forms. Tanner, a Georgia chicken farmer, never in his life fully comprehended the importance of the bridge he and his wild band of musical geniuses known as the Skillet Lickers built between traditional folk and modern popular music.

They not only gave respectability and popularity to what previously had been derided as "hillbilly" music but also served as the initial catalyst in the sweeping electronic evolution that helped mix of country, jazz, blues, and urban pop and give commonality to American music as we know it today.

Had it not been for the lure of the burgeoning music recording and radio broadcasting industries, James Gideon Tanner probably would have been content to limit his musical activities to occasional forays out of his Walton County farm to joust with the likes of Fiddlin' John Carson, his senior, and Clayton McMichen, his junior, in the fiddling competitions of the time, which he sometimes won and in which he always placed.

But then Frank Walker of Columbia Records invited him at the age of thirty-eight to come to New York to help that company catch up with Okeh Records' highly successful issues of Carson's country recordings. He took with him his blind friend, Riley Puckett, who was to gain fame as the first of the crooners and rhythm guitarists, and on March 7, 1924, they became the first Southern rural artists to record for Columbia.

Further at Walker's request, Tanner came home and assembled the Skillet Lickers, which, with periodic shifts in membership, was to become one of the most highly respected and popular names in the field of string band music. From 1926 until their final disbandment in 1934, they made a phenomenal total of 565 recordings combining hillbilly with popular music, including the forever popular "John Henry" and the classic "Down Yonder," which was one of the first instrumental records to sell a million copies. They also introduced comedy to the recording industry with their rural skits borrowed from the minstrel show format of humorous dialogue interspersed with snatches from previously recorded songs and instrumentals.

Gid Tanner

Besides Tanner and Puckett, the Skillet Lickers originally included McMichen and his brother-in-law Bert Layne as fiddlers and Fate Norris on the banjo and the harmonica. Layne was replaced by McMichen's brilliant young protege, Lowe Stokes, from Rome, Georgia, whose contest with Carson for the Fiddlin' Championship was the subject of Stephen Vincent Benet's "The Mountain Whippoorwill." Tanner's younger brother Arthur sat in on earlier sessions, and his son Gordon played on the last one in 1934. Also with the group at one time or another were Ted Hawkins on the fiddle and mandolin and Mike Whitten and Hoke Rice on the guitar.

Because of personal predilections, conflicts, and musical preferences, most of these men recorded and performed from time to time with different groups of their own or others and sometimes under different names.

The differences revolved mainly around the tendency of McMichen to veer off into progressive and experimental styles as opposed to the conservatism of Norris and the middle-of-the-road traditional inclination of Gid Tanner.

Tanner had an intuitive sense of what would please the public, and he remained the undisputed leader and pacesetter of the group because of his capacity to warm up audiences, together with his recognition that the success of the band lay in featuring Puckett's singing.

The recordings from the first session in April 1926 were labeled "Gid Tanner and his Skillet Lickers, with Riley Puckett," but because of McMichen's objections, based on the argument that the original Lick the Skillet Band had been his, all subsequent records added "and Clayton McMichen." For many years it was believed the band featured a two-fiddle lead, but research has demonstrated that it was a three-fiddle band from the beginning, with McMichen and Tanner playing the high parts while Stokes added the baritone. The confusion arose from the fact that McMichen insisted that Tanner be kept off mike and Stokes play with a mute so that McMichen was certain to be heard. Critics agree, however, that it was Stokes's brilliant fiddle, added to Puckett's strong contrapuntal bass runs on the guitar, that gave them the exciting, wild sound that set them apart as a string band. Their incorporation of elements we know today as jazz, bluegrass, western swing, and R&B gave their music broad appeal.

Tragedy, in the form of an accident that cost Stokes his right hand, and the Depression, which left people with no money to spend for music, forced the dissolution of the band in 1931. Tanner, who never ceased being a farmer first and a musician second, went back to his chicken farm and also worked at several radio stations. He and McMichen never got back together, but he did reassemble the band in March 1934 to record twenty-four sides for RCA Victor. The band, comprised of Tanner and his son Gordon on the fiddles, Puckett on the guitar, and Hawkins on the mandolin, turned out a different sound with the mandolin carrying the musical lead and Gid singing the vocal lead. The numbers were almost entirely traditional dance tunes, fiddle songs, and instrumentals with several duets by Tanner and Pucket.

Gid continued to make appearances and to compete in fiddling contests until his death in 1960. He won his last Old Time Fiddler's Contest at age seventy-one in 1955. He married twice and had five sons. Gordon, who followed in his footsteps, died in 1982 while attending an Old-Time Music Festival in Delaware. Gid Tanner was inducted into the Georgia Music Hall of Fame in 1988.

TLC

To the uncool and those who are uninformed about the rap and hip-hop worlds, TLC probably stands for "tender loving care," but to those who are with it the acronym means T-Boz, Left-Eye, and Chilli, the performing names of Tionne Watkins, Lisa Lopes, and Rozonda Thomas, who make up the irrepressible female performing trio, TLC. TLC has, according to LaFace Records (for which they are Platinum-selling stars), "successfully combined that comically witty and intuitive lyrical direction and the undeniable groove, swagger, and thump of urban life into one persona that is theirs alone."

TLC has cut a wide swath since its debut in 1992 and has succeeded in redefining what R&B and rap listeners can expect from a female rap act, not only in records and videos but also in movies, television, and style. Although they have toned down their more exaggerated look, which they wore when they splashed onto the performing scene, they emphasize that they have not contradicted their original and continuing message, that "women can wear whatever they want."

The group's first album, *Ooooooohhh . . . On the TLC Tip*, sold more than three-million units, producing Top Three Platinum-selling singles in "Ain't 2 Proud 2 Beg" and "Baby Baby Baby" and a Gold hit in "What about Your Friends." Their second album, which followed two years later, *Crazysexycool*, went five times Platinum and produced the sizzling single "Creep," which not only was certified Platinum but also was Number One on the R&B charts for nine weeks and Number One on the Pop charts for five weeks. A second single, "Red Light Special," went Gold, as subsequently did "Waterfalls," which soared from Number Seven to Number One on the *Billboard* Pop Chart in one week. "Waterfalls" was a 1996 Grammy nominee for Record of the Year, and *Crazysexycool* won the 1996 Grammy for Best R&B Album.

"People never know what to expect from TLC as far as how they're going to look or what they'll do; but, when it comes to music, you should expect quality," said President Antonio "L. A." Reid of LaFace Records whose wife, Perri "Pebbles" Reid, first brought the group to the label's attention. "TLC is what I call the epitome of entertainment. . . . These girls know how to entertain and their appeal is so broad."

The group's capacity to be both outrageous and entertaining got its members co-starring roles in the motion picture, *House Party 3*, and an invitation to cover the Time's "Get It Up" for the soundtrack of the film, *Poetic Justice*.

"I look at TLC and I see more than singers, I see characters," says filmmaker John Singleton, who wrote and directed *Poetic Justice*.

TLC also wrote the theme for the Nickelodeon television show, *All That*; was on the Patti Labelle sitcom, *Out All Night*; was featured in a pro-literacy episode of the *CBS Schoolbreak Special*; contributed the rollicking single "Sleigh Ride" to the soundtrack of the movie *Home Alone II*; performed on the *MTV Movie Awards* and *Saturday Night Live*; and toured the nation with Boyz II Men in the spring of 1995. Lopes's rat-a-tat rhyming skills were lent to Keith Sweat's Top Ten single, "How Do You Like It?"

The range of their collective talents has attracted some of the top producers of the recording industry. On their *Crazysexycool* album, "Kick Your Game" was produced by Jermaine Dupre, "Waterfalls" by Organized Noize, "Red Light Special" and "Let's Do It Again" by Kenneth "Babyface" Edmonds, and the cover of Prince's hit,

TLC

"If I Was Your Girlfriend," by Dallas Austin and Sean "Puffy" Combs.

"We can do anything," Lopes says. "Everyone from little girls to young women our age and older look at us and see themselves. They can relate. . . . We're human . . . and going after our dreams on our own terms."

Travis Tritt

The only thing that can be said with certainty about Travis Tritt and his music is that both defy categorization. To some he is a mainstream country artist; to others, a Southern-fried rock 'n' roller. He is equally at home at the Grand Ole Opry, where he has been the youngest member since 1992, and in concert halls or arenas, where he consistently demonstrates a rare ability to achieve intimacy with thousands of fans who are turned on by his hot licks.

Whatever the individual judgment of his musical genre, most critics agree he is an entertainer nonpareil who demonstrated in convincing fashion with his fourth album, *Ten Feet Tall and Bullet Proof,* that he has an uncanny and unerring ability to walk the narrow path between his country heritage and his rock leanings to the acclaim of the devotees of both.

This very talented Georgia native began as a soloist performing in the children's choir of his church. He had taught himself to play the guitar by the age of eight and wrote his first song when he was fourteen. (When he finally went to Nashville, he carried five hundred songs he had written.)

He has been performing his skills as a hybrid performer since his graduation from high school in 1981. He was influenced by James Taylor and John Denver but also by Hank Williams, Jr., the Allman Brothers, and Lynyrd Skynyrd. He honed his unique amalgam of their disparate styles in six years of playing in every bar and VFW hall within reaching distance of his home of Marietta that would book him. He readily admits he was more interested in the exposure and experience of such gigs than the sparse remuneration they brought him.

He did not quit his daytime job working in the heating and air conditioning business, but rather was inspired by his boss who encouraged him with his own stories of regrets about passing up his chance at becoming a rock 'n' roll guitarist. He vowed he would be ready to seize his chance when, and if, it came.

It came in the person of Danny Davenport, a Warner Brothers field representative working out of Atlanta, who chanced to catch one of Tritt's local performances. He allowed Tritt to use his home studio to make the demonstration tapes they pitched to Warner Brothers, which sent representatives to Atlanta to sign him and arranged for superagent Ken Kragen, the manager of such greats as Kenny Rogers and Lionel Ritchie and the discoverer of fellow Georgian Trish Yearwood, to manage him.

Tritt's first commercial effort was "Country Club," described as a "semi-hokey novelty tune" that no one took seriously despite the fact that it made the Top Ten in 1989. But he followed it up in 1990 with an album bearing the same title that went Platinum and set the tone for his future efforts of mainstream country spiced by potent strains of Southern rock with hints of rhythm and blues thrown in. The titles of two of the tracks—"Put Some Drive in Your Country" and "Son of the New South" —described the import and impact of Tritt's work better than anything the critics could say.

Porter Wagoner and Travis Tritt

His cowritten "Help Me Hold On" went to Number One and stayed on the charts for six weeks, and his second single of that year, "I'm Gonna Be Somebody," reached the Top Three, all of which prompted *Billboard* magazine to name him Top New Male Country Music Artist of the Year.

His second album in 1991, *It's All About to Change,* also went to Platinum and firmly established the expansive vocal and stylistic range he was struggling to define and perfect. It also demonstrated his imaginative and wicked wit as a songwriter, expanding on traditional country themes of hard-drinking and somebody-done-somebody-wrong with four Number One hits, including the spirited duet with Marty Stuart, "The Whiskey Ain't Working," and the ultimate putdown of love-gone-wrong, "Here's a Quarter (Call Someone Who Cares)." These earned him the highest accolade for a new artist, the Country Music Association's Horizon award.

His first single of 1992, "Nothing Short of Dying," went to Number Five, and its flip side, "Bible Belt," was featured on the movie *My Cousin Vinnie.* He and Stuart did a Top Ten single, "This One's Gonna Hurt You (For a Long, Long Time)," and embarked on their hirsute "No Hats" Tour, which marked them as one of the most popular and compatible duos in the business. His third album, *T-R-O-U-B-L-E,* went Gold that year and Platinum the next, and his Christmas album, *A Travis Tritt Christmas— Loving Time of the Year,* was a crossover in the Top Twenty-five country category and the Top Seventy-five pop classification. His single covering the Elvis Presley hit of the album title reached the Top Fifteen.

Travis Tritt

He and Stuart won the Vocal Event of the Year award of the Country Music Association, and Tritt was named TNN/*Music City News* Star of Tomorrow. The two won a Grammy for Best Country Vocal Collaboration in 1993.

Tritt has followed the lead of Kenny Rogers and Randy Travis in venturing into western movies, appearing with Kenny in *Rio Diablo* and with Keifer Sutherland and Woody Harrelson in *The Cowboy Way,* for which he wrote the theme song. He was named a permanent host of VH1's country music show, *Country Countdown,* and, with Michael Bane, has published his autobiography, which bears the title of his fourth album, *Ten Feet Tall and Bullet Proof.*

He did a rhythm and blues duet with Patti LaBelle, "When Something Is Wrong with My Baby," and another with David Lee Roth. He also appeared with Madonna, the Red Hot Chili Peppers, and Tom Petty on a tribute album to George Harrison. He brought the fabled Eagles together to film a video for "Take It Easy," a cut from the chart-topping album *Common Thread: The Songs of the Eagles,* and starred with Wynonna, Tanya Tucker, and Clint Black on the half-time show when the Super Bowl was played in Atlanta.

But of all the cuts on his *Ten Feet Tall* album, the one which Tritt is the proudest of is "Outlaws Like Us," in which he was joined by his idols, Waylon Jennings and Hank Williams, Jr., as well as the guitar work of the irrepressible Stuart. The critics have stated that it "captures perfectly Tritt's depth of feeling and gut-level understanding of Southern music" and pronounced it "destined to stand as a classic."

He realized his dream of having his own country home located in rural Georgia, not too far from his hometown of Marietta, which he still claims as home.

PHIL WALDEN

Georgia's Phil Walden can attest to the elation Lazarus must have felt when he was called forth from the tomb because he has had the experience almost as many times as a cat has lives and still is on his feet managing and recording away.

Walden got into the business as a student at Mercer University in Macon when he discovered Otis Redding and guided the talented and charismatic singer/songwriter into becoming a rhythm-and-blues legend in his own time. His stock soared as he groomed and led a talent stable, which not only was headed by Redding but also included Sam and Dave, Al Green, and Percy Sledge. His stock, however, crashed just as fast and disastrously as the plane in which Redding perished in 1967.

His second incarnation came the following year when he bought the contract Jerry Wexler of Atlantic Records had signed with Duane Allman and proceeded to act on the dream he and Redding had had to build their own record label. Part of the deal was that Walden was to establish Capricorn Records as a custom label to be distributed by Atlantic, but things got off to a slow start until he inked a contract with the second Allman Brother, Gregg, to be organist and vocalist for the group to be known as the Allman Brothers Band.

The Allman's sold only thirty-three thousand copies of their first album, and it was not until 1971 that they had their breakthrough with the album, *Fillmore East*. Atlantic balked at Walden's ambitious plans for the group, so he took the label to Warner Brothers in 1972, and things went straight up from there, not only with the Allman Brothers but also with the other Southern rock talents Walden signed up—the Marshall Tucker Band, Wet Willie, Elvin Bishop, and the Dixie Dregs.

But, following the deaths of Duane and Berry Oakley in almost identical motorcycle accidents in 1971 and 1972, and disputes that erupted among band members as to the group's musical direction, high-flying lifestyles, Gregg's marriage to Cher Bono, and Walden's decision to take Capricorn to PolyGram (after he and Warner Brothers were unable to agree on a buyout), the band disbanded in 1975 and PolyGram pulled the plug on Capricorn in 1979.

Capricorn went into Chapter 11 bankruptcy proceedings. While Walden struggled to continue recording operations at its studio, he gave up and moved to Nashville in 1984, where his nose for talent led him to comedian Jim Varney, the hapless Ernest P. Worrell of television commercial and movie fame, for whom he became manager.

Once again he "rose from the dead" and negotiated another deal with Warner Brothers, a joint venture agreement that allowed him to revive Capricorn, this time as an extension of Warner Brothers Nashville division. He issued his first release in twelve years in 1991—an album by the Athens, Georgia-based band, Widespread Panic—and since then has gotten into high gear pursuing his original goal of discovering, developing, and recording Southern rock acts on a Southern-based label. He admits his return to and resurrection by Warner Brothers has been "beyond my wildest dreams."

Phil Walden

This is what Jim Ed Norman, president of the Warner Brothers Nashville Division, had to say about it:

"The music that has been born out of the traditions of the Southeast is really America's contribution to world culture. . . . Phil certainly has been associated with some of the most dramatic examples of that kind of music development over the last thirty years."

Walden was inducted into the Georgia Music Hall of Fame in 1986.

FREDDY WELLER

"Prodigy" is the word often used to describe Atlanta's multitalented Freddy Weller. His incomparable career, which began when he was fifteen, spanned the spectrum from lead guitarist with the hit-parading rock group Paul Revere and the Raiders to writer and recorder of a string of the greatest country hits of the late 1960s and 1970s.

Born September 9, 1947, Weller came to the attention of Joe South, Ray Stevens, and their mentor Bill Lowery, when he won the Georgia Jubilee Talent Contest in East Point at the age of fifteen. By the time he graduated from high school, he was playing bass and rhythm guitar for South's band, the Believers. He backed South on his great popular hit "Games People Play" and Billy Joe Royal on his million-seller "Down in the Boondocks." While Weller was sharing a bill in Birmingham, Alabama, with the teenage Revere organization, Revere was so impressed that he invited young Weller to join his group and, after his refusal, persisted with offers until he finally found them impossible to refuse.

Freddy confounded Raider fans with the country numbers he interspersed with their rock renditions and occupied his spare time on the road teaming with Tommy Roe to write a series of "bubble gum" hits, which included million sellers "Dizzy" in 1968 and "Jam Up and Jelly Tight" in 1969. When Weller made an appearance on the *Ed Sullivan Show*, the exposure boosted Weller's popularity and his fame took off in inverse proportion to the declining fortunes of the Raiders. Revere, sensing Weller's great country potential, persuaded Columbia Records to put him under contract.

Beginning with his country version of "Games People Play," which went to Number One in 1968, Weller scored with successive hits with "Down in the Boondocks," "The Promised Land," "Indian Lake," and "Another Night of Love" as well as smash albums bearing the first three titles. Although he caught some flack from a few country fans because of his long hair, the criticism dissipated with the rise of older contemporaries like Kris Kristofferson and Waylon Jennings. He had other chart records with "These Are Not My People," "Listen to the Young Folks," "Ballad of a Hillbilly Singer," "The Perfect Stranger," "She Loves Me Right out of

My Mind," "The Roadmaster," "I've Just Got to Know," "Sexy Lady," "You're Not Getting Older," "Liquor, Love and Life," and others.

He had eleven albums with Columbia and more than thirty hit singles. On his 1979 hit, "Love Got in the Way," his partner was an unknown at that time, a receptionist for the Acuff-Rose Publishing Company named Lorrie Morgan. Since then, of course, Lorrie has become a superstar.

He also had his own songs recorded not only by his old buddies, Joe South, Tommy Roe, Billy Joe Royal, and Paul Revere but also by such superstars as George Jones, Barbara Mandrell, Del Reeves, Judy Miller, and Hugo Montenegro.

With friend Tommy Roe, they turned out "Dizzy" and "Jam Up and Jelly Tight," superhits in the 1970s. In 1991 "Dizzy" became a hit all over again when Vic Reeves and the Wanda Stuff recorded it and it became the Number One record in England.

Freddy Weller

Another Weller song that became a hit twice was "Lonely Women Make Good Lovers," which he cowrote with Spencer Oldam. Bob Lunan and Steve Wariner had hits with it. In the 1987 movie *Rain Man*, the Lunan version is played while Tom Cruise and Dustin Hoffman sit at a diner with a jukebox at their table.

Hits keep coming: "She Never Cried When Old Yeller Died" on a Confederate Railroad album, "The Garden" for Vern Gosden," and "Don't Make Years Like They Used To" for Doug Stone.

Weller finds no contradiction or conflict between his country roots and early rock inclinations. He is proud of his role in the development of the contemporary country sound. His idols are George Jones and Merle Haggard, and he insists that "home is where the heart is and my heart has always been set on becoming a country music recording artist."

HEDY WEST

Hedy West, born April 6, 1938, in Cartersville, Georgia, is a folk singer in the classic tradition who, now living in London, is better known in Europe than in her native Georgia.

She sings the traditional songs of Appalachia exactly as they were handed down for generations from her great grandparents, Asberry Kimsey and Talitha Prudence Sparks Mulkey of Gilmer County, Georgia, and as they were taught to her by her banjo-playing grandmother, Lillie Mulkey West, and her poet father, Don West. Don West lived for many years in Pickens and Union Counties in North Georgia and is the founder and director of the Appalachian Folklife Center in Pikestem, West Virginia.

Hedy's musical education was a melange of the classical piano lessons insisted upon by her parents and the self-taught banjo picking of the songs learned from her grandmother. Her local fame as a singer of old songs led to applause as a singer at a festival in Boone, North Carolina, in 1956 and the winning of first prize in a folk song contest in Nashville, Tennessee, two years later.

She pursued her education in symphonic music at Columbia University while also performing the traditional songs of her family in coffeehouses from New York to Chicago and, by invitation of *Sing Out!* magazine, at Carnegie Hall. By the mid-1960s she had performed at most major folk festivals in the United States, recorded two albums of her songs for Vanguard Records, composed music to go with her father's poem "Anger to the Land," and joined Bobby Bare and Charlie Williams in writing the 1963 country hit recorded by Bare, "500 Miles Away from Home."

Disillusioned by American politics, the nuclear arms race, and the Vietnam war, she moved to London at the end of the 1960s and recorded extensively and performed widely throughout Europe. By the end of the 1970s only one of her albums, *Old Times and Hard Times* on the Folk-Legacy label, remained in general distribution in the United States. In the accompanying notes for that LP, A. L. Lloyd calls Hedy "among the best women singers in the American folksong revival" and notes that she is one of the few performers belonging to "that happy band who are entirely at home in either . . . the world of fine arts or that of folk arts." He points out that she performs the repertoire of her family songs in a straightforward, unpretentious manner and is "not the kind of singer who acts the 'country-cousin' and wears a cotton bonnet and makes a nasal caricature of her 'down-home' vocal style just to charm city audiences."

Her uncle, Harold West, was editor and publisher of *The Towns County Herald* and *North Georgia News* in Union County for many years.

James S. "Big Chief" Wetherington

He was called "Big Chief" because he could hit notes lower and hold them longer than any of his contemporaries on the gospel-singing circuit. Hovie Lister might have been the showman, but bass singer Jim Wetherington was the crowd-pleaser and show-stopper of Georgia's renowned Statesmen quartet for twenty-four years.

Born on a tobacco farm in 1922 and raised by his grandparents in Ty Ty, Georgia, James Stephen Wetherington and his older brother, Gerald Austin Wetherington, were tutored by their grandfather, Professor Solomon Swett, a music teacher of some note, and grew up playing several instruments and singing solos and duets all over South Georgia and North Florida.

Jim "Big Chief" Wetherington

The brothers moved to Lakeland, Florida, where Jim went to work for the Atlantic Coastline Railroad in 1939. He also became a featured soloist in the Lakeland Presbyterian Church and Sunday Night choir director for a small nondenominational church where he met his future wife, pianist Elizabeth Huguley.

After serving in the U.S. Navy in both the Atlantic and the Pacific during World War II, Wetherington returned to work with the Atlantic Coastline Railroad until he and several friends formed the Melody Masters quartet and moved first to Greenville, South Carolina, and later to Lincoln, Nebraska, where he also worked for radio station WFAB.

In July of 1949 he followed Melody Masters tenor Jake Hess to Atlanta, where both joined Hovie Lister and the Statesmen quartet, which gained a nationwide reputation as performing and recording artists. The quartet earned several Grammy nominations and were named Georgia's Ambassadors of Good Will by succeeding Georgia governors.

The "Big Chief" was a leader in the North Atlanta community and in the 1960s became choir director of Atlanta's Assembly of God Tabernacle, where he formed that church's acclaimed Golden Stairs Choir. He also became an active and prolific writer of gospel music for publication and recording, his best-known songs including "Lord, I Want to Go to Heaven," "At the Roll Call," "This Was Almost Mine," and "Little Boy Lost."

He died of a massive heart attack while participating in the National Quartet Convention in Nashville, Tennessee, on October 3, 1973. He was inducted into the Gospel Music Hall of Fame— Deceased Category in 1977. His widow, daughter, and two granddaughters live in Norcross, Georgia.

Wetherington always said he lived his life doing what he loved best and felt called by God to do: "using my singing gift to share my faith in God and encourage and inspire people."

CHUCK WILLIS

The legend is larger than the life of Chuck Willis, the "King of the Stroll," who was born and died in Atlanta and whose death at the age of thirty cost him the personal fame later enjoyed by his successors such as James Brown and Otis Redding.

But the supreme irony of his brief career as one of the most influential black rhythm and blues singers was that the song "What Am I Living For?" became a best-seller one month after his death and earned him a posthumous Gold record. He was inducted into the Georgia Music Hall of Fame in 1994.

He was born January 31, 1928, in what was described as a "ghetto situation," began singing in neighborhood joints at the age of eighteen, became vocalist for Red McAllister's band in 1950, and, under the management of Zenas "Daddy" Sears, the white guru of Atlanta R&B, signed a contract in 1951 to record for Okeh, the "race" label of Columbia Records.

His first success came with the double-sided hit, "Caledonia" and "My Story," in October 1952, followed by other Southern best-sellers like "Don't Deceive Me" and "I Feel So Bad" in 1953 and 1954. He did not achieve national fame, however, until Sears arranged a new contract with Atlantic Records, where Willis scored with "Juanita" and "It's Too Late" in 1956 and followed with the biggie, "C. C. Rider," which went pop and established him as a major rock 'n' roll artist with both white and black audiences. He followed with another hit, "Betty and Dupree."

Chuck went on the road wearing a turban and doing the dance that dubbed him the "King of the Stroll" and sometimes the "Sheik of the Shake"; but illness overtook him and he died in the hospital on April 1, 1958, from what Sears said were complications from a stomach ulcer and his failure to follow doctor's orders. Others claim, however, that he died in an automobile accident. Recording industry rumors said that his death was the result of a brain tumor and that the reason he wore a turban was to hide the scars of brain surgery.

In addition to the huge success of "What Am I Living For?" which became Number One on the American R&B charts and was a hit in England, several other fine Willis blues performances turned up on the

Atlantic label, and no one ever was able to trace the date and place of their production, although they generally are attributed to the session at which he collapsed. In later years, Columbia reissued much of the material on an Epic Album, and most of the songs he wrote that became hits are included in a current Atco album.

Sears, who regarded Willis as a better songwriter than a performer, agrees with the assessment of Willis's potential for stardom had he lived but points out his life was not as glamorous as legend would have it.

Willis was inducted into the Georgia Music Hall of Fame in 1994.

TRISHA YEARWOOD

Trisha Yearwood knows just how satisfying it can be to start one's singing career at the top. She did just that when she belted out her first single record, the up-tempo ballad "She's in Love with the Boy," and it became an overnight megahit that soared to the top of the charts.

But she also quickly found out that such an achievement immediately creates the problem of what so fortunate an artist does for an encore. The critics, as she learned, are not hesitant to apply the "one-hit wonder" label to the one who falls short of the ultimate with subsequent performances.

She is a mercurial interpreter of songs who insists on doing things her way, and fortunately for her, she also had friends in high places such as rising superstar Garth Brooks, with whom she had toured as an opening act and recorded the duet "Like We Never Had a Broken Heart," and superagent Ken Kragen, who managed Kenny Rogers, Lionel Ritchie, and Travis Tritt and who signed up Discover Card as one of her sponsors, Revlon Cosmetics as the marketer of her own perfume, and Chevrolet cars and pickup trucks for which she became a spokeswoman in the tradition of that Southern songbird of the preceding generation, Dinah Shore.

But she got a handle on the situation with the decision that, since she alone in the final analysis would be responsible for the success or failure of her career, she alone should and would make the decisions about what she did and the songs she sang. MCA Records grudgingly came to the conclusion that "that is the kind of artist she really is."

Since Yearwood is a selector, rather than a writer, of songs, she has proved her instincts to be correct with five succeeding albums, beginning with *Trisha Yearwood* in 1991, each better than its predecessor. Her fifth, *Thinking about You*, spun off two Number One singles, a most unusual achievement for a female singer.

Country Music magazine's Patrick Carr lauded her choice for that album of such songs as Melissa Etheridge's "You Can Sleep While I Drive," Gretchen Peters's "On a Bus to St. Cloud," and Larry Henley's and Red Lane's "'Til I Get It Right." He called the album "a truly stellar example of the interpretative singer's art," concluding it was "so well created and so well fitted to her sophisticated but passionate post-country sensibility."

"I'm very song-driven as an artist," Yearwood explains. "As a listener of music and a fan of music, I've always been very true to myself as far as what moves me to sing, and I've never recorded a song I didn't believe in."

In making her choices of material, she said she always asks herself if she would be "able to hold my head up" if she passed Emmylou Harris on the street.

"Emmylou's pretty much the integrity police for me. I think about artists like her whom I respect, the choices they've made in their careers, and that's really the criterion: Is this what I believe in? And that means that every song doesn't go Number One, . . . but I'm sleeping really good at night."

Yearwood has been described as a "white-bread success," born and reared in Monticello, Georgia, as the "banker's and school teacher's"—not the "coal miner's"—daughter. She did not have to struggle, starve, or perform in a succession of seedy nightclubs or disreputable honky-tonks to pay her dues or get her big break.

In fact, unlike most of her contemporaries, she achieved success through the education route. She graduated from Young Harris College and was pursuing a music-business degree at Belmont College in Nashville when she was accepted for an internship in the publicity department of MTM Records. While working there, she began doing demo and studio work and met another young unknown, Garth Brooks. As Brooks's career took off, he invited her to be a backup singer for his first albums and then to be his opening act on the road.

The rest, as they say in show business, is history. She was signed to a solo deal in 1991 and hit it big with "She's in Love with the Boy," which she followed up with the sultry "Wrong Side of Memphis" and the duet with Brooks.

Her first album was called "the most important new-artist release since Randy Travis' first back in 1986." But her next one, *Hearts of Armor*, was panned by critics despite its duet with Don Henley on the "Walkaway Joe" track being well received. In 1995 she won a Grammy for her duet with Aaron Neville, "I Fall to Pieces," and, beginning with Atlanta, has won high praise for a succession of performances with full symphony orchestras around the country.

She married Robert Reynolds, the bassist with the Mavericks, and they have bought themselves a log-and-rock home so far back in the woods north of Nashville that they had to get a four-wheel-drive vehicle to get to it. She says she is happy and adores her spouse, whom she calls "a good

. . . and funny . . . person" who has caused her to lose her cynicism and decide that "I really do like men."

Her new spirit was described by Carr as "one of confidence, security, poise, and resolve lightened by good humor." He concluded in his *Country Music* profile of her: "That's not a bad four-year report card, really. I'd say it shows continuing potential—which was obvious right from the start— plus character development, too."

Trisha Yearwood

DENNIS YOST
AND THE CLASSICS IV

Dennis Yost was born in Detroit, Michigan, and grew up and learned music in Jacksonville, Florida, but it was in Atlanta, Georgia, that he and his group achieved fame as Dennis Yost and the Classics IV.

During a five-year period beginning in 1968, they had thirteen consecutive chart singles, including three that reached Number Two nationally, and an album that remained in the Top Fifty for twenty weeks.

With Yost's vocals, and the sensational songwriting and production talents of J. R. Cobb and Buddy Buie, who went on to found the even more successful Atlanta Rhythm Section, the group was one of the most popular soft-rock sounds of the late sixties and was featured on most major television network shows. It had several highly acclaimed European tours before Yost went back to Florida to go into business.

As lead singer and drummer, with his high school classmate Wally Eaton as rhythm guitarist and songwriter, Yost established his rock group in Jacksonville in 1962 and switched to Atlanta to take advantage of the growing popular recording business there. By 1967, with Cobb on lead guitar, they gained a club following and recorded the Cobb-Buie classic "Spooky," which scored hits both as a single and as an album of the same title the following year.

Although Cobb and Buie left to pursue their individual and collective careers, they continued to write and produce for the group billed as Dennis Yost and the Classics IV after realignment with the singing of Auburn Burrell as guitarist and Dean Daugherty as keyboardist. Their "Spooky," which became the Number One hit of 1968, sold more than two million copies and was followed by two more Cobb-Buie best-sellers, "Traces" and "Every Day with You, Girl."

From 1968 to 1970, the group was one of the hottest and most sought after in the country; they appeared on *American Bandstand* and the *Tonight, David Frost,* and *Mike Douglas* shows and were honored by a party given by Nancy Sinatra.

In 1970 they changed record labels from the Imperial to the Liberty/VA and then to MGM, and, in a two-year period, had hit singles with "The Funniest Things," "Midnight," "Where Did All the Good Times

Go," "It's Time for Love" and "What Am I Crying For" as well as top albums titled "Traces" and "Golden Greats—Vol. 1."

Tiring of the pressures, depressed by the departure of talented associates to the Cobb-Buie organization, and searching for a less complicated lifestyle, Yost disbanded the group in 1972 and returned to Florida to indulge his passion for fishing and to go into the retail floor covering business.

However, by 1977 he decided singing was in his blood and organized another group to play the Holiday Inn circuit, to cut albums of "oldies" for television marketing, and to try a comeback with Robox Records for which, in May 1981, he issued the album *Going through the Motions,* featuring the title song by Hal Bynum, the coauthor of "Lucille." In his search for a second musical career as a solo artist, he billed himself as "The Classic One."

Dennis Yost and the Classic IV was inducted into the Georgia Music Hall of Fame in 1993.

Dennis Yost and the Classics IV (top: Kim Venable,
Wally Eaton; bottom: J. R. Cobb, Yost, and Joe Wilson)

AND MANY MORE . . .

The overriding dilemma of anyone undertaking to list the greats in any field is not whom to include but whom to omit. There are always more success stories than can be told within the limits of a single printed volume. This is especially true in the field of music. Determining which of the many talented individuals whose contributions to Georgia's musical greatness should have sections in this book was particularly difficult.

In this chapter I want to list those worthy of inclusion on any list of Georgia musicians and to whom I would have devoted more detailed sketches had space and time permitted. But, before doing that, there are several special Georgians of whom I wish to make separate mention because, while not musicians themselves, their many contributions to Georgia Music are deserving of particular recognition.

Don Rhodes has been of immense help to me both with the first edition and with this revised one. He has worked to correct errors, asked probing questions, and submitted sketches and many names of those persons he thought should be included. I'm deeply grateful for this. Don is the publications editor of Morris Communications Corporation in Augusta and the longest running country music columnist in America. His weekly "Ramblin' Rhodes" column marked its twenty-fifth anniversary in October of 1995. He has authored stories for *Country Music Magazine*, *Music City News*, *Bluegrass Unlimited*, *Pickin'*, and *Frets* national magazines. In 1995 he was asked to write entries for the Country Music Association's books about country and bluegrass music. He was inducted into the Atlanta Country Music Hall of Fame and has been nominated several times to the Georgia Music Hall of Fame. He has authored several songs including "Bluegrass Music All the Time," sung on the Grand Ole Opry House stage. The introductions for his book, *Down Country Roads with Ramblin' Rhodes*, were written by Minnie Pearl, Barbara Mandrell, and Brenda Lee.

Russ DeVault, **Bill King**, and **Steve Dollar**, three very talented writers with the Atlanta Newspapers, have reported in depth on the Georgia music scene for many years.

With his pen, **J. Garland Pembroke** (Jack Tarver, Jr.), has opened the door of country music to many who would not otherwise have read about it.

Lee Walburn, present editor of *Atlanta Magazine*, has written some of the best country music columns I've ever read, as did our friend, Lewis Grizzard, who also tried his hand at songwriting.

Billy Dilworth, newspaper columnist, for more than thirty years has emceed a country music show on radio and television stations in Northeast Georgia and has consistently won awards as one of the nation's top country disc jockeys.

Paul Hemphill, Atlanta author, whose book, *The Nashville Sound,* was one of the first good books on country music.

The late **Jim Wilder** of Marietta, the owner until his death in 1982 of country music station WBIE in Marietta, was beloved by all country music artists for his continuing support of the business and for his understanding and generosity in encouraging and giving free air time to new songwriters and performers.

In making the above and following listing, I acknowledge that un-doubtedly many others should be on the list, and I urge readers to let me know of omissions. And now alphabetically, here are some very notable Georgia artists.

Rhett Akins is one of Nashville's most talented new "hunks." But he has more than the physique of a football player—which he was at Valdosta High and the University of Georgia. He can also write and sing with the best of them. His debut album on Decca Records was A *Thousand Memories,* and he wrote every song on it except one. Among them are "Old Dirt Road," about a road in Brooks County; "My Truck," a true story of finding another guy's truck in his girlfriend's driveway; "Those Hands," about his grandmother; "She Said Yes," about a shy boy getting a date; and "Kay Brought My Guitar Back Today," about a couple breaking up.

Dorothy Alexander, Georgia's grand dame of the dance world, was the founder of the Atlanta Ballet, the oldest continuous dance company in America.

Bobby and **Mac Atcheson** of Atlanta, fiddle and steel guitar duo, played for WSB on both Radio Barn Dance and with the WSB-TV Peachtree Cowboys, and subsequently worked as scenic designer and floor manager respectively for WSB-TV.

Atlanta, a country music group that has scored early success with two Top Twenty hits, was nominated by the Country Music Association in 1984 for Group of the Year.

Avalanche is a popular North Georgia bluegrass band that has head-lined concerts throughout the state. The band consists of bassist Chris Black, fiddler David Blackmon (a veteran of Jerry Reed's band and a member of Mercury Records act, the Normaltown Flyers), mandolinist Doug Flowers, banjoist Eddie Hoyle, and guitarist Jim Iler.

Doce and **Lucy Barnes** of Athens exemplify the vitality of black sacred singing in the South and have performed for decades throughout the area. Doc played on a "quill," an instrument made from a reed, notched and tuned with wood plugs, and used by slaves on the antebellum plantations.

Marcus Bartlett of Atlanta, retired Cox Broadcasting Company execu-tive, was staff pianist, organist, and member of the staff orchestra of radio station WSB. He also retired from a second career as professor of broadcast journalism at the University of Georgia Henry W. Grady School of Journalism and Mass Communication.

Debbie Bass was a local star in Atlanta nightclubs for a long time.

Edgar W. (Puddinghead) Battle was an outstanding musician and composer born in Atlanta in the early 1900s. He organized the Cosmopoli-tan Record Company that specialized in recording and releasing works of outstanding black musicians who did not have the opportunity to record with larger white companies. Some of the artists who performed his works were Fats Waller, Count Basie, and Cab Calloway.

Danny Beard of Atlanta, is co-owner with British partner Peter Dyer of independent Atlanta recording label DB Records, specializing in recording the "Athens Sound" of bands like Pylon, B-52s, Love Tractors, and Swimming Pool Qs.

Jackey Beavers of Cartersville, was a successful songwriter for Motown Records. He wrote the Supreme's hit, "Some Day, We'll Be Together."

William Bell, based in Atlanta, penned the classic "Born under a Bad Sign" and in the 1960s worked with all the great blues singers out of Memphis. Rod Stewart, Lou Rawls, Albert King, and others have recorded his tunes.

Thomas Greene Bethune or "Blind Tom" was the first black pianist to win national fame. He was born a slave in Columbus in 1849. A Colonel Bethune purchased him when he was a baby and soon recognized that Tom was a child prodigy. He made his debut in Savannah and for more than forty years amazed audiences all over the world. He had total recall of more than 700 songs and composed many himself. He died in 1909.

Buddy Blackmon of Washington, was a former player in the bluegrass group Rocky Mountain Strings and former leader of Jerry Reed's band. He cowrote Randy Travis's first hit, "1982."

Lee L. Blair was a banjoist and guitarist who was born in Savannah, Georgia, in 1903, and played with Charlie Skeets and Louis Armstrong.

Brenda Boozer, a mezzosoprano who is as famous in Europe as in her native Atlanta, debuted with the Metropolitan Opera Company in 1979.

Roger Bowling of Dillard was a major country songwriter who wrote "Lucille," "The Coward of the County," "Blanket on the Ground," and other hits before his death in 1983.

Helen Bickers, young Atlanta soprano and finalist in Metropolitan Opera auditions, sang in *Carmen* with the Summer Opera Theater Company in Washington, D.C.

B-52s is an Athens rock 'n' roll dance group that recorded the single "Rock Lobster" with DB Records of Atlanta. This led to a major recording contract with Warner Brothers Records and then later with Reprise Records. The band includes members Fred Schneider, Cindy Wilson, Keith Strickland, and Kate Pierson. Other hits by this dynamic group include: "Love Shack," "Hot Pants Explosion," "Dreamline," "Good Stuff," "Revolution Earth," "The World's Green Laughter," and "Breezin'."

The Blue Sky Boys, **Earl** and **Bill Bolick**, with their haunting and unique harmony, although not from Georgia, appeared all over the state and recorded for Bluebird, the early Victor label.

McHenry Boatwright, a baritone soloist who toured the United States and Europe, was born in Washington County, Georgia, in 1928. He received his training at the New England Conservatory of Music and appeared with the New York Philharmonic and the Philadelphia Symphony Orchestras.

Catherine Boswell was a blues singer and recording artist of note in the 1920s and 1930s in Atlanta. She was another popular WSB star.

Steve Brantley of Augusta is a well-known Nashville session musician and backup player for Barbara Mandrell and Ronnie Milsap.

Harold J. Brown was a notable music teacher, composer, and arranger who was born in Shellman, Georgia. He taught at a number of colleges in Florida and the Midwest. His choral works include "The African Chief" and a collection of spirituals published in 1925.

Lillian Brown or "Lillyn" as she was known by many, was born in Fulton Country, Georgia, in 1885. Her father was Indian, and her mother an African-American. When she was a teenager, she toured in vaudeville and performed with the Queen City Minstrels tent show as a singer and dancer. She was often billed as the Youngest Interlocutor in the World.

Uze Brown, a member of the Morehouse College faculty, has been a frequent soloist with the Atlanta Symphony and has arranged spirituals for renowned soprano Jessye Norman.

W. Gary Bruce, of Trion, at eighty-five years of age was invited to pick old timey banjo at the Smithsonian Festival of American Folklife in Washington, D.C. He also did some ballad singing, told a few tall tales, and recited a few bawdy toasts learned from his Scottish and Irish ancestors.

Jimmy Bryant, in the 1950s, was one of the most recorded guitarists in the world. One of twelve children, he was born to a sharecropper in Moultrie, Georgia, in 1925. Wounded in World War II, he learned how to play the guitar while recuperating. Later he made his way to Hollywood and became an extra in movies and played the guitar in bars at night. He met Speedy West, the great steel guitarist, and they did a lot of innovative, complex instrumentals. He was a sought-after session musician and had hits himself: "Stratosphere Boogie" and "Whistle Stop." He also wrote "The Only Daddy That Will Walk the Line" for Waylon Jennings. He moved to Nashville in the 1970s, discovered he had lung cancer, and returned to Georgia to live until his death in 1983.

The Burch Sisters have had several excellent albums on the Mercury label. These South Georgia artists had a big hit single and video, "Old Flame, New Fire," produced by the talented Doug Johnson, another Georgian.

Bill Carlisle is a legendary Opry star who played in his early years in Atlanta and on WSB.

Flo Carter was one of the first rockabilly singers and became nationally known as a highly successful gospel artist with such hits as "He Said He Would" and "Mama Please Don't Cry (I'm with Jesus)." She sang with Brenda Lee and in the 1950s had a daily TV show with Jim Nabors on WJBF television in Augusta.

Pete Cassell was an early Jim Reeves-type who sang and performed on WSB radio and was very popular throughout the South.

Cedar Hill is an Atlanta-based bluegrass group that won the McIntosh Country Music Award in 1981. An album, *Ruff 'n' Ready*, did well.

Steve Chappell is one of Augusta's most popular entertainers and packs them in at the Honky Tonk. His biggest claim to fame is that he was the winner of the National Elvis Impersonation contest in Memphis, Tennessee.

Lew Childre was a popular country comedian and Hawaiian-style guitarist on Atlanta radio during the 1930s and 1940s before moving on to the Grand Ole Opry where he was a regular for many years.

Edgar Rogie Clark, a singer, composer, and arranger, was born in Atlanta and graduated from Clark College. He served as the chairman of the music department at Fort Valley State College and director of the Harlan Recreation Center in New York City.

Wayne Cochran, white rock and soul singer, lived in various parts of Middle and South Georgia before hitting it big on the Las Vegas circuit with his group, the C. C. Riders.

Grady and **Hazel Cole** were Atlanta recording stars in the 1930s and 1940s. Grady was also a successful songwriter, his best known song being the classic "Tramp on the Street."

Peter David Conlon, a native Atlantan, is president of Concert/Southern Promotions, one of the South's premier entertainment promotion companies. Among the musical events he has personally coordinated are the Atlanta Jazz Festival and the Montreaux Music Festival. His company has also jointly promoted and produced the Chastain Park Summer Concerts, a nationally renowned series bringing to Atlanta some of the world's most famous acts. One of his greatest feats was organizing and setting up the 1989 Rolling Stones concert. He got his start at age twenty-six when he organized benefit concerts across the country for President Jimmy Carter's 1980 reelection campaign.

Alex Cooley has been involved in most of the big musical events that have happened in Atlanta during the last thirty years. In 1968, the Atlanta Pop Festival, the first major rock event in the South, attracted 700,000 people, and the Champagne Jam later drew more than 100,000. He operated the Alex Cooley's Electric Ballroom and the Great Southeast Music Hall, which hosted the likes of Steve Martin, Jimmy Buffet, and Bruce Springsteen. He became a member of the Georgia Music Hall of Fame in 1987.

Alex Cooley

Cousin Emmy, a star on WSB Radio in the 1930s and 1940s before she moved on to St. Louis, was one of the first female country music artists to have her own band. She had a national reputation and was a great fiddler who could also play banjo and guitar. In addition she had a "show-stopper" where she blew up a rubber glove and then played "You Are My

Sunshine" on it as she let out the air. During the folk music revival of the sixties, she made a big comeback performing for a new urban audience. She appeared in some western movies and first brought the song "Ruby" to national attention.

Dock D. Crawford was a musician and educator born in Norcross, Georgia. He taught in numerous colleges around the country, and many of his students played in the bands of Lionel Hampton, Count Basie, Bennie Carter, and other notables.

Mike Curb is a Savannah, Georgia, native, born there in 1944, who has made it big in both Los Angeles and Nashville. He was a twenty-year-old boy wonder who made a big splash with the Madison Avenue and Hollywood types when he created the Honda jingle, "You Meet the Nicest People on a Honda." He took over the MGM label in 1970 and hit it big with a youthful audience with Donny and Marie Osmond. He also entered politics and was elected lieutenant governor of California. Later he moved to Nashville and started Curb Records, where he has been successful with Sawyer Brown, the Bellamy Brothers, Debbie Boone, and others. He has also been involved in the success of the Judds.

Crossroads was a leading Augusta rock band of the mid-1970s that featured Robbie Ducey, Jimmy Burch, and the late Tommy Witcher, who also founded the Georgia Prophets.

Raoul J. Daggett, a native of Augusta, has sung in both the Metropolitan Opera House and Carnegie Hall.

Wayne Daniel, a professor at Georgia State University, is a prolific bluegrass and country music writer. His "Pickin on Peachtree" is an excellent work.

Tom Darby, born in Columbus, Georgia, in 1884, joined with South Carolinian Jimmy Tarlton to make up the pair of Darby and Tarlton, the two most famous white blues men of the 1920s. In 1927, they had a two-sided hit, "Birmingham Jail" and "Columbus Stockade Blues." It sold more than 200,000 copies—a megahit at that time.

Paul Davis is from Mississippi but made Atlanta his home for several years. Singer, songwriter, keyboardist, and coproducer with Ed Seay, he has many pop hits like "I Go Crazy," "Cool Night," "Sweet Life," and "65 Love Affair." He rarely tours and doesn't record too often, but his talent is recognized universally. In 1984, he was named Top Male Vocalist at the first Atlanta Music Awards.

Danny Dawson is a black country singer along the lines of Charley Pride. He is managed by Terry Jennings, son of Waylon. He also fronts the

Georgia Heartbeat that has appeared on the Nashville Network with Waylon and Alan Jackson.

Billy Dean, Nashville artist, big in height and talent, got his first major break when he came up from Florida and won a True Value talent contest in Valdosta.

Bruce Dees of Augusta, is a well-known Nashville session musician and backup player for Barbara Mandrell and Ronnie Milsap.

Mike Dekel, from Athens, was recognized as Songwriter of the Year in 1983. He wrote "Scarlet Fever" for Kenny Rogers and numerous other hits for various artists.

John Dilleshaw recorded on the early Okeh label and was a popular guitarist and performer on WSB in the 1920s and 1930s.

Joey Douglas of Douglasville, a singer who was born Joanne Blodgett, has been successful as a club singer in Atlanta, Las Vegas, and on the West Coast with a crossover sound combining pop, country, and rock.

Reese LaMarr Dupree wrote "Shortenin' Bread," "You're Always Mine," "Friendless Blues," and many others. This Macon native was born in 1884 and is probably most famous for building the Roseland Ballroom in 1922.

Elmo Ellis was given the Mary Tallent Pioneer award in 1995 for his nearly four decades as the program director and manager of WSB, where he encouraged many artists and helped make their songs into hits. He was an author, (*Opportunities in Broadcasting*) and a songwriter ("They Locked God Outside the Iron Curtain").

Ray Eberly, one of the top male vocalists of the Big Band era, lived in Georgia after his retirement and was buried here after his death. He was named to the Georgia Music Hall of Fame in 1995.

The Eller Brothers, **Lawrence** and **Vaughn**, with their partner on the fiddle, **Ross Brown**, lived in Towns County but took their traditional Appalachian music repertoire of two hundred songs to the Smithsonian in Washington, D.C., and the Edinburgh International Festival in Scotland, where they stole the show.

Phil and **Nancy Erickson** founded the Wits End Players and created some of the zaniest songs, satire, and skits found anywhere. They not only heard Georgia singing, they kept Georgia laughing for twenty-five years.

Leon Everette, who at one time lived in Oglethorpe County, was nominated for a Grammy for his "The World's Greatest Star Has Gone Home," and had such hits as "Giving Up Easy," "Don't Feel Like the Lone Ranger," "Over," and "Hurricane."

Betty Fisher's Dixie Bluegrass Band has performed at bluegrass festivals across the country and on the Grand Ole Opry stage.

Jim Fogelsong, a president of MCA Records, played guitar in Augusta's Broad Street USO while stationed at Fort Gordon and signed Terri Gibbs to her MCA recording contract.

Tony Ford, a Young Harris resident known as "The Piano Kid," has been playing and singing since the age of seven. He has averaged two hundred appearances a year, including trips to Mexico and Canada, even before leaving high school. He sings a variety of music and plays piano, drums, saxophone, and harmonica. He has been seen on the *Star Search*, *The Statler Brothers*, *Joan Rivers*, and *Crook & Chase* TV shows, and has torn up the crowds at Nashville's annual Fan Fair celebration.

Jerry Foster, singer and award-winning country music songwriter, first performed on station WSAV-TV and at the Bamboo Ranch in Savannah while stationed with the Marine Corps at Paris Island, South Carolina. He went on to write hits like "When You Say Love" for Sonny and Cher, "Would You Take Another Chance on Me" for Jerry Lee Lewis, and "The Easy Part's Over" for Charley Pride.

Kelly Foxton of Athens was a country singer who was born Joyce Sanders. Under the name Dixie Lee, she was the star baton twirler for Georgia Tech. She then became the singing partner of country music great Hank Snow for four years. Besides the Opry, she appeared on *Hee Haw* and *Nashville Now*.

Randall Franks is seen regularly on television on the *In the Heat of the Night* series, but he first became known as a very talented fiddler with Bill Monroe and Jim and Jesse. He also had his own band, Peachtree Pickers, and has produced a very good Christmas album featuring singing by the *In the Heat of the Night* cast.

Georgia, a Gainesville-based group, in 1984 was voted the Most Promising Male Group of the Year by the Southern Gospel Music Association. Members include **Mike David, Terry Dale, Lee Burke**, and **Phil Satterfield**.

The Georgia Mountain Fair has for more than forty years provided excellent music in Hiawassee, which is billed as the Country Music Capital of Georgia. The legendary **Fiddlin' Howard Cunningham** has been in charge of the event. He began with local musicians playing under a tree on a hill; he then moved the show to the high school auditorium and then to a big tent; now performances are held in the comfortable million-dollar Robert Anderson Music Hall on Lake Chatuge.

Pop Eckler and the Younguns were big stars in Georgia as members of WSB's Cross Roads Follies. Their most popular recording was "Money, Marbles, and Chalk."

Edwin Gerschefski, a noted composer and performer, is a professor of music at the University of Georgia.

Wycliffe Gordon grew up in Waynesboro and Augusta. He is the trombonist with jazz artist Wynton Marsalis and can be heard on many of this septet's albums.

Warren Gowers of Augusta is a well-known Nashville session musician, member of Terri Gibbs' original trio, and former backup player for Barbara Mandrell and Ronnie Milsap.

A. A. "Ahaz" Gray was a legendary fiddler who appeared on WSB radio and Okeh Records. Between 1919 and 1938, he won the Georgia fiddling championship eight times.

Mike Greene has been president of NARAS, the National Academy of Recording Arts and Sciences and a leader in the annual Georgia Music Festival.

Cortez Greer rose from baggage handler for Delta Air Lines to be a star rock and soul singer known as "Tez" before his accidental death from carbon monoxide poisoning in 1976.

Fred Guy, a Burkeville, Georgia, native, was a guitarist with the Duke Ellington band from the 1920s through the 1940s.

Conner Hall was born in South Carolina but joined the great Georgia gospel group, the LeFevres, in 1943. He also was an original member and manager of another great Georgia group, the Homeland Harmony quartet. He was inducted into the Gospel Hall of Fame in 1979.

Fredrick Douglas Hall was the founder of the Association of Music Teachers in Negro Schools. An Atlanta native, he attended Clark College and later taught there. He also taught at Morris Brown College.

Theresa Hamm, at twenty years of age, was awarded the Most Promising Young Singer award at the Metropolitan Opera Southeastern National Auditions in 1983. She is from Conyers, Georgia.

Bob Hannah, an Atlanta actor, played Patsy Cline's husband in *Coal Miner's Daughter* and Nick Nolte's stepfather in *Prince of Tides*.

Linda Hargrove was born in Florida but lived with her grandmother in Macon for several years. Not only did she later write a song about that experience, but this very talented singer and songwriter wrote "Tennessee Whiskey" for George Jones; "Just Get up and Close the Door" for John

Rodriguez; and others for the likes of Olivia Newton John, Julie Andrews, and Dionne Warwick.

Lucille Hegamin, also known as Fannie Baker, was born in Macon in 1894. She toured with the Leonard Harper Minstrel Stock Company as a singer. She entertained throughout the country before finally settling in Chicago where she was billed as the "Georgia Peach" in clubs throughout the area.

Horace Henderson, the brother of Fletcher Henderson, was born in Cuthbert, Georgia. He composed many songs including "Dear Old Southland" and "I Found a New Baby." He worked closely with band leader Benny Goodman.

John Hill Hewitt, called the "Bard of the Confederacy" and "the father of the American ballad," was born in New York in 1801 and came South to Augusta about 1820 to join his father's theatrical troupe. It failed, but Hewitt stayed on to teach music. He moved to South Carolina briefly before returning to Augusta in the mid-1820s, where he published his first and famous ballad, "The Minstrel's Return from War." He moved North in 1827 and worked on various newspapers and taught school. He founded philharmonic groups in Norfolk and Richmond, Virginia, and moved to Savannah in 1863, where he taught music. He wrote more than 300 songs, published several cantatas, and wrote more than fifty dramatic works under various pseudonyms. He died in Baltimore.

Jack Higginbotham, jazz trombonist from Atlanta, played with Fletcher Henderson and Louis Armstrong.

Yvonne Hodger of Metter has been a backup singer for Lynn Anderson, Reba McEntire, Janie Fricke, and Spanish singer Clay Corelli.

Hugh Hodgson founded the University of Georgia music department and was its chairman for many years. He composed the "Bulldog Fight Song," but he did much more than that for a generation of students who had their musical horizons broadened by this remarkable man who died in 1969. He was a pianist, an organist, and an arranger. He had a talent for explaining music to those with no previous understanding. Ralph McGill called him "Johnny Appleseed of Music in Georgia."

Greg Holland is a Warner Brothers artist best known for a big single and a successful video, "When I Come Back I Want to Be My Dog." Another hit single for this Douglas, Georgia, native was "Slide Over Honey (and Let Me Drive)."

Randy Howard is a musician from Milledgeville who has taken top honors throughout the South in bluegrass festival contests.

Dean Hudson of Atlanta was a leader of one of the larger and better known big bands of the pre- and post-World War II.

Larry G. Hudson, a country singer born in Hawkinsville and raised in Unadilla, charted singles "Just Out of Reach" (with Willie Nelson in the Capricorn Studio in Macon), "Loving You Is a Natural High," "I Can't Cheat," and "I'm Still in Love with You."

Elizabeth Maddox Huntley of Eaton, Georgia, composed the song "Behold Thy Mother," which was voted as the official Mother's Day song in 1951 by the U.S. Congress.

Ed Hurst, fiddler from Augusta, has emceed the world's largest bluegrass festival at Union Grove, North Carolina, and several other festivals throughout Georgia.

Graham Jackson

Graham Jackson lived in Atlanta from 1924 until his death in 1983. He taught at Washington High School and performed at Pittypat's Porch for years. What made this versatile musician known around the world was his role as President Franklin Delano Roosevelt's favorite musician. Jackson hung out with him and played at the Little White House at Warm Springs. He became world famous when he appeared on the cover of *Life* magazine playing the accordian at FDR's death. He was inducted into the Georgia Music Hall of Fame in 1985.

Harry James

Harry James, one of the most popular big band leaders and trumpeters in the big band era was a Georgian. That's right, he was born in Albany, Georgia, where his family came through with the Mighty Haig circus. He once had Frank Sinatra in one of his bands, did dozens of successful recordings, and was on the *Jerry Lewis Television Show*. He was inducted into the Georgia Music Hall of Fame in 1983 posthumously.

Willis Laurence James was on the faculties of Leland College in Baker, Louisiana, where he wrote Leland's "Alma Mater," and of Alabama State Teachers College in Montgomery, where he wrote the school's fight song. He directed the Spelman College Glee Club and the Morehouse College Band in Atlanta. He became chairman of Spelman's music department and director of the Atlanta-Morehouse-Spelman Chorus. In 1940, he cofounded the Fort Valley State College Folk Music Festival, an annual event that continued for fifteen years. He became a recording fellow for the Library of Congress, and his field recordings are contained in the library's archives of folk songs. Before his death in 1966 he was a lecturer and panelist at the Newport Jazz Festival and the Newport Folk Festival.

Neal James, a native of Commerce and a favorite around Athens for years, had a nationally recognized album, *Living and Loving*, and a hit single, "Hurricane Shoals."

Hugh Jarrett, the disc jockey on many stations over the years, was with the excellent gospel group, the Jordanaires, who provided the backup on many of the Elvis Presley recordings.

Sammy Johns, another very successful member of the Lowery Group, had a hit record, "Chevy Van," in 1974, selling close to three million copies and going to Number Two in the national charts. "Early Morning Love" and "Rag Doll" were mid-chart singles. With Elektra Records, his singles "Common Man" and "Love Me Off the Road" garnered considerable pop and country air play. The former song later became a smash for John Conlee.

Bobby Johnson and the Swinging Gentlemen for years entertained audiences all over Georgia, particularly at the old WPLO Shower of Stars programs and the Georgia Mountain Fair in Hiawassee. Regulars included **Jerry Hall**, and **Houston** and **James Childers**.

Hall Johnson wrote songs that will live forever: "Sometimes I Feel Like a Motherless Child," "Roll Jerd'n Roll," "I've Been Buked." His choir performed for the Broadway shows *The Green Pastures* and *Run Little Children*. It has been said that he was the first Negro to organize a professional chorus that received international fame. He was born in Athens, Georgia in 1888.

Bessi Jones grew up in Southeast Georgia in Terrell County. There she learned many traditional songs as a child, which she later used as the lead vocalist for the Georgia Sea Island Singers, the renowned coastal folk group.

Rubarb Jones for over a decade has played records, told jokes, waxed philosophical, and promoted country music and humanitarian projects every morning on radio station Y106. Countless industry awards have been bestowed upon him including Disc Jockey of the Year by the Academy of Country Music in 1983, Broadcast Personality of the Year by the Country Music Association in 1987, and Country Radio Air Personality by *Billboard* in 1988 and 1989. In 1991 he was inducted into the Atlanta Country Music Hall of Fame.

Samuel Porter Jones was born in 1847 and died in 1906. The only singing Jones did probably was at his theatrical evangelistic crusades, but he inspired the building of the place that became world famous as the "Mother Church of Country Music." Alabama-born Jones was a lawyer with a drinking problem. He promised his dad on his deathbed that he would reform and become a pastor with the North Georgia Conference of the Methodist Episcopal Church. He led huge revivals throughout the nation from his life-long home base in Cartersville, Georgia. One revival converted a river boat captain, Thomas Ryman, who built a tabernacle in downtown Nashville for Jones in the late 1800s. The church became a theater and then the home of the Grand Ole Opry in 1941. It remained the Opry's home until 1974 when the show cast moved to Opryland. Ryman Auditorium, now remodeled, is often used for concerts. The Nashville Network cable TV system remembered the reason for its founding in creating the *Sam's Place* program for gospel music performances by Opry members and other music stars.

Archie Jordan, country song writer who was born in Augusta and lived eight years in Metter, wrote the hits "What a Difference You Made in My Life" and "Let's Take the Long Way around the World" for Ronnie Milsap, "Drifter" for Sylvia, and "It's All I Can Do" for Anne Murray.

Carole Joyner of Decatur composed, with Ric Carty, the hit song "Young Love," which has sold more than fifteen million copies. She also wrote smash hits for four artists: Sonny James, Tab Hunter, Lesley Gore, and Donny Osmond.

Gwen Kesler was inducted into the Georgia Music Hall of Fame in 1994, and well she should have been. This Carnesville native managed King Records and owned Tara Records. She was instrumental in James Brown signing his first contract and opened doors for many artists.

Tom Key is known internationally for his award-winning off-Broadway musical hit, *Cotton Patch Gospel,* which he conceived and coauthored with the late songwriter Harry Chapin. Based on Clarence Jordan's distinctive present-day, South-Georgia version of the New Testament, this jubilant retelling of the gospel story has won numerous awards and was the subject of an NBC special. A highly acclaimed actor, Key has made numerous film and television appearances and continues to hear Georgia singing with productions such as *Appalachian Christmas Homecoming.*

Harpo Kidwell of Atlanta was the harmonica-playing "Kentucky Colonel" on the original Barn Dance of Atlanta's radio station WSB.

Chick Kimball of Atlanta was a star of the original Barn Dance on Atlanta's radio station WSB and was particularly known for his Wildroot Hair Tonic commercials.

Ron Kimball had a large following for many years playing his special brand of country-rock in the metro area.

Chuck Leavell, who lives in Twiggs County, Georgia, on his tree farm, has made music all over the world with many of the superstars of the musical world. He was a key member with the Allman Brothers in Macon and later formed Sea Level, a band that released several successful albums in the late 1970s. In 1982 he joined the Rolling Stones in their "Tatoo You" tour in Europe. Later he recorded *Dirty Work,* an album with the Stones, and coauthored "Back to Zero" with Mick Jagger and Keith Richards. In 1986 he was chosen to play with Jagger on his first solo album *She's the Boss.* The next year he was chosen by Keith Richards to be a member of Chuck Berry's all star backup band for the movie *Hail, Hail Rock 'n' Roll* and Aretha Franklin's hit single and video "Jumpin' Jack Flash." In the 1990s he was still touring with the Stones all over the world, and with Eric Clapton. That's him on keyboards on the Stones' *Voodoo Lounge* and *Stripped.* It's not all rock either. He's played with Kitty Welles and was in Hank Williams Jr.'s breakthrough album *Friends.*

Calvin Lewis is a classical violinist who was born in Augusta and whose parents live in Hephzibah. He is also a nephew of the Lewis Family from Lincolnton. He played in the American-Soviet Youth Orchestra and with the New York String Orchestra in Carnegie Hall in 1988.

The Li'l General and General Cloggers perform in harmony with the goal of preserving the rich heritage of mountain folk culture. They dance the authentic mountain "clog" and have performed on the Grand Ole Opry many times.

Sonny Limbo of Atlanta is a songwriter and record producer who cowrote the Gladys Knight hit, "Midnight Train to Georgia," with Jim Weatherly and the Bertie Higgins's hit, "Key Largo," with Higgins. Before coming to Atlanta, he worked with Sun Records in Memphis, where he helped produce recordings by Elvis Presley, Jerry Lee Lewis, and Carl Perkins. He was then with Fame Studios in Muscle Shoals, Alabama, where he worked with Rick Hall and became executive president of that firm.

LaWanda Lindsey started singing on her father's country music radio station in Savannah when she was only five years old. Discovered at the age of fourteen by Conway Twitty's business manager, she signed her first recording contract with Chart Records and moved to Nashville. Her first record, "Beggars Can't Be Choosers," and all of her thirty-seven singles released through 1975 charted in all three trade magazines, and her duet, "Wild Mountain Berries," with Kenny Vernon, reached the highest levels. When invited by Buck Owens to succeed Susan Raye as the featured singer with the Buckaroos, she moved to Bakersfield, California, in the mid-1970s and switched to recording for Capitol Records, which issued her hits "Today Will Be the First Day of My Life," "Sunshine Feeling," "Hello Trouble," "Hello Out There," and "I Ain't Hangin' Round."

Mosie Lister worked in Georgia in the 1940s and 1950s, and in 1976 was elected to the Gospel Music Hall of Fame. He is not related to Hovie, another famous name in Gospel music, but did work some with the Statesmen. He wrote many songs, including "How Long Has It Been?" "Then I Met the Master," and "Till the Storm Passes By." He was also involved in the music publishing business.

Buddy Livingston had a popular Savannah band that at one time included Billy Joe Royal, Joe South, and Ray Stevens.

Charles Mann, singer, actor, and composer, has had his work recorded by B. B. King, Roberta Flack, Donny Hataway, and others. He has made television appearances on *Soul Train* and *The Mike Douglas Show*. He directed the music for the Atlanta production of *The Wiz* and has composed a musical entitled *Savannah*.

Mario Martin is a young Georgian from Bonaire who at age seventeen had a single, "Keep It on the Country Side," that did well. Mae Boren Axton, author of *Heartbreak Hotel* became interested in him when she heard one of his tapes, but urged him to finish high school before going to Nashville. He did and then ended up in the National finals of the 1990 True Value talent contest.

Lowell Mason (1792-1872), organist and music director at Savannah's Independent Presbyterian Church, published his first collection of music in Georgia. He became a nationally recognized leader in promoting good church music and a solid music education for all children. He wrote and arranged more than 1,200 hymns including "Nearer My God to Thee" and "My Faith Looks up to Thee."

Melanie Massell of Atlanta, daughter of former Atlanta mayor Sam Massell, is a nightclub singer in the modes of Bette Midler, Patsy Cline, and Pat Benetar.

Anita Sorralls Wheeler Mathis was Georgia fiddle champion in 1934, the first and only woman to win that honor. Her artistry was recognized throughout the South in the 1930s.

Tim McCabe, one of the leaders in the music industry in Georgia, makes money writing commercial jingles for leading businesses but is best known for his sensitive "Springtime in Atlanta" and other songs about Georgia, its people, and places.

Thelma "Butterfly" McQueen of Augusta, acclaimed for her role as Prissy in *Gone With the Wind,* also performed the role of "Queenie" in traveling productions of the musical *Showboat,* and had an opening role in *The Wiz* on Broadway. She died in a fire in 1996 in her home in Augusta.

"Blind Willie" McTell

Willis Samuel "Blind Willie" McTell, called "one of the greatest twelve-string guitar players of all time" was born in McDuffie County and lived in Statesboro, Georgia. He wrote "Statesboro Blues," which later became a hit for the Allman Brothers. In 1981 he received a posthumous Grammy nomination for his 1933 album *Atlanta Blues.* This great blues singer, writer, and musician died in 1959 and was buried back home in McDuffie County where he is remembered each year with a musical festival. He was made a member of the Georgia Music Hall of Fame in 1990.

Bob Melton is a Metter, Georgia, entertainer who toured with Gary Stewart's band for years and cowrote songs with him. He was also a good friend of fellow Georgian Gram Parsons. He cowrote with Dean Dillion "Whiskey Ain't the Answer," a big song for superstar George Straight.

Jesse Mercer, for whom Mercer University is named, was a hymn writer and publisher of hymnals. To meet the need for hymn books in the early 1800s, he collected "spiritual songs, divine hymns, and sacred poems" in a volume known as *The Cluster.* The hymn book went through numerous editions and revisions and by 1829 had sold more than 33,000 copies. The student newspaper at Mercer University, *The Mercer Cluster*, is named for this hymnal.

Leonard Boyd "Snuffy" Miller was an Atlanta-born drummer for Bill Anderson, Dottie West, and Nat Stuckey. He was also a producer of MCA Records albums and hit singles for Mary Lou Turner, Kenny Starr, Jerry Clower, and Bill Monroe.

Leroy Miller of Macon had a song, "Hook Me, Then Reel Me In," that got in Billboard's Top One Hundred charts.

Paul Mitchell headed a jazz trio that entertained Atlantans at Dante's Down the Hatch for many years.

Ruth Mitchell, a veteran of Broadway musicals, is credited with introducing jazz dance to Atlanta. She is from Decatur.

Henry (Hank) Mobley is a tenor saxophonist from Eastman, Georgia, with the technique of Charles Parker. Mobley performed with many of the greats including Dizzy Gillespie and Max Roach.

James Moody of Savannah, Georgia, was a fine jazz artist who toured Europe, had his own band, and recorded several albums, including the most popular *I'm in the Mood for Love*.

Jeff Mosier is much more than just a fine bluegrass musician who performs with the band Good Medicine. He has also produced and hosted the popular radio show, Born in a Barn, on WRFG FM, and the Great Southwest Music Show, on WQXI AM, which featured a mix of American-roots music, including bluegrass, vintage country, traditional American folk, old-time string band, and gospel. In 1993, Jeff produced and hosted the WSB Barndance Reunion, which showcased radio entertainers who were popular in the 1930s and 1940s. He also collaborated with Tom Key in recreating a revival of the off-Broadway hit, *Cotton Patch Gospel*, and, along with Mark Nelson, produced the musical theme for *Appalachian Christmas Homecoming*, in which he also acted and played the banjo.

Jim Nabors, comedian and singer, best known as television's *Gomer Pyle*, worked for Station WJBF-TV in Augusta before becoming a television and recording star.

Jimmy Nalls of Macon became famous with "Wet Willie" and Sea Level, a successful jazz-flavored group.

Normaltown Flyers is a great Athens band that put out some albums with Mercury Records. They also did some interesting videos.

Sammy O'Banion is another native of Augusta who went on to Nashville and has been very successful with a beach music band.

King Joe Oliver, famous blues singer, died in poverty in Savannah, Georgia.

Bert Parks from Atlanta was a national television personality, star of *The Music Man* and other Broadway musicals, and for many years the singing master of ceremonies for the *Miss America Pageant*.

Uncle John Patterson, the self-proclaimed "Banjo King" from Carrollton once served in the Georgia General Assembly and picked with Gordon Tanner, Gid's son, and Smokey Joe Miller from Walton County.

Minnie Pearl (Sara Ophelia Colley Cannon), Country Music Hall of Fame member and legendary performer on the Grand Ole Opry, once lived in Newnan.

Duke Pearson of Atlanta was one of the nation's greatest jazzmen. He was an excellent composer, pianist, conductor, and arranger. His original compositions number in the scores: "Cristo Redentor," "New Time Shuffle," "Chant" and "Sweet Honey Bee." He appeared at the Apollo Theater in New York and all over the world. He died in 1980 at the age of forty-eight from multiple sclerosis.

Ojeda Penn has been one of the principal leaders of the growing jazz recording industry in Atlanta. This innovator and developer of talent came to Capitol City in 1967 and released his first highly acclaimed album *Happiness* through Aapogee Studio in 1980. A virtuoso on both acoustic and electric pianos, as well as the synthesizer, Ojeda combines the three in easy transitions to produce melodic styles ranked among the best in contemporary jazz. His technique has been compared to those of artists Duke and McCoy Tyne.

Ojeda Penn

Margaret Perrin, Elbert County native and Atlanta institution, played piano at Noel Coward's birthday party and entertained legions of Atlantans in a kiddie review in the early days of WSB Radio.

Ivey Peterson was a country music comedian in Atlanta known to radio listeners as "Herman Horsehair Bugfuzz."

The Pine Ridge Boys had the distinction of being the first to record the classic, "You Are My Sunshine." The two, Marvin Taylor and Doug Spivey, appeared on the Cross Roads Follies.

Diane Pfeiffer studied to be a chemist at Merrimee College in Missouri, but the only formula she discovered was how to write and sing country songs, which she used when she moved to Marietta, Georgia. She won an invitation to perform at Opryland in a contest sponsored by Atlanta country music station WPLO. This led to a job singing backup for Tammy Wynette, a songwriting and recording contract with Capitol Records, and an award as Georgia Songwriter of the Year in 1982. Her single, "Free to Be Lonely Again," was on the national country charts in 1980, and her songs have been recorded by Roy Clark, Dottie West, Billy Jo Spears, Debby Boone, and Johnny Mathis.

Joel Price, a Lavonia native known as a talented comedian, for many years also played bass for Judy Lynn and Little Jimmy Dickens.

Faith Prince, was nominated for a Tony in 1992 when she appeared on Broadway as Miss Adelaide in *Guy's and Doll's*. She was born in St. Joseph Hospital in Augusta and moved to Virginia as a child.

The Georgia Prophets, a rock group founded in Augusta in the mid-1960s by the late Tommy Witcher, recorded "Nobody Loves Me Like You" for Capricorn Records and featured the husband and wife duo, Billy and Barbara Scott, as harmonizing vocalists.

Pylon is the Athens band that had a popular album, *Chomps*, produced by Atlanta's independent DB Records.

Robert Ray, New York's 1980 Entertainer of the Year, moved to Atlanta where he and his group, the Rayettes, became hits on the night and supper club circuits.

The Revelairs were a popular gospel group in the 1950s. Bob Shaw, who became Georgia's Republican chairman, was a member.

Danny Rhea is a talented Augusta performer who won the regional True Value talent contest and put out a CD country album.

Hoke and **Paul Rice** were a popular radio act in the Atlanta area during the 1920s, 1930s, and 1940s. Hoke was an influential guitarist who did session work for several record companies.

Bob and **"Babs" Richardson** built the first state-of-the-art recording studio in the Southeast with Master Sound in Atlanta. Music producer Bob Richardson engineered recording sessions for the Tams, James Brown, Prince, Shelia E., the Swinging Medallions, Billy Joe Royal, Isaac Hayes, Little Richard, and countless others. Bob also was a sales manager for Columbia and Mercury Records and was inducted into the Georgia Music Hall of Fame in 1987.

Ace Richman and the Sunshine Boys of Atlanta were a country and western singing group that performed on the WSB Radio Barn Dance and on the first television program of station WEB-TV.

Josephine Robinson from Augusta, Georgia, composed some giants, including "Don't Let Anyone Turn You Around" and "Give Me That Old Time Religion."

Ernest Rogers of Atlanta was a columnist and amusements writer for *The Atlanta Journal* and an original performing personality on radio station WSB, whose song, "Tune in My Heart," recorded by Ernie Hare, was one of the first recordings played on radio.

Gamble Rogers, well liked and respected Lithia Springs resident, has been called the "Daddy of Bluegrass Music in Georgia." *Bluegrass Unlimited*, in a profile stated, "His contribution to Bluegrass has been equaled by few, if any, anywhere in the country."

Pam Rose, a former Atlanta nightclub vocalist, had some highly acclaimed albums on Capitol Records before coforming the popular all-girl band Calamity Jane. She and fellow band member Mary Ann Kennedy cowrote the giant country hits "Ring on Her Finger, Time on Her Hands" (recorded by Reba McEntire and Lee Greenwood), "I'll Still Be Loving You" (recorded by Restless Heart), "The First Word in Memory Is Me" (recorded by Janie Fricke), and "Safe in the Arms of Love" (recorded by Gail Davies and Martina McBride). She and Kennedy later formed the duo Kennedy Rose and put out more highly acclaimed albums on rock singer Sting's Pangea Records label.

Art Rosenbaum is a nationally recognized scholar on folk music and has written an excellent book, *Folk Visions and Voices* about the traditional music of North Georgia. His wife and collaborator, Margo Newmark Rosenbaum, has photographed many folk singers in Georgia and throughout the world. Art, an artist and instructor at the University of Georgia, is a skilled banjo picker and has written an excellent book on that art.

Aunt Sarie (Sara Wilson) was part of an act on the Grand Ole Opry with her sister, Sallie, in the 1930s. The act broke up in the 1940s, and Aunt Sarie came to Atlanta to entertain thousands.

Savannah, a group reminiscent of Alabama, formed by two brothers from Albany, **Jay** and **Gene Willis**, had charted songs, including "Back Street Ballet."

John Schneider, country singer and star of *The Dukes of Hazzard*, got his start as a teenaged star at Six Flags over Georgia.

Martha Scott, mezzosoprano, Atlanta native, and Clark College faculty member, is rated by many as one of the best soloists around.

Tommy Scott of Toccoa, operator of the last old-time medicine show on the road, got into the business during the Depression when he joined the show of "Doc" M. F. Chamberlain in Elberton. He employed such western movie stars as Johnny Mac Brown, Kit Carson, Fuzzy St. John, and Tim McCoy in his shows, and has been inducted into the Country Music Association's Walkway of Stars.

Sea Level, a six-man aggregation featuring many of Macon's finest performers, had five excellent albums.

Zenas "Daddy" Sears was one of the first persons to be inducted into the Georgia Music Hall of Fame in 1980. Few nonperformers have had more influence on so many notable careers. He was a great personality on Atlanta radio stations WGST and WAOK. He helped launch the careers of Ray Charles, James Brown, "Piano Red" Perryman, Fats Domino, Gladys Knight, Little Richard, and countless others. He, more than anyone else, introduced black music to an Atlanta radio audience. He died in 1988.

Zenas Sears

Arthur Lee Simpkins, from South Carolina, first sang publicly at Augusta's Thankful Baptist church. He later had a local band called Night Hawks and then traveled to Hollywood where he appeared in several movies before dying in 1972. He appeared at the London Palladium and recorded several albums. His musical version of "Trees," the poem by Joyce Kilmer, is outstanding.

Daryle Singletary is a former farm boy from the Southwest Georgia town of Whigham. He burned up the country charts with his ballad, "I Let Her Lie." Singletary arrived in Nashville in 1990 at the age of nineteen as one of Tanya Tucker's roadies. He met a bus driver for Randy Travis, who introduced him to Travis' wife and business manager, Lib Hatcher. One thing led to another with Mr. and Mrs. Travis taking Singletary under their wing and getting him a deal with Giant Records.

Arthur Q. Smith may be one of the most interesting Georgians of them all. Certainly, he was very talented. He was a songwriter born in Georgia, but he grew up in Harlan, Kentucky. This man never became famous because he sold the songs he wrote for ten to twenty-five dollars each. His clients included Roy Acuff, Hank Williams, Bill Monroe, Maybelle Carter, and countless others. His hit songs never had his name on them, but it has been established that he wrote "I Overlooked an Orchid," "If Teardrops Were Pennies," "Wedding Bells," "I Wouldn't Change You If I Could," and no one knows how many others. He died in 1963 without ever getting any recognition, much less money, for his work.

Betty Smith appears at concerts of Georgia traditional Appalachian music, playing the dulcimer and other instruments.

Carrie Smith, a native of Fort Gaines, Georgia, is a singer "blessed with a rich vibrant contralto voice" who has performed with the Carnegie Hall New York Jazz Repertory Company throughout the world. Her music has been greatly influenced by Ella Fitzgerald and Billie Holiday.

Gerald Smith. The Statesboro native became known as the "Georgia Quacker" from his numerous *Hee Haw* TV appearances and his Donald Duck-like talking/singing. He has become a top songwriter in recent years with his successes including cowriting "What Part of No (Don't You Understand?)," recorded by Lorrie Morgan, and "Every Second," recorded by Colin Raye.

Trixie Smith, also known as Tessie Ames and Bessie Lee, was a native Georgian, born in Atlanta in 1895 and was one of the earliest of the vaudeville-styled blues singers to record. She was on Decca in 1938–1939 and toured as a featured singer for TOBA (Theater Owner's Booking Association).

Charles Smithgall, Sr., of Gainesville, was one of the first morning disc jockeys on America radio and was a star on Atlanta radio station WSB with the popular characters he created: "Daisy, the Calf" and "Professor Early Q. Wormcatcher," whose antics were interspersed with the playing of country music records.

Herman Spears of Atlanta was a crooning singer on the original Barn Dance of Atlanta radio station WSB.

.38 Special had as one of its founders, Jeff Carlise of Atlanta, but most of this fine rock group grew up playing together in Jacksonville, Florida.

Roba Stanley in 1924 was country music's first "sweetheart"—the forerunner of Loretta Lynn and other women of that caliber. She was the first female to sing solo on radio and on record. She was only a teenager at the time when she performed on radio station WSB and Okeh Records. Married at an early age, she went to Florida and gave up performing. Her records were rediscovered by old-time music lovers, and she became a hit all over again with the "purists." She was the daughter of Rob Stanley, who was inducted into the Atlanta Country Music Hall of Fame in its second year. Roba was inducted during the first year. Her father was a champion fiddler who lived in Gwinnett County.

Starbuck, a premier rock group out of Atlanta, has had many hit records, and the band's albums have sold well.

The Swanee Quintet was identified by comedian Bill Cosby during a nationwide event honoring the restoration of New York's Apollo Theater as one of his favorite Apollo acts. They are a gospel group founded in Augusta in 1940. The group's original members were James Anderson, Jr., Charlie Barnwell, Rufus Washington, William Crawford, and Floyd Fouch. Newer members have carried on the quintet's tradition with extensive nationwide appearances.

Carl Talton was an Atlanta radio performer for many years in the 1930s, 1940s, and 1950s.

Ann Tant, daughter of the legendary Mama Wynett, represented Warner Brothers for many years in the Southeast and was a close friend of Patsy Cline.

Dub Taylor, as he was billed, was one of filmdom's most beloved character actors when he died in 1994. Walter Clarence Taylor, Jr., was his name, and he spent his boyhood in Augusta. He played drums at the old Summerville Academy and took dancing lessons at Miss Petite's dancing school. He launched his show business career in vaudeville playing a harmonica and xylophone. In 1936, he was discovered by the legendary film director, Frank Capra, who signed him for the film classic, *You Can't Take It with You*, with James Stewart. He acted in other Capra movies, and in two hundred westerns. He was also in *The Cincinnati Kid* and *How the West Was Won*.

Maude Thacker was a ballad singer from Tate who had a repertoire of British-American folk songs, which she learned from her father in the 1920s.

Susan Thomas of Mountain Park sang backup for Tammy Wynette and wrote "The Woman in Me," which went to Number Three in the charts for Crystal Gayle.

Willis Mae Thomas of Atlanta starred as Little Nehi on the WSB Barn Dance.

Bobby Thompson, bearded banjo player on *Hee Haw,* worked for station WFBJ-TV in Augusta before becoming a much-in-demand session, backup, and performing banjoist in Nashville.

Charles Davis Tillman was an ordained minister in the Methodist Episcopal Church South, but he never served as the pastor of a church. His ministry was as a hymn writer, publisher, and song leader for evangelists who traveled the South. Operating out of his Atlanta home on Murphy Avenue in southwest Atlanta, he led the singing at revivals held by well-known evangelists such as the Reverends Sam P. Jones, W. A. Dodge, and Charles M. Dunaway. A self-taught musician who played the organ, he was born in 1861 and died in 1943. He was the author of numerous popular hymns, including "Life's Railroad to Heaven," "When I Get to the End of the Way," "Ready," "My Mother's Bibles," "Save One Soul for Jesus," "The Broken Vase," "You Can Shine," and many, many more. He also published many well-known hymns by other writers, includ-

Charlie D. Tillman

ing "Love Lifted Me." He was also the first person to transcribe the words and music to the popular spiritual, "Old Time Religion." One of his collections of songs, *Little Light Songs*, was adopted by the Georgia State Board of Education in 1936 for use in public schools.

Bob Van Camp of Atlanta was music director of radio station WSB, succeeding Albert Coleman. He was a virtuoso organist best known for his performances on "Mighty Mo," the Moler organ in Atlanta's Fox Theater, which is the world's largest theater organ.

Joe Williams was an actor, a musician, a performer, and a great jazz and blues singer during the 1930s into the 1950s. He was also on some of the biggest television shows: *The Tonight Show*, *The Bill Cosby Show*, and *As the World Turns*. Voted five times the Best Male Singer by *Down Beat* magazine, he received a star in the Hollywood Walk of Fame in 1983 and became a member of the Georgia Music Hall of Fame in 1988.

Johnny Walker of Waycross wrote several hundred songs and has a dozen or more recorded by country music stars such as Roy Acuff, Jack Greene, and Ben Colter.

Agnes Ward of Columbus was a singer and dancer with Lena Horne.

Byron Warner of Atlanta was leader of the Seven Aces Orchestra, which appeared regularly on Atlanta's radio station WSB, before he moved to Athens to become professor of voice at the University of Georgia.

George Washington was a trombonist born in Brunswick in 1907 who played with many of the greats, including Fletcher Henderson, Louis Armstrong, and Bennie Carter.

Charles Wesley (1707–1788) was the first published songwriter in Georgia. A Methodist preacher, he was also the Secretary for Indian Affairs to Georgia founder James Edward Oglethorpe. His stay in the colony in 1736 with his brother, John, was brief, but Charles is said to have written several hymns and published a hymnbook while on Georgia soil. He composed 6,500 hymns in his lifetime—many composed on horseback.

Belinda West of Augusta was a backup singer for Ronnie Milsap, a recording artist under contract to RCA, and a singer of soul and gospel versions of commercials.

Benji Whilhoite of Cartersville is a talented young singer who has appeared in a number of films, including *Six Pack* with Kenny Rogers.

Ray Whitley

Ray Whitley was born in Columbus, Georgia, and had his first band when he was fourteen. Felton Jarvis discovered him in an Atlanta high school and put him on tour with Bill Lowery, who signed him to a contract. He wrote songs recorded by Billy Joe Royal, the Tams, Tommy Roe, the Swinging Medallions, and many others. Some of his megahits include "Be Young, Be Foolish, Be Happy," "What Kind of Fool Do You Think I Am," "Hey Girl, Don't Bother Me," and "I've Been Hurt." A great performer as well as a songwriter, he toured throughout the country and was inducted into the Georgia Music Hall of Fame in 1992.

Another **Ray Whitley** from Georgia also made it big in music as the "Singing Cowboy." Born in Atlanta in 1901, this Ray Whitley wrote "Back in the Saddle Again" (with Fred Rose) for Gene Autry. He left Georgia to serve in the Navy and then went to New York and cohosted the WHN Barn Dance with Tex Ritter in the mid-1930s. He was one of the first singing cowboys to head to Hollywood in 1936. There he made many movies, including *Giant*. He also cowrote with Fred Rose some of the great western classics including "I Hang My Head and Cry" and "Ages and Ages Ago." He also sang with the Sons of the Pioneers and died in 1979.

Larry Jon Wilson is a country singer and songwriter who was born on the Ohoopee River near Swainsboro and lived in North Augusta, South Carolina, before going to Nashville, where he wrote and recorded his hit single, "Kindred Spirit," and the songs on his album, *Let Me Sing My Song for You,* issued by Monument Records.

Eric Weisberg and **Steve Mandel** composed the banjo duo who performed the classic "Dueling Banjos" for the soundtrack of the movie *Deliverance,* which was filmed on Georgia's wild, scenic Chattooga River.

Mac Wiseman was appearing on the WSB Barn Dance when asked to join Bill Monroe.

Fletcher Wolfe is founder of the world-famous Atlanta Boys Choir. The group has performed concerts in Georgia for thirty-five years and annually tours Europe.

Randy Wood of Savannah was born in Douglas and is the designer and builder of custom guitars, mandolins, and banjos. Users of his instruments and services include Jerry Reed, Michael "Wildfire" Murphy, J. J. Cale, Chet Atkins, Bill Monroe, Byron Berline, Roland White, Keith Richard, and Eric Clapton.

Boots Woodall and the TV Wranglers, a country and western group, performed during the early days of television on station WAGA-TV.

Ginny Wright, one of the only two female artists to record major hits with the late Jim Reeves during his lifetime, was born in Twin City, Georgia, near Swainsboro, and graduated from Emmanuel County Institute. She and Reeves recorded "I Love You," which was Number One on the country charts for twenty-three weeks in 1953. She did "Are You Mine" with Tom T. Hall, which was Number One for twenty-six weeks. Her hits include the solo "I've Got Somebody New," "I Want You to Want Me" (with Tom T. Hall), and "I'm in Heaven" (with Tom Bearden).

Steve Young, who lived for some time in Newnan, Georgia, and played in Georgia honky-tonks before moving to Nashville during the 1970s, was called by Waylon Jennings "the second greatest country singer—to George Jones, of course." Jennings used Young's "Lonesome, Orn'ry, and Mean" as the title track of one of his best albums. Young's own album, *Renegade Picker,* done for RCA in 1976, was praised by critics, but major recognition eluded him. His "Seven Bridges Road" was recorded by Eddie Arnold, Rita Coolidge, Joan Baez, and Tracy Nelson of Mother Earth. He bounced around on several labels and maintained a strong cult following before he died an early death.

And there are many, many more talented artists whom I don't know about but should. I know that I would admire them and put them in this book if our paths had crossed or if I had heard their music.

INDEX TO *AND MANY MORE*